The Evolution of Teaching

The Evolution of Teaching

A Guidebook to the Advancement of Teaching, Teacher Education, and Happier Careers for Early Career Teachers

Rich Waters

ROWMAN & LITTLEFIELD
Lanham • Boulder • New York • London

Published by Rowman & Littlefield
A wholly owned subsidiary of The Rowman & Littlefield Publishing Group, Inc.
4501 Forbes Boulevard, Suite 200, Lanham, Maryland 20706
www.rowman.com

16 Carlisle Street, London W1D 3BT, United Kingdom

Copyright © 2014 by Rich Waters

All rights reserved. No part of this book may be reproduced in any form or by any electronic or mechanical means, including information storage and retrieval systems, without written permission from the publisher, except by a reviewer who may quote passages in a review.

British Library Cataloguing in Publication Information Available

Library of Congress Cataloging-in-Publication Data Available

978-1-4758-1379-1 (cloth : alk. paper)
978-1-4758-1380-7 (pbk. : alk. paper)
978-1-4758-1381-4 (electronic)

Contents

Acknowledgments		vii
Preface		ix
Prologue: Background on Why Teachers Need New Schools for New Learning		xv
Introduction		xxv

I: Make a Choice: The Industrial Age School or New Kinds of Schools? — 1

1. Guiding Step 1: Get Perspective on the Career of Teaching and the Possibilities for Change — 3
2. Guiding Step 2: Question the Assumptions and Practices of Traditional Schools — 21
3. Guiding Step 3: Face Traditional School Culture—The Game of School and Strategic Learning — 39

II: Embrace Positive Forces for Change: Twenty-First-Century Learning Will Be Different — 53

4. Guiding Step 4: Focus on Learning Engagement—A Premise for New Schools — 55
5. Guiding Step 5: Reconsider the Emerging Marketplace of Educational Experiences — 79
6. Guiding Step 6: Start Seeing Students as Independent, Voluntary Customers — 91
7. Guiding Step 7: Understand Two Related Concepts—Twenty-First-Century Skills and the Learning Organization — 101

III: New Schools for New Learning — 117

8. Guiding Step 8: Envision a New Kind of School — 119
9. Guiding Step 9: Envision New Roles for Youths and Adults in a New Kind of School — 139
10. Guiding Step 10: Begin the Journey to New Schools and Happier Careers by Making Connections — 159

Index — 171

Acknowledgments

Becoming able to write this book was the outcome of learning to listen. Thus, I am indebted to the fine qualitative researchers and teachers of listening who guided me. Valerie Jansick, Kathy Charmaz, and Brene Brown were primary in helping me understand how a researcher listens.

My growth as a listener led to trying to hear everything and accept feedback in all its forms. That feedback came to me primarily from students and their teachers while I was teaching and later as a researcher. Often it was the most offhanded and unrehearsed remarks from both groups that translated into important concepts and ideas. I am deeply appreciative to the students, whom I may not name, who earnestly took it upon themselves to tell this old man what was really going on in school and how they really experienced it. Likewise, I am indebted to teachers who spoke frankly with me about the sometimes unflattering realities of life as a teacher. From this sometimes risky and frank testimony emerged one overriding concept, which was at once quiet but loud: Everything about school could be so much better if only it were more personal.

Finding that message in all of my data and then translating it into this manuscript was also an outcome of learning to listen to others who inhabit schools. My hat is again tipped to Dr. Linda Crawford, who guided a sometimes difficult student in the completion of his research and dissertation. Also of special mention are two colleagues with whom I worked to develop a professional development school, Marie Toto and Pat Lasko. Apart from being an inspiration as a colleague, Marie was instrumental in helping me launch and complete the research project that provided much of the data important to this work and another one in press. She also provided important feedback on the manuscript itself. I am especially appreciative of Pat Lasko, a reader's reader, who in several iterations undertook not only providing insightful feedback but also the refinement of this manuscript in each and every word. She worked on it as if it were her own.

My appreciation is also extended to Ed Dirkswager, co-author of *Trusting Teachers with School Success: What Happens When Teachers Call the Shots*, for his important research, which I see as foundational to the outlook expressed in this book. I believe his feedback on my manuscript probably had more impact than he imagines.

Finally, I extend deep appreciation to Rowman & Littlefield editor Dr. Tom Koerner, who, much to my inspiration, rejected a manuscript in a way that encouraged and invited a better one. In the process I began to see Tom not as a gatekeeper but as a fine teacher and grower of writers.

Preface

This book has a premise: The career of teaching is on hard times. Teachers are increasingly unhappy with their work. That unhappiness is not a good fit in schools. By their very nature, schools must be happy places, and the students and teachers must be happy people.

This book, then, is a response to that teacher unhappiness. Its purpose is to help early career teachers move away from their sense of powerlessness over their work and the resulting frustrations they endure in contemporary schools. It advances the idea that our traditional notion of who teachers are and what teachers do needs to change. The very concept of what it means to be a teacher needs to evolve. With the right leadership—teacher leadership—that evolution could bring early career teachers the happy, satisfying careers they seek.

To be developed later, this book is addressed to early career teachers because as a group they have the best opportunity to advance the evolution of teaching. They can guide teaching in such a way that teachers will feel increased control over their work as they experience ongoing professional growth and the personal, human rewards all teachers want. Readers, in fact, may consider this book an attempt to sell them on change because the right change will offer early career teachers something much better than what they have now.

Readers need to know this because they will never lead change unless they believe change will lead them to something *much* better. Readers should consider the contrasts developed in the following table as they begin to think about change, the profession of teaching, and the quality of their future careers.

If, now, readers think they would prefer the satisfying career described on the right-hand side, they will want to read this book.

However, because this book is addressed to early career teachers and their teachers, it is important to make a clarification. Although similar to a small number of other books, this book is very different from the vast majority of advice books for novice teachers. Most books published for teacher education make recommendations to early career teachers, or their teachers, on how to be successful working within existing schools, most of which are of industrial age design.

The term used here, "industrial age design," refers to most people's notion of a traditional school. It is probably the kind of school readers

What's in It for Teachers? What's in It for Me?

A Career of Frustration Today	A Satisfying Career in the Future
Lack of Self-Determination You lack a sense of control over your work. For the most part the nature and design of student work and its implementation and evaluation are dictated by legacy practices of federal, state, or local officials or publishers with whom you have little contact and who do not ask your opinion.	*Self-Determination* You have a sense of purpose and feel control over your work. You make important choices and play a key role in the design, execution, and evaluation of your work.
Sortive Evaluation You feel little power over your own evaluation. You believe there are factors included that should not be there and other important factors left out. You see the process as a way of sorting teachers and not very helpful in supporting your improvement as a professional.	*Supportive Evaluation* You inform how you are evaluated. You have helped design the evaluation process. You play a critical role in how the process is applied. You believe the others involved in your evaluation care about you and are supporting your growth as a professional.
Teacher Technician You see yourself as a worker/technician tasked with implementing standards, goals, curricula, lesson design, and even scripts dictating what you should say in delivering lessons to students. You are never asked to reflect on or give judgment about what is being taught, how it is taught, or the overall assumptions and practices of your school.	*Teacher Professional* You are a member/stakeholder: you feel like a respected member of a professional team. You help the team create a vision for optimal functioning, and you work collectively with it to learn and to take action to apply that learning. As part of this, you are often called upon to bring your judgment and imagination to important decision making.
Lack of Community The school you work in is large: there are many hundreds, maybe more than a thousand, students and over a hundred staff. Many people don't know or care about each other. The friendships that form are part of cliques that are unrelated to the school's goals and culture. There is often animosity between groups. Student and adult behavior often shows disconnection and disregard for others. There is a lot of negative gossiping and complaining. Students' achievement is usually the outcome of compliance or competition, not high engagement.	*Caring Community* The school you work in is a deliberately designed small community with the stated purpose of creating a culture of caring where both adults and students are committed to a high level of kindness and respect for all members. Members feel connected and cared about. They believe that such a caring community is the foundation for human engagement in life and learning. Caring and engagement are seen as the basis for high expectations and high achievement.

Technical Learning	Professional Learning
Your professional learning is focused on the implementation of standards created by others and preparing students for success on an array of standardized proficiency assessments and year-end standardized tests created by others. Neither you nor other teachers are asked to reflect on the value of these standardized tools nor many of the other assumptions and practices of your school. If you disagree with their use, you are regarded with suspicion. A lot of research, including research suggesting the ill effects of standardized testing is ignored. You experience a high level of frustration as you realize that your thoughtfulness and its role in your professional growth are being ignored.	You are aware that your school community is heavily invested in your professional learning. There is ongoing reflection on the effectiveness of a broad array of learning and schooling strategies for both students and teachers. Professional learning is embedded in your everyday routines. Research is happening everywhere. There is a collective eagerness to consider imaginative and entrepreneurial ideas for change and improvement. You enjoy your continual growth in competence within this culture as you take on new challenges and ever greater responsibilities.

remember from their own primary and secondary education or the kind of school they are teaching in now or about to teach in soon.

Readers should know, then, that this book will not make any such recommendations. Instead, it joins with the small but growing number of other books that maintain that what everyone thinks of as a traditional school is a deeply flawed model, a model that is, in fact, hurtful to student learning and will be hurtful to readers' careers as teachers. Thus, *this book is about helping readers enrich their careers and student learning by moving away from that toxic model from the industrial age and toward many newly conceived models for schooling.*

Readers are also asked to reflect on the fact that all of those other books, and the teacher preparation programs that use them, that do offer advice about classroom control, presentation of lessons, motivation, curriculum design, and many other aspects of traditional teaching rarely even allude to an important but unstated assumption: The advice offered applies within the context of a teacher working in a traditional school of industrial age design. That is, the advice is given without discussing or questioning the difficult issue of that context and its effects on students and teachers.

As this book will demonstrate, this is an extraordinary omission in light of the research and writing that have clarified the importance of context and culture in learning and, thereby, have exposed the deep flaws of the industrial age model and how it stands to pervert learning for teachers and students.

With this clarification made, this book takes the author's perspective of a full career in teaching, twenty-five to forty years. His intent is for readers to consider its meaning in anticipation of their own full careers.

The author wrote this book to help early career teachers to think long term about their careers and to help them fully satisfy their career dreams. As the author will explain later, those dreams are now at risk. Making those dreams a reality will likely require early career teachers to embrace change like never before and to assert themselves in ways no other generation of teachers has ever done.

Again, what is at issue is teachers' professional learning and career satisfaction. As stewards of schools and learning, teachers are entitled to their own high-quality professional learning. That professional learning is a core element of career satisfaction. Teachers' entitlement to it leads to a simple issue. Teachers (and students) cannot learn what they need to learn for the twenty-first century while working in schools committed to industrial age assumptions, practices, and culture. It is a fundamental impossibility.

Equally fundamental is the proposition in learning theory and organizational theory that people learn what they do. Research verifies that context and culture dominate in learning. Thus, working in industrial age schools, teachers and students will learn the ways of the industrial age. They will not learn about new structures for schools, new models for teacher and student learning, or new concepts in school organization and organizational learning.

Early career teachers may ask, if schools are so out of touch with twenty-first-century thinking, why don't they just change? The answer to this question is complicated and confusing. Basically, change is not happening because the people who lead and maintain our schools do not want change. While this sounds harsh and hard to believe, for a variety of reasons to be developed throughout this book, most educators see it as in their interest to keep schools the way they are. In fact, this book is going to inform readers that many educators not only resist change, but they actively fight against it.

This situation is complicated even more by the fact that these people who are resisting change are good and decent people. They are not some perverse enemy. They are likely people who are teaching readers in college or supervising them in a school right now. These people are very accomplished, with years of excellent performance behind them. They probably entered the field of education for the same reason readers have: They have a special care for young people. What's more, they are accustomed to being treated with respect. They believe in their work. Confronting them now with an indictment of failing to change must be a very delicate venture.

At some point, early career teachers will need the support of these veterans. As the change process unfolds, early career teachers will someday have to turn to them and say, "We believe schools need to change. We want to try something new. This is why we want to try it. We are asking for your support." This moment may be a difficult one for many veteran educators. Change for them will imply on some level an invalidation of what they have done or are doing in schools and in teacher education.

The author would like to consider this issue of implied invalidation head on. He would submit to his fellow veterans that the threat of invalidation is, in fact, overestimated. But, let's be very clear. The message of this book does invalidate some current and past approaches to schooling and teacher education just as it has invalidated much of the author's career. Writing this book has clarified for him that during most of his seemingly successful career, he was on the wrong path. And, even during times when he thought he was looking for a better path, through acts of rationalization, he chose to continue on the wrong path.

So, this book is not about indicting others. Rather, it is the outcome of realization and self-indictment. The author has had to face the invalidation of much of what he did throughout his career. He has come to recognize that over the years, his mind-set was the problem. In that mind-set, he accepted the ways of a traditional school as if they were immutable, God given, infallible, or beyond question.

Thus, he spent his entire career acting like, thinking like, and performing his duties like a traditional teacher. His thoughts and behavior did not evolve toward something new but stayed within the confines of what it meant to be a traditional teacher in a traditional school. He stayed in the box. *This book is about improving the career of teaching by helping teachers get out of that mind-set, that trap.* The concept of teaching must evolve.

Having experienced this invalidation, the author appeals to other veterans to consider the upside of supporting change. Veterans are implicitly leaders, and all leaders must at some time face the invalidation of change. Something new is always coming at us. Everything and everybody gets replaced. Still, veterans will survive. They will survive best if they find their own place in the future. There is in the acceptance of new ideas an opportunity to take the high road. If veterans admit some mistakes, they will be recognized by their students for their magnanimity, and their stature as leaders will be enhanced.

Add to this that becoming part of the change process opens up new opportunities for veteran leadership, and it will serve as an example to peer veterans who may not be as open as others. The author asks the veteran readers, as one veteran to others, for their consideration of ideas for change, change that may appear threatening and invalidating. He does this, however, recognizing that teaching as a career has now become very troubled. Most educators recognize that this is true because they are in the schools and hear the complaining. Hence, early career teachers will need the support of everyone in leading the evolution of teaching to a happier place.

So, how will change come about? One purpose of this book is to clarify those circumstances. It will lay out the reasons for change, the look of change, and how to start change. However, it will stipulate that the right change will not happen unless teachers make it happen. The process will require personal initiative and effort, daily small steps as teachers experiment with a new premise for schooling and new models for learning.

The profession of teaching is now on the wrong course. Teachers, themselves, need to right that course. The failure to change will hurt teachers and students. This book, *The Evolution of Teaching: A Guidebook to the Advancement of Teaching, Teacher Education, and Happier Careers for Early Career Teachers*, is about teachers taking charge of their collective destiny. The end result will be teachers thinking more, questioning more, and imagining more. It will especially mean teachers following less and leading more. Such teacher leadership will be about getting better, newly conceived schools, places where teachers and students will learn in satisfying ways appropriate to the ever-new conditions and the ever-new capacities of the twenty-first century.

If readers would like to contact me, please send me an email at wrich1273@gmail.com.

Prologue

Background on Why Teachers Need New Schools for New Learning

This book is about students and teachers needing and getting new kinds of schools. These new kinds of schools are necessary to change how teachers and students experience schooling and, for teachers, how they experience their careers.

There is also a companion book for students, *The Evolution of Learning: A Guidebook to School Change, Authentic Learning, and Leadership for High School Students*. Both books convey the same idea: Schools are best thought of as places where two groups learn, teachers and students. Neither of these two groups can do its best learning for the twenty-first century in schools committed to the assumptions, practices, and cultures of the industrial age. It is a logical impossibility.

In making this assertion, this book works from a principle: The real places where teachers learn how to teach is in the schools where they work, not in teacher preparation programs. Yes, there are many innovative teacher preparation programs with high-minded objectives and effective programs, all well informed by research (Darling-Hammond, 2006). They likely contribute a great deal to the lives of prospective teachers on many levels, but there is still a hard reality that everyone involved in teacher preparation must face: Teachers get their real education as teachers in the schools where they teach, not from teacher preparation programs.

When new teachers enter the culture of a school to begin teaching, over time that context will become the primary source of their learning about the work of teaching. The source will not be the theory or practical advice they received in college. In every school they enter, new teachers will learn "the way we do things around here" in a local school. In effect, those new teachers will become acculturated. They will fit in and extend the legacy of traditional schooling. As Peter Drucker famously said, "Culture eats strategy for breakfast."

It is from this understanding of how school culture dominates the learning of teachers (and students) that the need for new schools becomes clear. If schools are the places where teachers really learn to teach, then providing appropriate professional learning for teachers requires that we provide teachers with schools where they are going to learn a repertoire of principles and practices that are grounded in twenty-first-century knowledge and capacities. These principles and practices cannot be learned in schools that are committed to industrial age assumptions, practices, and cultures. It is, again, a logical impossibility.

What readers must understand is that the fulfillment of their careers depends on that redesign of schools. If the profession of teaching does not undergo some evolution, the career of teaching is going to remain mired in the frustrations teachers now endure, most of which are directly attributable to the industrial age thinking in our schools. Readers should be very clear. The need to advance the evolution of schools and teaching is about better careers for teachers.

As this book will show, new schools will be very different from the schools of today. They will have a different premise, and they will be based on different assumptions, practices, and cultures. Because of this, participation in these new schools will result in different learning. Teachers will think about their role in schools and their work with students differently. Teachers in new schools will, as a result, have very different careers marked by three experiences that satisfy: self-determination, stakeholder membership, and professional growth and effectiveness.

HAPPINESS AT WORK HAS BEEN INFORMED BY SCIENCE

How work can make people happy has been informed by research. There are, in fact, several strands of research that have examined the conditions under which people become happy in general and more specifically under which people become happy at work. One of the most interesting insights to come out of this research about a happy life in general is that it requires happiness in one's work. To be happy, people must derive satisfaction in their love relationships with spouses, family, and friends, and they must derive satisfaction in their work. In effect, happiness at work is a necessary condition for general happiness in life (Haidt, 2006, p. 219).

So, what makes work satisfying? The markers of happiness in work, described in Textbox P.1, have been adapted from a number of fields of research, including self-determination theory (Deci, 1995; Deci & Ryan, 1985), social psychology (Haidt, 2006), positive psychology (Ben-Shahar, 2007; Csikszentmihalyi, 1990, 1997; Seligman, 2002), and human potential psychology (Maslow, 1968). These concepts will be revisited again and again in this book as the case for change and happier careers in teaching is made.

THREE EXPERIENCES THAT LEAD TO HAPPINESS IN A CAREER

1. Self-Determination: You have a sense of personal purpose and ownership in your work and a sense of control over what and how you do things in that work. You play a key role in the design, execution, and evaluation of your work. Your work feels like a personal mission and you feel deeply about it.
2. Stakeholder/Membership: You feel like a respected member of a professional team. You helped the team create a vision for optimal functioning and you work collectively with your team to learn and to take action to apply that learning. As part of the team, you are often called upon to bring your judgment and imagination to important decision making.
3. Professional Learning and Effectiveness: You are aware of how your work and professional growth have resulted in the achievement of personal and organizational goals. You know that your professional growth is supported by your school community. There is ongoing reflection on the effectiveness of a broad array of learning and schooling strategies for both students and teachers. Professional learning is embedded in your everyday routines. Research is happening everywhere. There is a collective eagerness to consider imaginative and entrepreneurial ideas for change and improvement. You enjoy your continual growth in competence within this culture as you take on new challenges and ever greater responsibilities.

It is important for early career teachers to reflect on these markers of satisfaction because it is now becoming increasingly clear that these three experiences are on the wane for teachers. That is why this book for teachers approaches this need for new schools from the standpoint of the career of teaching.

This book will clarify that the career of teaching is being threatened now by forces outside of schools that are dictating standards, goals, curricula, lesson design, and even what teachers should say in delivering a lesson. There is even talk of "teacher proofing" instruction, and a recent Phi Delta Kappa/Gallop poll indicated that "among all occupations tracked in their survey, teachers were the least likely to say that their opinions counted at work" (Blad, 2014).

Add to this condition teachers' deep unhappiness with a variety of new evaluation systems, which they see as unfair, the plummeting career satisfaction data reported by the Met Life Foundation (2012); the recent observations of the famed classroom teacher Rafe Esquith, who complained of teachers being "the scapegoat for factors beyond their control . . . and the unfair, often ridiculous expectations being placed on teachers" (2014, p. 20); and the old but persistent statistic: nearly 50 percent of all new teachers leave the profession within their first five years of teaching (Ingersoll, 2012).

As outside forces look to control more and more of what teachers do, teachers are feeling more and more dissatisfied with their careers. Like all professionals, teachers want to have control over their work so they may be thoughtful and creative and use judgment as they do it. They do not want to be just technicians following the commands of people who are not even present in their schools. Neither do they want their professional judgment to be focused solely on preparing students for standardized tests or following the other dictates coming from central authorities.

TEACHERS AS THINKERS, CREATORS, AND INNOVATORS

The influence of central planners imposing themselves on the teaching profession is compounded by a related issue. Readers may or may not be aware that in the 1990s there were two very positive developments in the professional lives of teachers and teacher education: professional development schools, PDSs, and professional learning communities, PLCs.

Both approaches are research-based concepts that signaled a departure from industrial age thinking focused on top-down controls, and both approaches looked to involve teachers in designing their own professional learning and the learning of students. In effect, these movements looked to make teacher thinking and creativity central to school operations. Both PDSs and PLCs are about teachers being involved in and leading schools' decision making about learning and schooling.

In the case of PDSs, local schools partner with universities and serve as sites for the induction of new teachers who would be under the supervision of both experienced teachers and university personnel while experiencing the everyday activity, practice, and culture of a school. In the case of PLCs, schools become places where teachers take responsibility for their professional development.

Briefly put, PLCs are formed when teachers get together on matters of learning: lesson design, lesson study, evaluation protocols, curriculum development, and/or ad hoc problem solving of all sorts. A PLC could be in a small-group situation where teachers exchange ideas about how social studies and English teachers might work together to teach a Victorian novel. Or, a PLC could be where teachers have come together to talk about how to insert emotional education into scientific lab work.

PLCs also can be large collectives, such as an entire school faculty. In these collectives teachers might discuss the standards, goals, and objectives of the school. PLCs are a very twenty-first-century concept because they invite thinking, reflection, imagination, and involvement. Most theorists would agree that PLCs are intended to invite not only teacher input but also teacher leadership (DuFour et al., 2006; Schlechty, 2002; Schmoker, 2006; Wenger et al., 2002).

Implicit in the creation of both PDSs and PLCs are two fundamental ideas. One is that professional learning is at its best when it is embedded in the work of teaching and participating in a community of practice (Lave & Wenger, 1991; Schlechty, 2009; Wenger et al., 2002).

This concept acknowledges that the real-world workplace is the real site of teacher learning. Yes, courses and degrees taken and earned at a college or university have a role, but the more important learning for teachers will come from what is embedded in their participation in a school. The greatest force for a teacher's professional development will come, then, on the job in a school, not from a degree program at a college or university.

The second guiding concept is that in a community of practice all members of a school should come together for collective learning and action as a result of that learning. In such communities teachers are expected to act as thinkers, creators, and innovators. Such a scenario acknowledges contemporary organizational theory, which sees all members of an organization as agents of change empowered to learn, reflect, and change the organization for continual improvement (Deming, 1986; Senge, 1990; Senge et al., 2000). It further recognizes the human need for continual learning and thoughtful, decisive participation in an organization. Such a scenario would promise very fulfilling careers to teachers as respected professionals charged with the continual improvement of their schools.

It is from this perspective that a problem presents itself. The problem is that in almost all cases, teacher educators send novice teachers to communities of practice that are situated in industrial age schools committed to top-down authority structures along with industrial age assumptions, practices, and culture.

By their very nature, schools of industrial age design do not see teachers as thinkers, creators, or innovators. They see teachers as technical workers whose job it is to convey information and skills to students in preparation for standardized testing. The most important decision making in these schools is taken away from teachers and given to central authorities not even present in the school or the district. In effect, the central premise of PDSs and PLCs of making teachers the thought leaders of schools is nullified.

Rick and Donna Adair Breault referred to this force of culture in their work, *Professional Development School: Researching Lessons from the Field*. In confronting issues of culture and the resulting implementation uncertainties in PDSs, they explain:

> This [implementation] is aggravated by the PDS typically being situated in a regular public school that is distracted by the necessity of its own technocratic preoccupation with state standards and high stakes testing. As a result, whatever idealistic potential there might have been

in the NCATE PDS standards is undermined by the bureaucratic, politically situated nature of their sponsoring organization, and the potential for critical reflections and naming PDSs through dialogic process is lost. (Breault & Breault, 2012, p. 23)

This circumstance forces many questions. Here are two: How can early career teachers enjoy and develop the ways of twenty-first-century learning and learning organizations in industrial age schools? How can teachers lead their own professional learning when their thinking is supplanted by the dictates of central planners who impose standards, goals, curricula, lesson design, and even scripts for what teachers should say as they deliver a lesson?

The answer to both of these questions is that teachers cannot. It is a logical impossibility. People learn what they do. When early career teachers begin their careers in industrial age schools, they will learn the industrial age assumptions, practices, and cultures of industrial age schools. As experienced teachers look to develop as professionals, they too will do so burdened with the assumptions, practices, and cultures of industrial age schools. They will not learn the assumptions and practices appropriate to a twenty-first-century learning organization. This conclusion has dark implications for teachers' professional development and their career satisfaction.

In the earliest stages, the advent of PDSs and PLCs appeared to be signs of change. Each appeared to be a movement toward new approaches in organizational thinking, but the truth is that both concepts have been perverted to fit into the cultures of industrial age schools. The primary indicator of this is, of course, that these programs are situated in schools of industrial age design with top-down authority structures that have an increasingly narrow focus on improving student scores on standardized tests and compliance with central planners.

More than likely readers are working in schools that employ the concept of PLCs. As a teacher in such a school, you probably know that when you work in a small PLC, there is an ardent focus on preparing students for taking standardized tests. Teacher input on topics other than test preparation is considered off topic. The assumptions, practices, and cultures of the industrial age receive no reconsideration.

But what if in the context of a PLC, a thoughtful young teacher were to say, "I don't think our emphasis on teaching to the test is a good approach"? What if another such thoughtful young teacher were to say, "I don't remember in any of the theory or research that I studied in college where it said that schools need an ardent focus on high-stakes, standardized testing"? How do readers think these observations would be received in their schools?

Forced into the restraints of industrial age schools, PDSs and PLCs will not function as they were intended. They will not engage teachers in thinking and reflecting on all of the factors of schooling and learning that need their attention. Instead, schools will treat teachers like factory workers and expect them to perform narrowly defined jobs in conveying information and skills to students for success on standardized tests. In doing this, the professional learning of teachers will be significantly diminished as well as their careers.

What is also very troublesome is that PDSs and PDCs, as they are now constituted in traditional schools, serve as props. They give the appearance of school leaders doing the right thing, of increasing teacher participation. PDSs and PDCs give the appearance of "change" and progressive thinking. But it is important to remember that as they currently exist in traditional schools, PDSs and PDCs are about appearances. They do not encourage teachers to think big picture or to question and reconsider the underlying assumptions, practices, or culture of their schools or the value of schools focusing on standardized test success.

THINKING FOR SCHOOLS SHOULD BE DONE IN SCHOOLS BY TEACHERS

It is in light of this condition that this book was written. As this book helps readers sort out what circumstances will make for a high-quality career, it will stipulate their fundamental need to be active learners, thinkers, creators, and innovators in all aspects of fully participating in a school.

This book will further stipulate that when learning, thoughtfulness, and creativity are diminished or removed from the work of teachers by outside forces, the career of teaching will be proportionately diminished. High-quality careers in teaching demand that the most important decision making about schooling be made by the people in the schools. A persistent theme of this book will be the rejection of teacher passivity and the need of teachers (and students) to assert control over their work and to act as learners, thinkers, creators, and innovators. Actions that minimize such participation will be seen as unhealthy for the career of teaching.

Readers who are familiar with Abraham Maslow's (1968) hierarchy of needs will remember that the need for self-actualization was the ultimate human need. This need drives people to seek out or create conditions that will allow for high levels of self-expression, creativity, and personal evolution. When this need is met, teachers will achieve a sense of fulfillment. When it is not, teachers will experience frustration, unhappiness, and a sense of incompleteness. In reaction to current conditions, this book is about teachers achieving fulfillment by creating, themselves, the conditions in schools for their own happiness and maximum evolution.

HOW TEACHER PREPARATION, PROFESSIONAL LEARNING, AND CAREERS IN TEACHING SHOULD EVOLVE

- Higher levels of education: more MAs, EdDs, and PhDs in local schools, where the greatest part of the degree work is done via research and program study *in* schools
- A focus on the techniques and mechanics of individualized learning
- Deeper psychological and developmental understanding of youths
- Deeper understanding of organizational design and self-organization in schooling
- Deeper understanding of the change process and its initiation in schools
- Greater involvement in research on learning and schooling
- Deeper subject/interdisciplinary expertise
- Knowledge of applications for interactive teaching machines, instructional software, online teaching, learning networks, open courseware and software, and other educational technology advances
- Deeper understanding of the nature and uses of collective learning
- Deeper understanding of community building for nurturing students and teachers
- Deeper understanding of the role of student voice in schools
- Deeper understanding of techniques in counseling learners
- Deeper understanding of how to assess and engage student interests
- Deeper understanding of scaffolding in human learning
- Deeper understanding of how to elicit intrinsic motivation in students
- Greater teacher leadership and responsibility for school success

WHY THE AUTHOR GOT INTERESTED IN READERS' CAREERS

Although the author has retired from teaching in an actual school, he has continued his focus on teaching by doing research in schools and completing a PhD. It was an easy transition because in the latter part of his career he got very involved in two areas: school reform and teacher education. During this period the author served on and chaired a site-based planning group that focused on school reform for a high school.

The objective of the committee was to create a better school. One of the reforms embraced by the committee was becoming a PDS. As with most schools, becoming a PDS involved partnering with a local university that prepared aspiring teachers for teaching.

Through this partnership, university students who believed they wanted to become teachers could begin visiting the high school for induction experiences as early as their sophomore year. These induction experiences would be many and varied and continue throughout college and right up to what is generally called "student teaching" and then into the early years of teaching. The committee and school staff wanted the induction process to be very thorough and thereby to increase the likelihood of new teachers' success and retention.

As in the development of any skill, the committee believed that situating novice teachers within a community of practice was the most reliable way to provide the full and sometimes tacit knowledge of teaching (Lave & Wenger, 1991) and the culture that surrounds it. One of the big benefits for our school was that staff members were able to observe and influence the growth of these young teachers, and the school often hired the most promising for positions that opened on the faculty. Everyone involved strongly believed then that situating teacher induction right in a school among those who practiced the art of teaching was a great idea. How could it not be?

Then the author began to see a problem in the late 1990s and early 2000s. My seeing the problem came from my involvement with the issue of high school reform, which was a popular issue at the time. What started to emerge was that in spite of all the committee's efforts, the school was not being reformed. Yes, over the years the school had improved its operations (and test scores) as the result of the attention of the site-based planning committee, but no changes had come in the basic structures of the school. No one was rethinking basic assumptions or practices.

This realization expanded as the author read more and more about the problems inherent in industrial age schools as well as the promise of changing them. There was more and more literature about new structures for and new assumptions about schooling and learning that could make for better schools. What was ultimately most troubling about all of this was what the author unavoidably concluded about his school as a PDS. It was, in effect, preparing teacher candidates, interns, and novice teachers for teaching in the *twentieth* century.

REFERENCES

Ben-Shahar, T. (2007). *Happier: Learn the secrets to daily joy and lasting fulfillment.* New York, NY: McGraw-Hill.

Blad, E. (2014). More than half of students "engaged" in school, says poll. Retrieved from http://www.edweek.org/ew/articles/2014/04/09/28gallup.h33.html?utm_source=fb&utm_medium=rss&utm_campaign=mrss&cmp=RSS-FEED.

Breault, R., & Breault, D. A. (2012). *Professional development schools: Researching lessons from the field.* Lanham, MD: Rowman & Littlefield Education.

Csikszentmihalyi, M. (1990). *Flow: The psychology of optimal experience.* New York, NY: Harper & Row.

Csikszentmihalyi, M. (1997). *Finding flow.* New York, NY: Basic Books.

Darling-Hammond, L. (2006). *Powerful teacher education: Lessons from exemplary programs.* San Francisco, CA: Jossey-Bass.

Deci, E. (1995). *Why we do what we do.* New York, NY: Penguin Books.

Deci, E., & Ryan, R. (1985). *Intrinsic motivation and self-determination in human behavior.* New York, NY: Plenum Press.

Deci, E., & Ryan, R. (2008). Self-determination theory: A macro-theory of human motivation, development, and health. *Canadian Psychology, 49*(3), 182–185.

Deming, W. E. (1986). *Out of crisis.* Cambridge, MA: Massachusetts Institute of Technology.

DuFour, R., DuFour, R., Eaker, R., & Many, T. (2006). *Learning by doing: A handbook for professional learning communities at work.* Bloomington, IN: Solution Tree.

Esquith, R. (2014). Can't wait for Monday. *Educational Leadership, 4*(5), p. 20.

Haidt, J. (2006). *The happiness hypothesis: Finding modern truth in ancient wisdom.* New York, NY: Basic Books.

Ingersoll, R. (2012). Beginning teacher induction: What the data tell us. Retrieved from http://www.edweek.org/ew/articles/2012/05/16/kappan_ingersoll.h31.html

Lave, J., & Wenger, E. (1991). *Situated learning: Legitimate peripheral participation.* New York, NY: Cambridge University Press.

Maslow, A. (1954). *Motivation and personality.* New York, NY: Harper & Row.

Maslow, A. (1968). *Toward a psychology of being* (2nd ed.). New York, NY: Van Nostrand Reinhold.

Met Life Foundation. (2012). The Met Life Survey of the American teacher: Challenges for school leadership. Retrieved from https://www.metlife.com/assets/cao/foundation/MetLife-Teacher-Survey-2012.pdf

Schlechty, P. C. (2002). *Working on the work: An action plan for teachers, principals, and superintendents.* San Francisco, CA: Jossey-Bass.

Schlechty, P. C. (2009). *Leading for learning: How to transform schools into learning organizations.* San Francisco, CA: Jossey-Bass.

Schmoker, M. (2006). *Results now: How we can achieve unprecedented improvement in teaching and learning.* Alexandria, VA: Association for Supervision and Curriculum Development.

Seligman, M. E. P. (2002). *Authentic happiness.* New York, NY: Free Press.

Senge, P. (1990). *The fifth discipline: The art and practice of the learning organization.* New York, NY: Doubleday.

Senge, P., Cambron-McCabe, N., Lucas, T., Smith, B., Dutton, J., & Kleiner, A. (2000). *Schools that learn: A fifth discipline fieldbook for educators, parents, and everyone who cares about education.* New York, NY: Doubleday.

Senge, P., Scharmer, C. O., Jaworski, J., & Flowers, B. S. (2004). *Presence: Exploring profound change in people, organizations, and society.* New York, NY: Currency Doubleday.

Wenger, E., McDermott, R., & Snyder, W. (2002). *Cultivating communities of practice.* Cambridge, MA: Harvard Business Review Press.

Introduction

A fantasy: The year is 2016. A young teacher is being interviewed by a school principal and a committee comprising other administrators, community members, teachers, and a student. The principal thinks of himself as progressive but also the leader of a tight ship, a smooth operation. The school has a reputation for high standards and academic achievement. The committee members have asked the young teacher candidate many questions trying to determine how well she will relate to teenagers and be an overall fit for their school.

As a courtesy, at the end of their questions, they ask the candidate whether she has any questions for them. She does: "I have a question that comes out of my concern for student learning but also for my own professional development. Does this school have a plan in place for moving away from the industrial age assumptions and practices of a traditional school and toward a twenty-first-century school? I mean, do you have something on paper? Do you have functioning committees? Could you cite for me some of the forward movement that your school has accomplished in the past few years?"

Everyone on the committee is speechless. They start looking at one another to see who might speak first. The candidate overhears one person whisper to another, "What does she mean industrial age assumptions and practices and twenty-first-century school?" After an awkward silence, the superintendent speaks up and gives a boilerplate statement about the school's sterling reputation and its high test scores. He thanks the candidate for her interest, and the meeting is concluded. As the candidate gets up, a book falls from her lap to the floor. It is this book, *Teaching Evolution: A Guidebook to the Advancement of Teaching, Teacher Education, and Happier Careers for Early Career Teachers.*

TAKE A PERSONAL STAKE IN TEACHING

The purpose of this book is to support the leadership of early career teachers in the creation of happier careers. In spite of this broad social-change agenda, the author's desire is for this book to be as personal as possible. His intent is that in the course of reading, early career teachers will be helped to sort things out so that in the end they have more clarity about how the current circumstances of the teaching profession are likely to affect them and their careers in personal ways. He intends for the book to stir them out of an old mind-set and toward thinking about how they would like to advance the teaching profession.

Asking readers to look at the teaching profession in this personal way will be a persistent theme in this book. In fact, readers will see later on in this book that the value of taking such a personal view of teaching is supported by a great deal of research. Expecting the profession of teaching to offer teachers personal rewards is not about being selfish. It is about wanting the right conditions for teachers to be fully alive and engaged as they facilitate strong personal connections with students and redirect schools away from distant, controlling, impersonal forces.

THREE PROBLEMS

There are, however, a few inherent problems in raising the issue of change with all educators. One problem is the idea of teacher learning itself. A common belief about schools is that they are places for students to learn. Although it is critical to the reconception of schools, the idea that schools are places for teachers to learn is much less common. The idea that schools are places where we grow teachers is not an industrial age concept.

Moreover, while the concepts of professional learning communities and professional development schools support the idea that schools are places for teachers to learn, the fact that both concepts have by and large been situated in industrial age schools has largely defeated the practical benefits of both. Getting readers and other educators to reconceive of schools as places specifically designed for teacher learning will mean abandoning long-held beliefs about the purpose of schools. That will not be easy. It might not be easy even for readers.

The second problem is that among educators the topic of change has a tendency to invite cynicism. Most educators have lived their careers dealing with this change and that change, most of which have passed away leaving very little changed. Add to this, as this book will demonstrate, that educators have resisted change while pretending to make it an urgent matter. Certainly readers know that educators are forever talking about change, new programs, and new policies. At the same time not much really changes. This book will describe this phenomenon in detail. Educator resistance to change will not be an easy concept to accept.

This brings us to the third and biggest problem. The author has been using terms such as "industrial age school" or "industrial age assumptions and practices." Most people don't know what these terms mean. Many educators don't know what they mean. Maybe readers don't know what they mean. It is very likely that most of the people on the principal's interview committee in the preceding fantasy didn't know what they meant.

However, in the opening fantasy scene there is the implication of something wrong, perhaps harmful, about the industrial age assumptions and practices of a traditional school. If that is the impression readers got, they got it right. This book will clarify for readers that becoming teachers in industrial age schools will be harmful to them, their students, and their careers.

Wow, that assertion is pretty out there. When the author makes it, he knows he is straining his credibility. Readers are likely thinking "How is that possible? Are people somehow damaged because they went to an industrial age school?" This author's credibility is further strained by the fact that most people went to industrial age schools and look back at them with some fond memories. Everyone accepts the schools they attended as what a school is.

Within this mind-set few people are aware of the industrial age heritage of our schools. They don't know that our schools were modeled after factories and that many of the common practices in schools, even today, were borrowed from factories. Still fewer know of any other kind of school that is experimenting with new ways of learning. People think "Schools are schools. It's those big buildings with the long hallways and teachers teaching in front of students sitting in rows. So, what is this idea of harm from industrial age schools?"

The answer to that question is what this book is about. The task of this book is to help readers understand the harm, leave behind the industrial age mind-set, and envision a new kind of schooling based on new ideas more appropriate to the twenty-first century. In doing this, this book will also clarify the need for teachers to take the lead in taking teaching to a new place.

After having read this book, readers, like the teacher candidate in the fantasy, will likely want to raise some of the following questions with school leaders:

- Is this school providing me with professional learning that embraces all of the new knowledge and capacities available in the twenty-first century?
- Is there a plan in place for moving away from industrial age organizational concepts and toward a new premise for schools and new structures for schooling?
- Are those leading my professional learning employing many of the new models for both teacher and student learning?

These questions raise yet another question for readers. What if readers raise these questions, and their answers are, in effect, no? The term "in effect" is used because the author doesn't believe readers will get a straight answer. There will be hemming and hawing, word parsing, and qualifying. Readers will probably be asked "What do you mean?" Their leaders will make an effort to justify themselves. But in the end, if readers realize that there is no plan to move away from industrial age thinking and toward newly conceived schools, where will that leave them? Where will it leave students? Where will it leave their careers?

THE LOOK OF LEADERSHIP

During the preparation of this book, there was a significant event in a Seattle, Washington, school district. Teachers made a decision to boycott the administration of a standardized test called MAP, Measure of Academic Progress. According to the *Seattle Times* newspaper, teachers at Garfield School made a decision to boycott the test because in the words of a leading teacher, Rachel Ells, "I don't want to spend my time or my students' time on something that is not useful or beneficial" (Shaw, 2013).

Later the boycott received the endorsement of the staffs of a number of nearby schools and the support of a number of high-profile education scholars. Whether readers agree with the position taken by these teachers does not matter. What readers are being asked to see is that some teachers in Garfield School had a point of view and they had enough confidence in that point of view to take a stand. They did not just go along to get along. It is offered to readers as an example of teacher leadership. This book is about readers getting intellectually ready to take a stand and guide the teaching profession.

BECOMING READY TO TAKE A STAND

In the course of reading this book, readers will be asked to consider a variety of educational issues related to schools. Broadly stated, this book will raise the issues of how schools use time, place, resources, and people along with what students should learn, how they should learn it, and how learning should be evaluated and certified for credit. At every juncture, there will be difficult decisions to be made about what is best for students and whether schools should change. Readers will be asked to make decisions about whether schools should continue doing what they have been doing or experiment and try something new.

In any case, there is an absolute at hand: Like many of our schools, the career of teaching is in crisis. As this crisis unfolds and begins to impinge on life inside schools, there are going to be people who attempt to manage or lead a response. It could be the politicians in federal, state, and local governments. It could be policy advocates from colleges and universities. It could be local or national unions. It could be readers' local school leaders. It could be outside for-profit or nonprofit contractors. Or, it could be teachers—teachers in individual, local schools making decisions for the unique conditions in their schools. This book is about teachers taking the lead.

TEACHERS SHOULD TAKE THE LEAD

An important consideration in why teachers should lead change has to do with why people become teachers in the first place. Why do people want to be teachers? Readers need to consider this speculation about teachers' answers and take time to answer this question for themselves.

Readers probably want to be teachers because they have a special empathy for young people. They perhaps have some deeper than average sensibility for the joys and difficulties of being a kid. They probably have memories of a number of teachers whose sensitivity to them proved crucial in their own development. That memory drives them to be there for young people. And they probably have a special feeling for the role of teachers in clarifying how learning advances personal development and a good life. They might say to people who ask why they wanted to be teachers that they "felt drawn to teaching."

With these motives readers are going to derive satisfaction from teaching when they see that their unique, personal interactions with students result in learning, mature decisions, and all-around better lives. And that satisfaction will be clearest and most gratifying when it happens in the context of a personal relationship. Yes, readers will find satisfaction in their grades and promotions, but they will see it most in the personal feedback they get from students.

It will be the times when students come to their door for extra help, just to have a talk, to get their opinion about a choice, to sign their yearbooks, to request a letter of recommendation, to apologize, to ask for their intervention, or to say thank-you that will satisfy the reasons readers have for being teachers.

REMEMBER: THIS IS PERSONAL

It is important that readers remember this moment in the reading of this book. It is important that they remember how they felt drawn to teaching. It is important to remember that they have personal reasons and purposes for becoming teachers, all of which have to do with being there for students. They must remember that their motivation for all of this was intrinsic. They always knew the primary rewards for teaching were going to be personal, not financial.

It should be injected at this point that when teachers enter the profession for these human rewards, they are doing so for precisely the right reasons. It is the enjoyment of the individual contacts with students and of being part of a caring community dedicated to learning that should be the motivation. The core of schooling should be the personal and caring support teachers give to learners. It is in the context of this thinking that teachers must take the lead.

If, however, teachers have come into the profession with the motives just described, they are not going to be happy if they don't get the human benefits they desire. Unfortunately, the possibility of teachers no longer being able to derive these personal satisfactions from their profession looms ever larger in the future of education. For many years now, teachers have been seeing that forces outside of themselves, outside of their classrooms, and outside of their schools are controlling what is happening in their schools and classrooms. These outside forces are dictating standards, curriculum choices, lesson design, evaluation methods, and more.

TEACHERS CONTROLLING THEIR OWN DESTINIES

In the face of these circumstances, this book will present readers with questions derived from their experience, the author's experience, and research. This will be done to provoke deep thought about what makes for a high-quality career experience. In so doing, this book will develop an important theme that revolves around concepts with which the author has close knowledge as a researcher. These include such concepts as agency, ownership of learning, self-determination, self-regulation, autonomy, independence, and intrinsic motivation.

All of these concepts come together in a notion of motivation that may be stated this way: Schools function best when they create the conditions whereby teachers and students motivate themselves in learning and building self-determined communities of caring and achievement.

In such schools it will be recognized that people are driven to various pursuits in life by intrinsic, personal motives. People like to make choices as they follow their pursuits. People like to control their choices and the paths they follow to enjoy the outcomes they want.

All people want to believe their actions come from inside them, not from outside, controlling forces. An underlying concept in this book about teaching is that teachers will need to assert self-determination in their work and will want ownership of their profession. If teachers don't have this ownership, they are not going to derive the intrinsic and personal rewards they are seeking, and they are not going to be happy. The developments in Seattle are just one example of this.

SOME PERSPECTIVE ON SCHOOL ACCOUNTABILITY

This is not a book about standardized testing, but it can't be ignored because the testing and all of the preparation associated with it frame the world of contemporary teachers. Thus, the example from Seattle is timely. As early career teachers, readers have entered the profession when school accountability and standardized testing issues are at a peak. The author would like to give some perspective on how these accountability issues have become such a dominating force in all levels of schooling.

The author has been a school teacher for a long time. He began teaching in 1969. From this experience he knows that standardized tests were used back in the 1950s and probably earlier. They were not used, however, by the state to monitor local schools. As an act of professionalism, local schools used them for their own purposes in measuring student learning. He should also explain that he went to public schools that were very smooth operations, very orderly, very purposeful. Most of the teachers were competent and committed, and the students were generally polite and obedient. If they were not, the consequences were usually severe.

The author graduated from high school in 1964. Five years later, he graduated from college and went looking for a teaching position. Shortly before he graduated, he had opportunities to observe a number of high schools in different states. One was the school from which he had graduated. In all of these schools, he noticed almost immediately that schools had changed in the five years since he had graduated. This was also true of the school where he landed his first teaching position, which, by the way, was quite similar to the one he had attended as a teenager.

Yet, it was different. It was now the late 1960s and kids seemed more restless and less compliant. The hallways were a little noisier. Student attire was a little rougher. Everybody's hair was longer. Foul language was more common. Rebellion was in vogue. Jimi Hendrix and The Rolling Stones were climbing the music charts, and rules did not have quite the same meaning as when he was younger. Consequently, teachers spent more time in the hallways and during instruction reprimanding students and trying to maintain order.

In the faculty lounge, as it was referred to then, amidst the cigarette smoke, there was incessant talk of discipline issues. Practically every day a teacher would come through the lounge door telling a story of some outrageous student behavior. One student had told a respected veteran teacher to go f— himself, and his response was to go around humming a famous Perry Como song, "It's Impossible." It always got a big laugh in the lounge. Another teacher loved telling his tale of a student who actually urinated in the classroom trash can when denied a bathroom pass.

Teachers constantly impugned the administrators for not properly holding kids accountable for their behavior. Administrators retorted that they couldn't suspend the whole school and added that setting a standard for an orderly classroom was the teacher's job. In all of this, it was becoming clear to this young teacher that many teachers were increasingly disenchanted with a position that in years past had been held in high regard. Add to this that this author had to deal with his own student discipline issues, which often shocked him and sent him home with a knot in his stomach.

In the faculty lounge discussions, teachers began to invoke cynical remarks, such as "You can lead a horse to water.... If the kids don't want to learn, you can't make 'em." One insisted, "My mantra is the 14th and the 28th [pay days]. That's what gets me through the day." Another achieved fame for saying "My main learning objective for today: get through without an incident." Teachers would say it to each other in the hallways—"Get through without an incident."

As year led to year, the author was seeing more and more that teachers had become discouraged, and he could see it in their classrooms. In response to what often seemed like impossible circumstances, many teachers developed techniques for maintaining control that involved less and less interaction with students and, sadly, less and less actual teaching.

Teachers created lessons such as outline the chapter here in class using the model on the board, no talking. Complete these worksheets and submit them before you leave today, no talking. Watch this movie and take notes to be submitted by the end of class, no talking. Read this story and do the questions at the end of the chapter, no talking. There was a lot of going through the motions of delivering lessons and doing the job without really doing the job. The author recalls that teachers' use of sick time became a big concern during this period, especially on Mondays and Fridays.

While all of this went on, with student behavior becoming more and more difficult, most students passed their classes and graduated. Teachers realized that if they failed a student, that would mean meetings, confrontations, investigation of their records, and lots of aggravation. If all the students passed, there was none of that. Add to this, that if a teacher took a stand and failed a nonperforming student, the principal would often assert what was called his "magic pen" in the final record book, and these students would pass and go on to graduate anyway.

In the face of all of this, many teachers, understandably, took the path of least resistance. Most teachers did the best they could but also agreed that they couldn't let the school defeat them. They couldn't let it drive them crazy. Meanwhile one of the most popular news stories of the era involved a young man who was suing his school district because he had graduated school without learning to read and write. Although this became a big, shocking topic on TV and radio, it is unlikely that people who worked in schools were surprised. They knew how the system worked.

The author must confess that he was not unaffected by all of this. As he began to get a feel for the school culture and how the game was played, he invented his own low-stress, high-control lessons and watched carefully what other teachers were doing to maintain a sense of well-being in what seemed like an environment out of control. Like most teachers, he began to use sick days strategically. He challenged student behavior less. He softened his grading standards and did the best he could with students who wanted to learn.

Looking back, he can see that this was an early stage of his induction into the game of school (a topic to be explored later). Yes, he knows now that he was very confused. He was a person who believed deeply in the value of schooling, and he wanted to be a great teacher like several who had touched him. He became a teacher probably for the same reasons readers have. Nevertheless, he saw himself beginning to give up a little. He was adopting cynical practices and feeling increasingly less satisfied with what he was doing. But what do people do when they feel no control?

When in the middle 1970s word came down from the state that there was going to be standardized testing to check whether students were actually learning in school, he was not at all surprised. It was quite evident to him that schools were in crisis. Standardized testing seemed reasonable. Fast-forward twenty-five years to the coming of the No Child Left Behind law and testing for annual yearly progress, and the whole accountability movement was in high gear. This has been intensified by the coming of Race to the Top, which now holds individual teachers accountable for the performance of their students.

THIS IS YOUR SCENE

It is in this era of ardent accountability schemes that early career teachers now find themselves. It is an era in which education leaders talk about change, twenty-first-century skills, and learning organizations while at the same time doubling down on industrial age concepts, such as central planning, top-down controls, standardization, and micromanaging teachers.

What is worse is that the accountability movement is basically a statement of distrust directed at teachers. The federal government and most states have, in effect, said that they will not trust local schools and their teachers to develop and judge the competencies of students so that when students graduate, they actually have those competencies. It's a less than inspiring message for teachers from their government.

But this situation forces a question. With a new mission and the right training and leadership, could teachers be empowered and entrusted to properly develop and accurately assess student competencies? Could teachers in local schools form contracts of trust with local municipalities to provide the best of both for youth? The answer is absolutely yes, they could. Teachers do have that capacity, and there is increasing evidence of it. The publication of *Schools That Learn* (Senge et al., 2000) documented a broad array of schools in which teachers were driving innovation and assuming more responsibility for school success.

More recent evidence of such teacher leadership is captured in the work *Trusting Teachers with School Success* by Farris-Berg, Dirkswager, and Junge (2012). One of the most forward-looking books of the past decade, it provides both a thorough rationale and many examples of how trusting teachers has resulted in school success while providing teachers opportunities for more fulfilling careers.

The fact is that with a new mission, teachers could do a better job and without the costly accountability bureaucracy, estimated at approaching $2 billion annually (Ujifusa, 2012), which has been imposed on schools so that central authorities may assert control from afar. Those central authorities steal professionalism from our teachers and cast a shadow over the career of teaching, a shadow any self-respecting professional should want to escape.

To address the issues of change and teachers' career quality, this book has three parts, each one prescribing steps that will provide early career teachers a sound basis for advancing the evolution of teaching.

Part I presents reasons for moving away from the industrial age school model. Step 1 involves an examination of the issue of change itself and how educators have dealt with it to this point. Step 2 involves examining the assumptions, structures, and practices that are common to industrial age schools and presents research that suggests the need for new assumptions, structures, and practices. Then, in step 3, readers are engaged in an examination of the industrial age school culture and how it is best captured in the concept of the game of school.

Part II involves steps in becoming aware of four positive forces in the twenty-first century that promise great change in educational thinking and will help readers envision new kinds of schools. Step 4 involves understanding the concept of school engagement; step 5, the emerging marketplace of educational experiences; step 6, the idea of students as voluntary customers; and step 7, the advent of twenty-first-century skills and learning organizations. All of these forces contribute greatly to building the rationale for new kinds of schools and better career experiences for teachers.

Part III addresses the issue of envisioning new kinds of schools. It presents how teachers can break away from the old mental models of school and the premise of standardization and move toward envisioning schools that operate from a different premise, individualization. Because the focus of this section is on envisioning new kinds of schools, steps 8 and 9 will be presented as a narrative description. Step 10 then focuses on concrete actions teachers can take to start and lead change toward better schools and happier careers.

There is a simple question for teachers: Is there a better way? This is the same question the author faced some twenty years ago when he got interested in school reform and teacher education. Can stakeholders conceive of new ways of schooling? Are there ways of schooling that are more satisfying to everybody involved and whereby teachers and students are really learning? Can educators conceive of schools in which teachers' evaluations of students are trusted and not challenged by costly state and federal bureaucracies? Can educators conceive of schools that are not micromanaged from afar but where teachers are empowered to think and innovate?

BACK TO THE FANTASY

The fantasy has an ending: Now the year is 2031. The woman being interviewed earlier has now been an educator for fifteen years. Her name is Rena Watson, and she will be part of the narrative in chapters 8 and 9. Most schools no longer have principals, but this educator does have a leadership role. She is referred to as a learning development coordinator (LDC). On this day she interviews a young man wanting to become a learning and development specialist in the Arts in the Sciences Community, which is part of a network of smaller schools that serves three contiguous municipalities. The interview is being conducted by Rena, two learning and development specialists, two parents, and six students.

The session is more of a conversation than an old-style interview, but as it concludes, the committee extends the courtesy of inviting any final questions from the candidate. The candidate takes a serious tone and explains, "Yes, I have a question that comes out of my concern for student learning and my own professional development. Could you give me specific examples of and, if possible, show me how your school has moved away from industrial age thinking and embraced new concepts in schooling and learning?"

Rena smiles at the question. Eager to respond, she then asks a student to use his mobile device to project the school's organic growth map onto the wall. When the candidate sees the map with lines and circles going in every direction, there is an expression of relief. What he sees does not reflect the old uniformity of structures, compartmentalization, standardization, or linear thinking. He explains, "Oh, it's great to see how learning communities grow organically. One connection leads to another and another, and so much of it is spontaneous. It looks like this school really does pay attention to new possibilities for learning."

Rena identifies immediately with the candidate's concerns. She thinks, "I like this person's outlook." She ponders for another moment, looks at her watch, and says, "We'd like to take you on a tour. Could we set something up for tomorrow?"

That tour will run through chapters 8 and 9. Seeing is believing.

REFERENCES

Farris-Berg, K., Dirkswager, E., & Junge, A. (2012). *Trusting teachers with school success: What happens when teachers call the shots.* Lanham, MD: Rowman & Littlefield Education.

Senge, P., Cambron-McCabe, N., Lucas, T., Smith, B., Dutton, J., & Kleiner, A. (2000). *Schools that learn: A fifth discipline fieldbook for educators, parents, and everyone who cares about education.* New York, NY: Doubleday.

Shaw, L. (2013). Teachers' test boycott draws growing support. Retrieved from http://seattletimes.com/html/education/2020185045_mapprotestxml.html

Ujifusa, A. (2012). Standardized testing costs states $1.7 billion a year, study says. Retrieved from http://www.edweek.org/ew/articles/2012/11/29/13testcosts.h32.html

I

Make a Choice: The Industrial Age School or New Kinds of Schools?

ONE

Guiding Step 1: Get Perspective on the Career of Teaching and the Possibilities for Change

Most early career teachers will start their careers in traditional schools of industrial age design. In this circumstance these teachers will be influenced by two competing forces. On the one hand, teachers will see outside of school that society and the world are changing rapidly. With the influence of new technology, along with new thinking about organizations, schools, and learning, the number of options for learning is expanding exponentially.

On the other hand, teachers may also observe that within schools there is a deep reluctance to change and to let go of industrial age thinking. Standardized testing keeps teachers focused on old learning models. Professional development is often limited to strategies for teaching to the standardized tests. Legacy comfort zones dispose our veteran educators and policy leaders to keep schools the way they have been. Early career teachers are caught between these two forces.

What follows in Part I is three chapters that guide readers through an examination of the assumptions, practices, and cultures of industrial age schools. This examination is structured so readers may see contrasts between the assumptions, practices, and cultures that drive society's industrial age schools now and new assumptions, practices, and cultures for the newly conceived schools of the future.

The question at hand is whether readers see the advantages of change. Do readers believe the existing assumptions, practices, and cultures of schools should be reconsidered and changed or should our society continue to rely on them? Can readers imagine teaching, learning, and schooling in ways that are very different from what they know and are used to? Can readers envision how change would translate into better student learning and better careers for teachers?

To help readers answer these questions, this chapter presents clear contrasts between existing traditional schools and newly conceived schools of the future. To achieve this contrast, readers are asked to recall the basic demands schools make on teachers by considering the lives of the teachers in the schools from which they graduated.

WHAT TEACHERS DO IN INDUSTRIAL AGE SCHOOLS

In these schools, for most teachers the average day started early in the morning. Teachers arrived at school sometime between 7:00 a.m. and 8:00 a.m. They probably began the day by grabbing a cup of coffee, having some quick conferences, and doing some preparation work. In short order they had a homeroom or other format for taking student attendance. There they took attendance, handled some absentee notes, and kept order so students could listen to some morning announcements on school media.

After this, most teachers began their teaching day of five or six classes, within which they would also have a prep period, duty period, and lunch break. As part of teaching these five or six classes, teachers would have to prepare lessons for two to five different courses. It was a lot of preparation. In each of the teachers' classes there would have likely been fifteen to thirty-five students. After teaching five or six hours during the day, most teachers would have had some sort of extracurricular activity that would keep them at school until 5:00 p.m. or 6:00 p.m.

Within this framework, the teachers' day was extremely complex. First there was instruction. Teachers would stand in front of a classroom full of students and guide them through a lesson. They already understood that it was a real challenge to keep the attention of the multitasking generation they faced, one that was used to doing and attending to many things at once. But they were prepared with a novel approach that kept students engaged. Still, there was the issue of who was ready for the lesson because they had done the homework and who wasn't because they hadn't.

While instructing, there would also be occasional interruptions from students with questions, some of which would be excellent. Some would be less inspiring requests: "Could you repeat that because I didn't get it," which the teacher knew meant somebody wasn't paying attention. Then there would have been hallway noise distractions and distractions out the window. There were building management distractions, such as fire drills, emergency intercom announcements, and administrators walking through classrooms. There were gum chewing distractions and general misbehavior distractions.

When the bell rang, a half-dozen students would go up to the teachers' desks to ask personal issue questions related or unrelated to the lesson. In that moment these teachers were probably thinking of many things at once: the answers to student questions, what they needed to be doing in the next few minutes, where they needed to go for the next class, a personal item overlooked at home, what's that ruckus in the hallway, and on and on.

Then there was the grading of student work and the preparation of yet more classes to teach. There was also paperwork required by administration for one good reason or another. Along the way still more students would come by to ask for meetings at times other than during class, perhaps during teachers' prep time or before or after school. These teachers would also be advised that parents had called and would like return calls or a meeting with the guidance counselor or an administrator.

And, sometime during the week these teachers would conference with their departments or a regular professional learning community, where they planned and developed lessons or curriculum together. Perhaps three or four times a month the entire faculty would meet to advance school priorities.

It also should be clear that in the course of the work these teachers did, they would apply some long-held beliefs and practices. Here are some of them. These teachers accepted and worked within the idea that all of the important, certifiable learning happened in the same building, the school. School was where students learned all the important things they needed to prepare for work or college and otherwise advance in life. Thus students were given credit for their work in school. They also accepted the idea that what students were supposed to learn was neatly separated into subjects, such as math, history, English, biology, and so on.

These teachers also accepted and applied the idea of using textbooks so everything the students had to learn was neatly put together in one place. They endorsed the idea of having a lot of required classes with just a few electives—there were just a lot of things people really needed to know, so they had better learn them in school.

Teachers also fully endorsed that students' important learning would come from classroom instruction. After all, research has shown that the most important factor in school learning was effective teaching (Gordon, Kane, & Staiger, 2006; Hanushek, 2011; Haycock, 1998; National Commission on Teaching and America's Future, 1996; Sanders & Rivers, 1996; Wright, Horn, & Sanders, 1997).

These teachers also endorsed the idea that schooling meant students would have a certain number of classes during school (five to eight) every day. In addition, they endorsed the idea of teachers evaluating students and giving students grades (A, B, C, D, F), giving students awards (e.g., for journalism, athletics, or scientific projects), and giving students a rank (top ten and so on). They believed all of this would make students work harder.

School leaders liked the idea that all of the classes were lined up along the hallways of the school so they were easy to check. Everyone liked the idea that teachers taught a certain number of classes each day and that everything they should teach was outlined in the school curriculum manual.

With this manual teachers knew what they were supposed to teach from day to day. Everyone endorsed the idea of school being exactly four years. Teachers also liked the idea that by teaching their classes every day, they would earn their salary, month by month, for the year. All personnel liked the idea that after thirty years or more, teachers and administrators could retire and get a good pension.

While engaging in these standard practices and asserting these beliefs, teachers would take time to meet with students individually, sometimes on a crisis basis. It was in those moments that they would get the intrinsic rewards of teaching. They would help students to understand. They would help students begin to enjoy important subjects. They would help them get over an emotional hurdle. They would play a critical adult role in affirming the value of students as people, and the students would never forget them for it.

> **A Career Diminished**
> **Working in industrial age schools, teachers will continue to think of themselves as conveyors of knowledge instead of stewards of full human development.**

Teachers with even minimal experience could probably add much more detail to what has been developed here. As a finishing touch, it might be added that this routine went on five days a week, except for holidays, for about 180 days each school year. One school year was separated from the next by a ten-week vacation during the summer months, from June to September.

Recalling all of this detail in the work of teachers will be helpful in understanding this book. On the one hand, it will serve most early career teachers as a frame of reference for what teachers do. On the other hand, it will help establish a contrast with things to come. As early career teachers consider this description of the lives of teachers, they might notice a couple of things. One, the schools that early career teachers went to were not that much different from those where they are teaching or about to teach right now.

Two, the schools they went to were not much different from the ones the author went to in the early 1960s. By a variety of accounts, the schools in the 1960s were not much different from those that existed at the turn of the twentieth century, more than a hundred years ago. In fact, the schools that society provides youths today have been about the same for more than a century (Hess, 1999; Senge et al., 2000; Tyack & Cuban, 1995).

Readers may respond, "So, is that a problem?" After all, many great people have graduated from such schools, and they have gone on to make magnificent contributions to society. So, what could be the problem?

As it turns out, yes, there is and has been a problem, and the problem was noticed decades ago. In the latter part of the twentieth century increasing evidence emerged that students were not learning like they should (Coleman, 1959; National Commission on Excellence in Education, 1983).

As indicated in the introduction, schools in the United States had been going through some turmoil about the time the author started teaching in the late 1960s. However, in the view of a growing number of educators, the problem with schools was not as simple as discipline or classroom instruction. There was a problem with the system itself (Acker-Hocevar et al., 2006; Davis, 2007; Goldspink, 2007; Goldspink & Kay, 2003; Senge et al., 2000; Wagner et al., 2006).

That system had been designed in a different era to accomplish different goals. Thus many observers forwarded the idea of changing schools as organizations. Some said schools needed to be reformed. Some said schools needed to be transformed. But there was general agreement that students needed to learn more and big changes needed to be made in schools to accomplish that.

What was wrong with the system? The fact is that schools as we know them were designed in the middle of the nineteenth century. Their design was intended to accommodate large numbers of immigrants to help them learn reading and writing and to increase the likelihood of their succeeding in and meeting the needs of American democratic society.

To do this, schools were modeled after an institution that was much admired at the time, the industrial age factory. Yes, our schools were modeled after factories. They attempted to produce as many people who could read and write as efficiently as possible and with as little expense as possible. In their work, *Schools That Learn*, Senge et al. (2000) gave the following description of such schools:

> [E]ducators of the mid-nineteenth century explicitly borrowed their new designs from the factory-builders they admired. The result was an industrial-age system fashioned in the image of the assembly line, the icon of the booming industrial age. In fact, school may be the starkest example in modern society of an entire institution modeled after the assembly line. Like any assembly line, the system was organized in discrete stages called grades that segregated children by age. Everyone was supposed to move from stage to stage together. Each stage had local supervisors—the teachers responsible for it. Classes of twenty to

forty students met for specified periods in a scheduled day to drill for tests. The whole school was designed to run at a uniform speed, complete with bells and rigid daily time schedules. Each teacher knew what had to be covered in order to keep the line moving, even though he or she had little influence on its preset speed, which was determined by school boards and standardized curricula. (p. 31)

Without taking readers through a lot of organizational theory, many observers came to believe that it was time to reconsider the design of our schools. In that spirit, many new designs for schools were advanced. Consider what follows.

SCHOOL REFORM: MAGIC OR REAL?

Having taken time to look carefully at the schools from which readers and the author graduated has helped in gaining some perspective. For more than a century, those leaders who have guided the practices of schools have never acted on the idea to change one of the previously cited practices—not one. That fact should lead to concern. How is it possible? Were all of the cited practices so perfect that no one ever saw the need to replace even one of them? Did neither experience nor research ever suggest a better way? The world is changing so rapidly, but schools don't change at all. How is that possible?

The reality is, however, that many fine thinkers and researchers have seen signs of failure in our schools. Over the past century numerous writers, researchers, and theorists have advanced many ideas about how schools should change. Numerous books and articles have been written. For whatever reason, however, large-scale change among our public schools never took hold.

Then came a turning point in 1983. Yet another study of American schools was conducted and a report was published. The report was called *A Nation at Risk: The Imperative for Educational Reform: A Report to the Nation and the Secretary of Education, United States Department of Education* (National Commission on Excellence in Education, 1983). This report came out not long after that difficult period in schools that the author discussed in the introduction. It explained that students were simply not learning enough in schools and that schools needed to change for many reasons. Since that report was published there has been a vigorous discussion among adults at all levels of government, in colleges and universities, and among school teachers and school leaders about how to change schools.

In the 1990s there was a huge push to reform schools through legislation as well as public and private initiatives. The primary legislation was called Goals 2000, and it provided many millions of dollars to schools to encourage reform. Many private endowments also provided millions for this purpose.

Also around this time an educator named Ted Sizer published a number of very popular books proposing compelling ideas for change in high schools, including *Horace's School: Redesigning the American High School* (1992) and *Horace's Compromise: The Dilemma of the American High School* (2004). Also, Sizer's work in a movement out of Brown University, called the Coalition of Essential Schools, contributed greatly to the thinking about how to change schools.

Additionally, in the 1990s and early 2000s, the National Association of Secondary School Principals (NASSP) published two fine works about school reform, *Breaking Ranks: Changing an American Institution* (1999) and *Breaking Ranks II: Strategies for Leading School Reform* (2004). Each work advanced thoughtful, research-based strategies for secondary school reform and provided guidelines for how educators working together should proceed. In the meantime there was an exhaustive literature published on the need for and the promise of school reform.

Now it is more than thirty years since the publication of *A Nation at Risk*. The outcome of all the research, all the writing, and all the discussion: no change in the vast majority of schools. Schools still operate in factory style, and the curricula and physical structure remain pretty much the way they were a century ago. The professionals, with all of their talk about reform, were unable to change schools. That, by the way, includes this author.

Mind you that the difficulty with schools changing was not lost on many education observers. What ensued was a spate of books on the difficulty with changing schools. These books included titles such as *The Predictable Failure of Educational Reform: Can We Change Course Before It Is Too Late?* (Sarason, 1990), *Tinkering Toward Utopia: A Century of Public School Reform* (Tyack & Cuban, 1995), *Spinning Wheels: The Politics of Urban School Reform* (Hess, 1999), and *Left Back: A Century of Failed School Reforms* (Ravitch, 2000).

There was also *Schools That Learn: A Fifth Discipline Fieldbook for Educators, Parents, and Everyone Who Cares about Education* (Senge et al., 2000); *So Much Reform, So Little Change: The Persistence of Failure in Urban Schools* (Payne, 2008); and *The Implementation Gap: Understanding Reform in High Schools* (Supovitz & Weinbaum, 2008).

MORE OF THE SAME CHANGE

Like the works just cited, many observers complained that when tasked with change, school leaders just could not do it. This included very competent and highly committed school leaders. Several patterns emerged, but one was most obvious. Often when new programs were initiated and lasted a few years, they would suddenly stop. The reason usually was loss of external funding. When the funding ran out on a new program intended to spur innovation, the receiving district would for a variety of reasons go back to doing what it had done before. The author personally witnessed this happen many times.

Other observers would see that when implemented over the course of years, innovative programs would slowly morph into something unintended and strongly resemble the traditional circumstance that the new program had been intended to replace. These failures of implementation eventually became the subject of many academic studies. Many of these studies, as well as their own, are brought together in the work of Supovitz and Weinbaum, *The Implementation Gap: Understanding Reform in High Schools* (2008).

In this work Supovitz and Weinbaum focused their attention on the long-standing problem of promising school reform initiatives failing to fulfill their intended goals. They gently referred to this phenomenon as "implementation variability" (p. 4), which was depicted as persistently thwarting the idea that "the introduction and spread of potentially powerful external reform ideas" (p. 1) could change schools on a national scale.

They also cited Dane and Schneider, 1998, who found that "in the messy real world, programs and policies are highly susceptible to adjustments and adaptations throughout the implementation process" (p. 5). They further cited Elmore, 1996, explaining how "powerful ideas tended to shrivel as they became widespread, replaced by more superficial and marginal rearrangements that were mere shadows of their former selves" (p. 6). So, even when local school districts were provided enormous amounts of grant money throughout the 1980s and 1990s, they were unable to find their way out of the industrial age school model.

The reasons for this persistent failure of schools to change developed an aura of mystery. Why couldn't the most capable and dedicated of school leaders accomplish real change? In his pivotal work, *The Fifth Discipline*, Senge (1990) attempted to address the mystery with a concept he called "mental models" (p. 163). Mental models are like pictures in a person's mind derived from past experience of what something is or should look like. By this line of thinking, when education leaders attempted to change, they began with the only mental models of a school they had, the traditional school. The outcome was that the new programs that leaders attempted to implement always came out looking like something from a traditional school.

The consequence was that anything innovative failed to materialize and merely reflected traditional concepts. Senge (1990) explained that "new insights fail to get put into practice because of the conflict with deeply held internal images of how the world works, images that limit us to familiar ways of thinking and acting. . . . Our mental models determine not only how we make sense of the world, but how we take action" (pp. 163–164). Thus, attempts to change most often resulted in more of the same.

What complicated the problem of leaders being constrained by old mental models was that few school leaders had a vision of what a school would look like that did not resemble a traditional school. Think about that. What would a school look like if it did not resemble the schools readers know from the past? On what basis would educators design such a different school? What assumptions and concepts would guide the design of a different kind of school?

These are no easy answers to these questions. But the fact remains that they do need to be considered. They need to be considered by everyone involved because to date student learning continues to lag. These questions stand to be especially important for early career teachers, because how they are answered stands to radically change the nature of teaching. The answers will affect their careers.

In this regard, some nuance needs to be injected into the discussion. In the broadest sense what is being explained here is true: Schools are not changing. There are, nevertheless, some important exceptions. Throughout our society, experimental schools, online schools, charter schools, and a variety of unique learning programs are springing up. Although these experiments serve a small percentage of all students, they are starting to have an impact on how people think about schools. Some of the programs are showing signs of success.

With these new programs in sight, there is increasing interest on the part of parents to be able to choose the schools to which their children go. This includes public schools. So, as consideration is given to the need for change and the rightness of change, there also must be consideration given to what is happening around traditional schools. Is the environment of our traditional schools changing? Are public schools encountering competition? How should teachers think about these developments?

In their work, *Teaching the Digital Generation: No More Cookie-Cutter High Schools*, Kelly, McCain, and Jukes (2009) are more pointed in attributing educators' inability to change to the force of habit. They capture this force of habit in a concept they call TTWWADI—That's the way we've always done it. They explain this concept as follows:

> How can you explain the steadfast refusal of most people in education to embrace anything more than superficial changes to the way schools operate? We perceived that the school system is under the influence of a powerful force that compels it to continue on its current course. This is a force so potent that few have been able to break free of its grasp. What is this force that makes education so impervious to change? It's TTWWADI, and it has awesome power over people . . . a mindset that develops as people form habits of behavior, both personally and professionally. (p. 3)

The application of this concept of habit rings true on a number of levels. Certainly most of us know this to be true in our personal lives. Habits are hard to break. New Year's resolutions are always a struggle, particularly when they come into conflict with habit. In the author's professional life, he has seen this to be equally true. He has seen so many innovative programs come and go, only to have schools return to long-standing practices that were established decades prior. Kelly, McCain, and Jukes are probably right that institutional habits are even harder to break than individual habits are. There are so many more wills resisting change.

THE ONLY REAL CHANGE: INTENSITY

Still, in spite of all of this evidence, if contemporary school leaders were asked whether they have responded to the call for change, most would likely respond that they have. But what the research shows is that much of the change attempted in the thirty years since *A Nation at Risk* might be called "more of the same change."

This is how it worked: While mountains of literature suggested that schools needed to change assumptions and practices, the outcome was that for most schools change meant getting better at what they already did (Wagner et al., 2006, p. 9). The changes were changes of intensity. School leaders tried to raise test scores by doing a better job at what they were already doing (although some observed that these leaders tried to do a better job at what was already not working). What did society get?

- More and harder standardized tests
- More school-wide focus on standardized tests
- More and harder required subjects
- More scripted teacher-centered, teacher-talk instruction
- More advance placement and baccalaureate programs
- More and bigger textbooks
- More homework
- More government oversight
- More government intervention
- More pressure
- More rules
- More penalties for failure to show adequate annual yearly progress

Society and students didn't get new schools guided by new assumptions and new designs. They got the same old schools with everybody working harder. Why didn't education leaders consider new guiding concepts and new designs? Again, without a vision for a new kind of school, most education leaders resorted to what they knew. They became more focused, and they worked themselves, their staffs, and their students harder. In some cases, this did raise test scores. From the perspective of many such leaders, they had instituted change. Still, in all of this, the cultural habits of the industrial age school persisted, and the traditional school looks and acts as it always did although with much more intensity.

THE COMPLEXITY OF NO CHANGE

Recently the author did research in a traditional school (Waters, 2012). After extensive interviews with students and discussions with the adults at the research site, he came away concerned. An impression was beginning to coalesce that schools didn't change because the adults in them didn't want them to change. That may sound harsh, but consider the logic. The adults are in charge of what schools do. The adults make decisions about the shape and structure of the building, the content of curricula, and all of the practices used to implement the curricula. If the adults are in charge and they design and implement the programs for learning, who or what else could be responsible?

As the author reflected on this logic, he felt more and more comfortable with at least holding adults responsible for the lack of change. He could reasonably write in this book that he held adults responsible for the lack of change and its negative effects on students and teachers. And, again, that included this author.

But then a question emerged. Was the adults' resistance to change an unconscious response because the adults, most of whom received the bulk of their schooling in the twentieth century, were unable to get past their mental models? Or, was their conscious and deliberate resistance because these adults just did not feel comfortable with the unfamiliar, with change? Were they protecting their comfort zones?

> **A Career Diminished**
> **Working in industrial age schools, teachers will continue to think of themselves as conveyors of knowledge instead of stewards of full human development.**

The author decided to check the research literature. He wanted to see whether there was evidence of conscious and deliberate resistance to change. There was. The following textbox is a list of books based on research that reports on educators consciously and actively resisting experiments in education. These reports usually included resistance to charter schools, online learning, changing customary time constraints, and more.

EDUCATORS' RESISTANCE TO CHANGE: A PRIMER REFERENCE LIST

Armstrong, T. (2006). *The best schools: How human development research should inform educational practice*. Alexandria, VA: Association for Supervision and Curriculum Development.

Bramante, F., & Colby, R. (2012). *Off the clock: Moving education from time to competency*. Thousand Oaks, CA: Corwin.

Chubb, J. (2012). Overcoming the governance challenge in K–12 online learning. In C. Finn & D. R. Fairchild (Eds.), *Education reform for the digital era* (pp. 99–133). Washington, DC: Thomas B. Fordham Institute.

Finn, C., & Fairchild, D. R. (Eds.). (2012). *Education reform for the digital era*. Washington, DC: Thomas B. Fordham Institute.

Hess, F. M., & Manno, B. (Eds.). (2011). *Customized schooling: Beyond whole-school reform*. Cambridge, MA: Harvard University Press.

Kelly, F., McCain, T., & Jukes, I. (2009). *Teaching the digital generation: No more cookie-cutter schools*. Thousand Oaks, CA: Corwin Press.

Moe, T. (2011). *Teachers unions and America's public schools*. Washington, DC: Brookings Institution Press.

Moe, T., & Chubb, J. (2009). *Liberating learning: Technology, politics, and the future of American education*. Thousand Oaks, CA: Jossey-Bass.

Schlechty, P. (2009). *Leading for learning: How to transform schools into learning organizations*. San Francisco, CA: Jossey-Bass.

Senge, P., Cambron-McCabe, N., Lucas, T., Smith, B., Dutton, J., & Kleiner, A. (2000). *Schools that learn: A fifth discipline fieldbook for educators, parents, and everyone who cares about education*. New York: Doubleday

Supovitz, E. H., & Weinbaum, E. H. (2008). *The implementation gap: Understanding reform in high schools*. New York, NY: Teachers College Press.

Wagner, T., Kegan, R., Lahey, L., Lemons, R. W., Garnier, J., Helsing, D., Howell, A., Rasmussen H. T. (2006). *Change leadership: A practical Guide to Transforming our schools*. San Francisco, CA: Jossey-Bass.

IT'S ABOUT A CHOICE FOR EARLY CAREER TEACHERS

It is into this era of change and change resistance that early career teachers are now entering the teaching profession. So readers must be asked to consider what these circumstances mean for schools and what they mean for early career teachers and their careers.

The very newest teachers might respond by asking whether they should even be thinking about change issues at all when their primary concern is getting in that classroom and showing superiors that they can establish order and deliver great lessons. These issues are complicated and confusing.

But remember, the focus on this book is not about early career teachers doing well in their first days of teaching. Performing well early on is very important, but that subject is a different book. This book is about the quality of early career teachers' professional learning and their career satisfaction over the long term. To offer even more clarity about these career conditions, consider the contrasts shown in Tables 1.1 and 1.2.

NEW DEPARTURES IN TEACHER PREPARATION

From Tables 1.1 and 1.2 on the next page, readers may observe how teacher preparation and professional development for the twenty-first century should be different. They should be able to contrast those areas of preparation they have received (in the left-hand column) with the areas they should have received if they were being prepared for teaching in the twenty-first century (in the right-hand column). It is certainly possible that readers' teacher preparation programs or professional development has provided preparation other than what has been cited, so to be fair, readers might fill this information in on the left-hand side.

The likelihood is that readers may now have noticed a lack of preparation in certain areas, as cited in the right-hand column. The point of the comparison is to clarify that teachers' skills in new schools will need to be different from those of the industrial age and teachers' perspectives on their work will be influenced by whether they work in an industrial age organization or in a twenty-first-century learning organization.

The point is that the contention that teachers need new schools for new learning is not just pie-in-the-sky, theoretical mumbo jumbo. It is about actual skills and perspectives that teachers will develop or not develop as they move through their careers. This comparison should provide for a fairly clear choice. Do readers want to develop a new outlook on learning or is staying with industrial age thinking acceptable? Add to this the question of what is right for students.

Table 1.1.

Industrial Age Teacher Preparation and Professional Development	Twenty-First-Century Teacher Preparation and Professional Development
My teacher preparation program in college and my professional development program where I teach have provided me with an academic background in and experiential knowledge of • My subject of expertise • Techniques of large-group classroom control and instruction • Teaching strategies for helping students understand complex material • Teaching strategies for helping students succeed on standardized tests	My teacher preparation program in college and my professional development program where I teach have provided me with an academic background in and experiential knowledge of • Human developmental stages • My subject of expertise • Understanding organizations as systems • The concept of self-organization in human systems • Understanding change in systems • Uses and applications of interactive teaching machines, instructional software, online teaching, open courseware and software, and other technology instructional advances • The nature and uses of collective learning • Techniques for listening to students • Techniques in counseling learners • Assessing and engaging students' interests • Scaffolding in human learning • Approaches to eliciting intrinsic motivation in students • Approaches to project learning • How to help students build twenty-first-century personal effectiveness skills • Group dynamics and leadership development • Facilitating effective group work • Using models and rubrics in supporting high standards in student work and competency achievement

EARLY CAREER TEACHERS ARE THE RIGHT CHOICE FOR LEADERSHIP

It is in the face of this choice that it would be helpful to revisit Kelly, McCain, and Jukes's (2009) work, *Teaching the Digital Generation: No More Cookie-Cutter High Schools*, where they make the following observation about the force of habit and TTWWADI. In the following remark, they

Table 1.2.   Organizational Structure Influences Professional Development and How Individual Teachers Will Think about Their Work

Teacher Thinking for the Industrial Age	Teacher Thinking for the Twenty-First Century
I am compliant. I do what I am told without a lot of resistance or questioning of authority. I go along to get along and internalize the frustration. I don't insist on enjoying my work.	I am a thinker, creator, and innovator. I question everything, and I demand participation in decision making that affects my work. I also insist on enjoying my work.
I am a subject expert, and I give classroom instruction about my subject. I am a member of a subject department, and I use a subject-specific textbook in teaching.	I am a human development expert and a subject expert, and I apply my human development expertise in facilitating learning about my subject of expertise using all sorts of learning models and tools.
My job is to present subject material to my students so they may master that material in preparation for learning other things later and for success on standardized testing.	My job is to create imaginative student work that will facilitate student learning in engaging and exciting ways and build students' desire to learn.
My primary mode of operation is large-group classroom instruction, whereby students spend most of their time listening to me explain the subject matter.	My primary mode of operation is frequently meeting with and listening to students individually and in small groups, understanding my students in a deep way, and using my knowledge of my students to help them pursue a personally satisfying program of learning using a broad array of learning models.
I evaluate primarily by testing student memory of the material I taught and the material in the textbook.	Evaluation of student work is a cooperative process between the student, the facilitator, and expert consultants as needed using previously agreed to models, rubrics, and competency indicators.
My subject is a requirement, and I believe all students should be expected to master the information in the grade that it is taught.	What and when students learn certain information and skills should be individualized depending on student development, talents, interests, and needs, not on arbitrary age or scheduling groups.
Most of the work students do is done individually in reading; writing compositions; and completing short-answer quizzes or tests and special projects, such as reports, illustrations, and model building.	Most of the learning students do is project based completed occasionally as individuals but more commonly in groups, with heavy emphasis on understanding group process, problem-solving skills, creative thinking, and innovation.

I give letter grades based on students' level of success on my tests, other student work, or tests provided by the publisher of the textbook my class uses.	Student evaluations by staff are qualitative and descriptive of student achievement in a variety of areas of subject mastery, skill competency, and personal development categories. Artifacts of student work, saved in an electronic portfolio, function as indicators of learning and achievement of standards.

clearly suggest that early career teachers have, like all new entrants into old cultures, a special role in supporting professional habit:

> Over time, TTWWADI becomes a powerful force that thwarts change as new people embrace doing things the way they have always been done without examining where the original decisions came from. People just accept the mindset because it is the path of least resistance. (p. 3)

Before considering the implications of this statement, the author asks whether it is even true that new teachers go into school systems and just accept the ways and habits of the school? Of course it is. When new teachers enter a school and begin to adapt to that school's culture, they are on overload. They are only in the early stages of learning to cope with high levels of intellectual and emotional complexity. They are primed to do one thing: prove themselves as effective classroom instructors. It would be unreasonable to expect them to immediately start taking stands at faculty meetings and asking for major departures from what everyone else is in the habit of doing. Nevertheless, the observation remains important. If new entrants don't ask questions, who will?

Many of the early career teachers who are reading this book have already entered or will soon enter the culture of a particular school. Now, they should be aware that by and large most schools have actively resisted change. They also should be aware that in the opinion of many, including this author, these change-resistant schools have become impediments to learning what needs to be learned for the twenty-first century (Davidson, 2013; Richardson, 2012; Schlechty, 2009; Wagner, 2012; Wagner et al., 2006; Zhao, 2012).

As this condition unfolds, many educators for many reasons continue to call for radical change in schools and for changing the system of schooling (Bramante & Colby, 2012; Davidson, 2013; Hess & Manno, 2011; Richardson, 2013; Wagner, 2012; Zhao, 2009, 2012). Still others warn of a coming wave of change that will disrupt schooling in unimaginable ways (Christensen, Horn, & Johnson, 2009). What are the implications of all this for student learning and teacher professional learning? What are the implications for readers' careers?

The idea being placed before early career teachers is that they may have a special role and a choice in the advancement and evolution of teaching. They can accept that role or reject it. Kelly, McCain, and Jukes (2009) said that out of all the people who might question the habits of a culture, it would be those who are new to it, those who have not yet become bound by it.

If early career teachers have this unique capacity, what should they do with it? What should leaders in schools do with these new entrants to facilitate use of their unique capacity? What should teacher preparation institutions do to clarify this dilemma and encourage early career teachers to participate in and lead change?

REFERENCES

Acker-Hocevar, M., Cruz-Janzen, M., Wilson, C., Schoon, P., & Walker, D. (2006). The need to reestablish schools as dynamic positive human energy systems that are non-linear and self-organizing. *International Journal of Learning, 12*(10), 255–268.

Christensen, C., Horn, M., & Johnson, C. (2009). *Disrupting class: How disruptive innovation will change the way the world learns.* New York, NY: McGraw-Hill.

Coleman, J. S. (1959). Academic achievement and the structure of competition. *Harvard Education Review, 29* (4), 330–331. Excerpts can be retrieved from http://educationnext.org/theadolescentsociety/

Davidson, C. N. (2013). *Now you see it: How technology and brain science will transform school and business for the 21st century.* New York: Penguin Books.

Davis, B. (2007). Expanding the space of the possible: Understanding knowledge, learning, and teaching as nested and recursively elaborated processes. In B. Després (Ed.), *Systems thinkers in action: A field guide for effective change leadership in education* (pp. 227–243). Lanham, MD: Rowman & Littlefield Publishers.

Goldspink, C. (2007). Transforming education: Evidential support for a complex systems approach. *Emergence: Complexity and Organization 9*(1-2), 77–92.

Goldspink, C., & Kay, R. (2003). Organization as self-organizing and sustaining systems: A complex and autopoietic systems perspective. *International Journal of General Systems, 32*(5), 459–474.

Gordon, R., Kane, J. K., & Staiger, D. O. (2006). Identifying effective teachers using performance on the job. Retrieved from http://www.brookings.edu/research/papers/2006/04/education-gordon

Hanushek, E. (2011). Recognizing the value of good teachers. Retrieved from http://www.edweek.org/ew/articles/2011/04/06/27hanushek.h30.html

Haycock, K. (1998). Good teaching matters . . . a lot. *Thinking K–16, 3*(2), 1–4.

Hess, F. (1999). *Spinning wheels: The politics of urban school reform.* Washington, DC: Brookings Institution Press.

Hess, F. M., & Manno, B. (Eds.). (2011). *Customized schooling: Beyond whole-school reform.* Cambridge, MA: Harvard University Press.

Jacobs, H. (2010). *Curriculum 21: Essential education for a changing world.* Alexandria VA: Association for Supervision and Curriculum Development.

Kelly, F., McCain, T., & Jukes, I. (2009). *Teaching the digital generation: No more cookie-cutter schools.* Thousand Oaks, CA: Corwin.

National Association of Secondary School Principals (NASSP). (1999). *Breaking ranks: Changing an American institution* (4th ed.). Reston, VA: NASSP.

National Association of Secondary School Principals (NASSP). (2004). *Breaking ranks II: Strategies for leading high school reform.* Providence, RI: The Education Alliance.

National Commission on Excellence in Education. (1983). *A nation at risk: The imperative for educational reform: A report to the nation and the Secretary of Education, United States Department of Education* (Vol. 2). Ann Arbor, MI: University of Michigan Library.

National Commission on Teaching and America's Future. (1996). *What matters most: Teaching for America's future*. New York, NY: Carnegie Foundation.
Payne, C. M. (2008). *So much reform, so little change: The persistence of failure in urban schools*. Cambridge, MA: Harvard Education Press.
Pettus, A. (2006). Grading teachers. *Harvard Magazine,* November/December.
Prensky, M. (2010). *Teaching digital natives: Partnering for real learning*. Thousand Oaks, CA: Corwin.
Ravitch, D. (2000). *Left back: A century of failed school reforms*. New York, NY: Simon & Schuster.
Richardson, W. (2012). *Why school? How education must change when learning and information are everywhere*. New York: Ted Conferences.
Sanders, W., & Rivers, J. (1996). Cumulative and residual effects of teachers on future student academic achievement: Research report. Knoxville, TN: University of Tennessee Value Added Research and Assessment Center.
Sarason, S. B. (1990). *The predictable failure of educational reform: Can we change before it is too late?* San Francisco, CA: Jossey-Bass.
Schlechty, P. (2009). *Leading for learning: How to transform schools into learning organizations*. San Francisco, CA: Jossey-Bass.
Senge, P. (1990). *The fifth discipline: The art and practice of the learning organization*. New York, NY: Doubleday.
Senge, P., Cambron-McCabe, N., Lucas, T., Smith, B., Dutton, J., & Kleiner, A. (2000). *Schools that learn: A fifth discipline fieldbook for educators, parents, and everyone who cares about education*. New York, NY: Doubleday.
Senge, P., Scharmer, C. O., Jaworski, J., & Flowers, B. S. (2004). *Presence: Exploring profound change in people, organizations, and society*. New York, NY: Currency Doubleday.
Sizer, T. (1984). *Horace's compromise: The dilemma of the American high school*. New York, NY: Houghton Mifflin Company.
Sizer, T. (1992). *Horace's school: Redesigning the American high school*. New York, NY: Houghton Mifflin Company.
Supovitz, E. H., & Weinbaum, E. H. (2008). *The implementation gap: Understanding reform in high schools*. New York, NY: Teachers College Press.
Tyack, D., & Cuban, L. (1995). *Tinkering toward utopia: A century of public school reform*. Cambridge, MA: Harvard University Press.
Wagner, T. (2012). *Creating innovators: The making of young people who will change the world*. New York: Scribner.
Wagner, T., Kegan, R., Lahey, L., Lemons, R. W., Garnier, J., Helsing, D., . . . Rasmussen H. T. (2006). *Change leadership: A practical guide to transforming our schools*. San Francisco, CA: Jossey-Bass.
Waters, R. (2012). *Secondary students' transitioning from compliance to intentional learning*. (Doctoral Dissertation). Retrieved from UMI ProQuest (Order No: 3504071)
Wright, S., Horn, S., & Sanders, W. (1997). Teacher and classroom context effects on students' achievement: Implications for teacher evaluation. *Journal of Personnel Evaluation in Education 11,* 57–67.
Zhao, Y. (2009). *Catching up or leading the way: American education in the age of globalization*. Alexandria, VA: Association for Supervision and Curriculum Development.
Zhao, Y. (2012). *World class learners: Educating creative and entrepreneurial students*. Thousand Oaks, CA: Corwin.

TWO
Guiding Step 2: Question the Assumptions and Practices of Traditional Schools

The focus of this chapter is questioning the assumptions and practices common to traditional schools. Ideally, leaders of schools and teacher preparation programs should encourage early career teachers to examine and question these long-held assumptions and practices. With this in mind, this chapter should be helpful to readers in developing the capacity to question and see with fresh eyes. It will lead to the possibility of using new assumptions, applying new practices, and imagining new schools for new learning.

> **A Career Diminished**
> Teaching in industrial age schools, early career teachers, like their predecessors, will become change resistant and stuck in the professional habits of the twentieth century.

Because the purpose of this book is to help readers sort out these issues and create better careers, let's again go back to basics. All of these people who urged schools to change, why did they do it? Is there something fundamentally wrong with the way schools are physically and programmatically structured? What exactly is the problem? As these questions are confronted, let's keep in mind readers' elementary and secondary schools, the author's old schools, and the ones where readers are now teaching or about to teach.

QUESTIONING ASSUMPTIONS

All organizations are based on assumptions. These are ideas that are held to be true. When ideas are accepted as basic truths, they create a basis for identifying and achieving goals. In the textbox below are the assumptions that underlie our traditional schools.

INDUSTRIAL AGE SCHOOLS ARE BASED ON ASSUMPTIONS

About **Time**: Credit for learning is based on teacher evaluation after a student has accumulated the required seat time in an approved course. School will run morning to afternoon, five days a week except for holidays and weekends, for 180 days per school year. There will be a vacation period of about 10 weeks during the summer months.

About **Place**: The primary place of learning is the school and its grounds.

About **Resources**: The school and its programs will be funded by the local board of education, as funds are provided by a local municipality via the raising of taxes. These funds may be supplemented by state and federal grants.

About **Teachers**: Teachers are the primary conveyors of knowledge and skills. Credit for learning will follow a student who receives instruction from a teacher in a classroom.

About **Students**: Students are inherently deficient and need to be coerced into having their deficiencies remediated by highly structured school programs.

About **Motivation**: Students will be offered a variety of extrinsic incentives, such as grades, rewards, praise, and recognition as the outcome of doing the work prescribed by the school.

About **Context**: The school is dedicated to serving its local community by developing students who are prepared for work, college, and participation in community government and city affairs.

About **How Students Learn**: Certifiable student learning comes primarily from classroom instruction with the use of approved curriculum and textbooks, and students fulfill required seat time in a classroom and successfully pass a teacher evaluation process.

About **Knowledge**: It may be thought of as an entity or thing that has quantity and mass. Knowledge can thus be transferred to students by teachers in the way water might be poured into an empty container.

> About **What Students Learn**: Students shall learn the approved school curriculum, including local- and state-required subjects as well as subjects required as stipulated by the many colleges and universities to which students apply. These required courses will be supplemented by elective courses and after school activities.
>
> About **How Students Are Evaluated**: Students will be evaluated by teachers on assignments and given letter grades (A, B, C, D, and F), which certify the completion of work and the level of achievement the work represents.
>
> About **How Learning Is Certified**: When students receive passing grades in their courses, they will be certified as having developed the necessary knowledge and skills for that particular course.

Having reviewed each of these assumptions, readers should see that in large measure they reflect teachers' thinking and practices that were identified in chapter 1. So let's ask some questions. Do the assumptions about *time* make sense, or is it possible that maybe time could be thought of and handled differently?

Now let's look at the assumption about *place*. Does it make sense that certifiable learning must take place only in the building called the school? Could such learning possibly happen somewhere else? In what other places could it reasonably happen?

Now let's look at the assumption about *teachers*. Are teachers the only facilitators of knowledge and skills? Could students acquire knowledge and skills from any other people?

Now let's look at the concept of the *student*. Are there any reasons to recast concepts of students as deficient and needing to be coerced into learning?

Now let's look at *motivation*. Is offering students extrinsic incentives the best way to motivate them? Is there research that suggests the need to change this Skinnerian view?

Now let's look at the assumptions about *resources*. Most local school districts fund their programs through local taxation along with some help from state and federal governments. Are there other means by which a school might expand what it has at its disposal?

What about *context*? Educators usually think of a school as serving its local community by providing young people prepared to enter the workforce or higher education. Might it be helpful to conceive of a school's context in a different and broader way?

What about *how students learn*? While most educators believe that students learn in a variety of ways, traditional schools tend to rely on one particular learning model, classroom instruction. Should schools maintain their emphasis on this single learning model, or should they consider other possibilities and diversify learning models?

What about *knowledge*? For a very long time people have thought about knowledge as something that has mass and can be transferred from teacher to student. Is there another way to think about knowledge that would suggest new approaches to learning?

What about *what students learn*? Most schools have a curriculum that is made up of a lot of required classes deemed necessary by the local board of education, the state, the federal government, and the colleges and universities to which the students apply. There are also a small number of electives. Should schools continue to maintain all of these required courses, or should there be more electives, including academic electives, which might be of importance in addressing the individual motivations, needs, talents, and ambitions of students?

What about the *evaluation* of students? It is commonly recognized that a mainstay of teachers' work is the evaluation of students' work and the application of a letter grade, A through F. Are there any problems with this approach? Why don't states and the federal government accept teachers' evaluations of student learning?

A Career Diminished
Working in industrial age schools, teachers will contribute little to youths' development of twenty-first-century skills.

What about the *certification* of learning? Local schools are usually the only place where students can go to get learning certified. Is that a good thing? Or, should society provide students with other ways to certify their learning that may happen in other places and with other people but which, nevertheless, results in important learning?

NEW ASSUMPTIONS FOR TWENTY-FIRST CENTURY LEARNING

The truth is that questions could be raised about all of these assumptions. What is more important here is what readers think. Readers will or will not lead change. Are these assumptions inadequate or inappropriate in some ways? Or, do readers feel that these assumptions have served pretty well so far, so why change? Now let's take a look at another set of assumptions in the following textbox, the assumptions of a new kind of school.

NEW SCHOOLS: WILL BE BASED ON DIFFERENT ASSUMPTIONS

About **Time**: Credit for learning any time and at any pace if a student can demonstrate the knowledge and competency.

About **Place**: Credit for learning any place, not just at the school, if a student can demonstrate the knowledge and competency.

About **Resources**: There is expanded use of resources beyond what can be provided by the local board of education to offerings from the city, county, state, and federal governments along with local citizens, nonprofits and corporations, and even national benefactors.

About **Teachers**: Not just licensed teachers but all kinds of community, regional, and distant experts are enlisted, who make themselves available to help young people develop knowledge and skills.

About **Students**: Students are people who volunteer to learn. They are customers, and their needs, desires, ambitions, preferences, and individual characteristics as learners should inform how and what they learn.

About **Motivation**: Schools will focus on eliciting intrinsic motivation in students and create the conditions where students will be self-motivated to complete the work of learning.

About **Context**: The entire world is the marketplace into which students will have to bring their knowledge and competencies. Schooling should prepare students for learning in the world and to consider global, cross-cultural conditions as they pursue learning.

About **How Students Learn**: Not just teacher-centered, classroom instruction is offered but lots of creative learning, personalized learning, active learning, discovery learning, problem-solving learning, adventure learning, reflective learning, real-world learning, action-research learning, community-development learning, student-presentation learning, and on and on.

About **Knowledge**: It is a tentative personal construction that results from participation in the world. It comes out of an individual's unique experiences doing things alone and doing things together with others. Knowledge is not stable. It changes. Knowledge emerges in individuals as an outcome of experience and reflection.

> About **What Students Learn**: The students get to influence and take responsibility for what and how they learn, how the school functions, and the role of teachers and how they teach. The knowledge and skills needed for the twenty-first century can be achieved in thousands of ways.
>
> About **How Students Are Evaluated**: Evaluation is viewed as a tool for student improvement, not for sorting. Rubrics and benchmarks are employed along with frequent formative assessment informed by student input and in consideration of a student's goals and desired outcomes.
>
> About **How Learning Is Certified**: Certification will be based not on seat time but on demonstrated competencies and knowledge whether or not they are an outcome of schooling.

Consider this summary of what these new assumptions are suggesting. American society should have schools where students learn at any time, at any place, on any path, and at any pace. Students are volunteers and should increasingly be thought of as customers shopping for great learning experiences in a world that has an ever-expanding marketplace of educational experiences.

Students' unique strengths, desires, ambitions, and talents will drive what they want to learn in the future in contrast to being dominated by school requirements. Students may do important learning with teachers but also with other well-qualified people, including but not limited to policemen, scout leaders, firemen, politicians, industry leaders, salespeople, doctors and nurses, tradesmen, collectors, writers and artists, peers, and all sorts of other professionals.

In fact, it will be recognized that students may acquire knowledge and skills in many ways from technology, peers, video, machines, programmed learning, and many other learning models. Knowledge will not be seen as a stable mass to simply be transferred to students but as a personal construct that comes from experience, reflection, and continual social interaction. What will matter is that students have learned and can demonstrate that learning.

Students will no longer be locked in by the clock doing seat time to earn credit for things they already know. Students will earn credit when they are able to demonstrate knowledge and skill. Students will advance at their own pace. Students will think of themselves as not only preparing for entry into their local communities but also into an increasingly flatter, global community, with many shared problems and opportunities.

This description, of course, presents a very different kind of school from the current schools, schools left over from the industrial age. When readers consider this summary and compare the new school assumptions to the earlier assumptions, what is their reaction? Does the summary of the new school assumptions sound sane or insane? Is it hard to envision teaching in such a school? Are the new assumptions in any way better or worse? Might they be more appropriate to our current historical period?

The value of these new school assumptions would probably be best developed in a big discussion with fellow students or colleagues. Such a discussion should probably go on for an extended period, months and years. It is likely that in the end, many would agree that, at least, some of the old assumptions need to be revised and some of the new assumptions might work well.

Still, many would also agree that it is hard to imagine how schools would be organized with these new assumptions and practices. On that note, it is important to emphasize that imagining these new organizations and applications would require that people step away from the traditional school frame of reference. That will not be easy, and how that might be accomplished will be explored in future chapters.

Having examined these two sets of assumptions should underscore the importance of early career teachers knowing what they think and why. In the future, there will come many times when teachers will be faced with choices related to these assumptions. At these times, they will need to know what they think. They will need to be able to present compelling explanations that show a deep understanding of the learning process and why one direction more than another is better for youths.

Although that clarity may not exist now, early career teachers should be developing an idea or vision for how schools will change. Considering these assumptions should help in developing some new ideas, perhaps the beginnings of a vision.

QUESTIONING PRACTICES

Now there is another step. To fully explore the need for change, let's take another look at practices. Readers should recognize by now that practices are often driven by habit. Some habits may serve well, but some may not. Again, with readers' earlier school experiences in mind, let's take another look at what teachers do in their practices.

Readers should want to know, is there really a compelling reason to change the practices of teaching and schooling? Some research suggests that there is. Consider Table 2.1, which designates the specific practices common in traditional schools in the left-hand column and then in the right cites scholarly writers and research that suggest the need for a change in practice.

Table 2.1.

What Industrial Age Schools Do	What the Research Says
1. Students spend a lot of time sitting and listening.	1. Students learn better when a variety of learning modes are employed, which include more activity, participation, and choice (Aldrich, 2005; Dewey, 1938; Lave & Wenger, 1991).
2. Schools put great emphasis on compliance and control. Teachers take great pride in tightly controlled classrooms. Students are rewarded for following directions, being quiet, and doing as they are told.	2. Student learning becomes more intentional in settings that encourage creative behavior, constructive interaction with others, problem solving, and participation in learning and schooling designs (Cook-Sather, 2006; Joselowsky, 2007; Mitra, 2008; Wagner, 2012; Zhao, 2009, 2012).
3. Schools place great emphasis on memorization, right answers, work completion, and short-answer/multiple-choice testing.	3. Remembering is only a small part of learning, and students should be challenged to employ higher level thinking modes. Students need to learn about the nature of thinking and its relationship to learning. As students learn about thinking, each needs to learn about his or her idiosyncrasies as a thinker and be able to explain them. Students also need to learn how mindful people gain control of their thinking (Decker & Davidson, 2006; Georghiades, 2004; Ritchhart et al., 2011).
4. Student learning is focused on mastering bodies of information, such as social studies, science, math, and English.	4. Students are better prepared for an ever-changing world when they learn how to learn instead of mastering information that will quickly become outdated (Black et al., 2006; Candy, 1991; Drew, 2001; James et al., 2006; Paige, 2007; Rawson, 2000).
5. Students are encouraged to learn for extrinsic rewards, such as social status, grades, awards, better jobs, and money.	5. Students learn more deeply when they are recognized for effort while pursuing learning for intrinsic purposes, such as enjoyment, curiosity, or challenge (Ames & Archer, 1988; Deci, 1995; Deci & Ryan, 1985; Dweck, 2006; Dweck & Leggett, 1988).
6. Student learning is dominated by requirements. Schools enforce a one-size-fits-all approach to learning so students are told what they must learn and everybody reads the same textbook,	6. Students learn more deeply when they have some control and influence over what and how they learn and when that learning is an expression of personal interests. There needs to be a lot of

does the same homework, and takes the same tests.

	choice in the process so students can customize their learning pursuits to their individual needs and strengths (Byrnes, 2005; Goyal, 2012; Guskey & Anderman, 2008; Holcomb, 2007).
7. Schools promote decontextualized learning. Decontextualized learning is learning that is enforced via required subjects even though students have not asked to learn it, and then students are asked to learn it apart from the actual real-world conditions they are learning about. For example, students must learn about government by reading a textbook and listening to the teacher but without a classroom election process or creating a student governing body for the classroom or participating in elections in the community. Students are asked to learn about erosion by reading about it, but the class never goes to the places that are eroding to witness causes and effects.	7. What a student learns should be in the context of the student having real personal questions about some topic. Also, when students are helped to learn the answers to questions, they should be helped to experience the context of the topic in the real world. For example, if students are interested in STDs, it would be best if students could go to a clinic for STDs and talk to medical professionals and their patients. If students are interested in the physics of flight, it would be best if students go out and examine planes and fly in planes. Learning is deepest when it happens in the context of a student's interests and out in the real world (Lave & Wenger, 1991; Wagner, 2012; Zhao, 2012).
8. Students have little influence over what and how they learn.	8. Student learning and student psychological development are improved when students reflect on and can influence what and how they learn (Armstrong, 2006; Cook-Sather, 2006; Holcomb, 2007; Joselowsky, 2007; Mitra, 2008).
9. There is little effort in schools to get to know students' strengths, talents, weaknesses, or ambitions in order to customize or individualize learning.	9. Learning is deepened and improved when students are able to apply their strengths and talents and connect their learning to personal interests, ambitions, and developmental stages (Armstrong, 2009; Gardner, 1985).
10. There is a heavy emphasis on following routines in highly structured learning with little emphasis on providing opportunities for creativity and innovation.	10. Students need opportunities for independent and unstructured learning and to present their findings. The marketplace circumstances of the twenty-first century will place high demands on the creativity of individuals and their ability to cope without neat structures and to still learn (Jacobs, 2010; Wagner, 2008, 2012; Zhao, 2012).
11. Course work involves little or no reflection on the relationship of effort, personal goals, or life purpose to	11. Students develop greater commitment to learning when helped to see it in terms of personal goals and a purpose in life

achievement.	(Damon, 2008; Deci, 1995; Pink, 2009; Thomas, 2009).
12. Few students are provided a relationship with an adult mentor.	12. Student learning is enhanced when it is in the context of a caring relationship with an adult (Beaudoin, 2008; DiMartino & Clarke, 2008; Rogers & Freiberg, 1994).
13. There is too much summative assessment and too little formative assessment that is informed by the student.	13. Learning is deeper when it involves periodic formative assessment that is informed by the student and provides many opportunities for errors and missteps followed by revision and improvement (Marzano, 2009; William, 2011).
14. Schools focus on learning as a linguistic activity dominated by teacher talk and "book learning" and the students that are good linguistic learners. Schools do this at the expense of most students whose learning strengths are not linguistic but may be logical-mathematical, spatial, bodily-kinesthetic, musical, interpersonal, intrapersonal, or some other learning strength.	14. Students learn best when that learning includes opportunities to express and employ their unique brand of intelligence. When a student's unique intelligence is overlooked in favor of traditional linguistic learning, that student is handicapped and subject to discouragement (Armstrong, 2009; Gardner, 1985).
15. Twentieth-century schools encourage the game of school, and the game of school dominates in the twentieth-century schooling model. In this game, students apply a complex set of behavioral norms to create the appearance of learning to get the grades they need while they covertly do the things they really want to do.	15. The game of school is diminished with the increased personalization of learning (Fried, 2001, 2005; Waters, 2012).
16. It is in the nature of twentieth-century schools to resist change and for leaders to think of schools as well-oiled machines that keep doing what they have done before over and over again.	16. Twenty-first-century schools will continually reflect on what they do with an eye to change and innovation to meet the needs of all stakeholders and respond to changes in their environment (Christensen & Raynor, 2003; Kelley et al., 2009; Senge et al., 2000).
17. School leaders delude themselves by thinking that bringing technology into their schools means that they have "changed" with the times, and these leaders typically misuse technology to support twentieth-century learning paradigms.	17. Use of twenty-first-century technologies in schools requires assumptions different from those of the twentieth century about what and how students learn (Aldrich, 2005; Kelly et al., 2009; Moe & Chubb, 2009; Richardson, 2010).

18. Schools focus on teaching students one-size-fits-all content information instead of focusing on the psychological development of individuals.	18. Learning happens best when encouraged in the context of an individual student's developmental stage (Armstrong, 2006; Bandura, 1997).
19. Students are not considered full stakeholders whose voices inform how and what they learn and the conditions of their school.	19. Students' psychological development and content learning are enhanced when they are listened to and are able to influence what and how they learn (Armstrong, 2006; Byrnes, 2005; Cook-Sather, 2006; Mitra, 2008).
20. School leaders have a misconception of schools as being factories or machine-like, where standardization serves the best interests of the functioning of the school.	20. Schools are better considered as being dynamic systems that change in response to the needs of their members and in relationship to their environment (Acker-Hocevar et al., 2006; Davis & Sumatra, 2006; Senge, 1990; Senge et al., 2000).
21. Teachers and school leaders do little to systematically measure student engagement.	21. Knowledge and understanding of student engagement guides the creation of learning opportunities. Without knowing about student engagement, school leaders cannot make meaningful decisions that will improve student learning (Senge et al., 2000; Waters, 2012; Yazzie-Mintz, 2007, 2009).
22. Grades are presented to students as the primary motive for learning, thus influencing students to value the grades above the learning and, more often than not, in place of the learning.	22. Evaluation of student work should be in the context of the students' chosen goals for learning and informed by learner-chosen rubrics, models, and benchmarks. The indicators of learning should not be grades but concrete evidence of knowledge and skill as represented in artifacts, presentations, modeling, and transference to real-world circumstances (Marzano, 2009; William, 2011).

When readers considered the implications of the list of assumptions underlying a new kind of school, it likely was hard for them to imagine how such a school could be organized. If, now, Table 2.1 impugns many of the most common practices of schools, what does that mean for the traditional concept of school, and what does it imply about new kinds of schools? Of course, the author cannot know for sure to what extent readers are surprised by the suggestion that current school practices are problematic.

Probably, many of these concerns have never been considered. It may even be that the courses taken as part of readers' teacher preparation programs even may have reinforced their faith in these common and familiar practices. So, again, readers are being confronted with difficult questions.

SHOULD CLASSROOM INSTRUCTION EVEN BE QUESTIONED?

Another issue that emerges from many of the practices cited on this list is the issue of classroom instruction. Some observers of this list rightly see that many of the cited problematic practices are practices related to classroom instruction. Therefore the question has been raised, is the nature of classroom instruction also problematic? How could that be? All that is heard nowadays is that the single most important factor in a school's promotion of learning is good instruction (Brill, 2011, pp. 150–154; Hanushek, 2011). So, how could classroom instruction be a problem?

Here is how readers might think about this. Certainly readers know that classroom instruction is sometimes great and inspiring, and sometimes it is boring and terrible. Schools are right to place a high priority on good classroom instruction, considering how much they use it. It is way better than poor instruction. And, yes, there is a great deal of research that shows that good classroom instruction plays a vital role in school learning (Gordon, Kane, & Staiger, 2008; Hanushek, 2011; Haycock, 1998; National Commission on Teaching and America's Future, 1996; Sanders & Rivers, 1996).

It is important to remember, however, that most of the research previously cited is saying that of all the factors that bear on learning in traditional schooling, it is good teaching that most supports learning. With this conclusion there is no debate. If a school is going to be primarily reliant on classroom instruction to spur learning, it would be best to have good instruction.

However, the cited research does not address how classroom instruction might compare to other models for learning if they were used, which they rarely are. In fact, one of the reasons schools should want to use a greater variety of learning models is because classroom instruction does have some inherent limitations. Knowing this is a sensitive subject for teachers, a question is offered: Could the following observations be considered fair about classroom instruction?

- **Most teachers are not top-notch instructors.** They may be very good in other aspects of their work, but by and large, high-quality instructors are in the minority.
- **Classroom instruction is overused.** In any given day students may be exposed to four to six hours of teacher-centered, teacher-talk instruction. Do kids get tired of so much classroom instruction? Yes. And adults do too, regardless of whether they are the teachers or the students.

- **Classroom instruction usually involves a lot of listening and very little activity.**
- **Classroom instruction favors students who are auditory/linguistic learners.** Students who learn in other ways are placed at a disadvantage.
- **Classroom instruction is subject to a lot of distractions**, especially with twenty to thirty students in the room (such large-group instruction is a manifestation of assembly-line production strategies), and all of the social and psychological implications of that. Among these implications consider the intensity and pressure of social networking and the deep distraction of youths coming from fractured homes plagued with divorce and unemployment. Add to that a wall of windows and what is happening outside, the intercom, noise in the hallway, and unruly behavior in the room.
- **Classroom instruction requires an unusually high level of control.** This control is asserted by teachers because of their awareness of possible distractions. This in turn inspires subversive responses from students (to be developed in a future chapter).
- **Classroom instruction tends to be one size fits all.** That is, there is often little effort or opportunity to individualize or differentiate. Everybody gets the same lesson, the same homework, and the same test.

Now, given these limitations, would readers consider that perhaps schools might include some other learning models that might address some of these limitations? What might those other learning models be? How about these models?

- Online learning
- Blended learning: Part teacher instruction, part guided learning online
- Adaptive learning machines
- Nings
- Learning from videos
- e-Game and simulations learning
- Community partner learning
- Independent research
- Action research
- Voice threads
- Student presentations
- Art creation learning (other than in art class)
- Tinkering and invention and innovation learning
- Cultural learning, whereby students observe or witness the playing of music; look at artwork; or watch a TV program, movie, play, or novel presentation and discuss it.
- Tutorial learning

- Conversational learning
- Travel learning
- On-the-job learning
- Apprenticeship learning
- Model-building learning
- Community-project learning
- Creating and conducting survey learning
- Interview learning

Readers probably have never even heard of some of these learning models and know little about the applications of most of them in facilitating learning. Still, there is literature that develops how each model is best employed. What readers do not know about these other learning models should provide some insight into what is being learned from a college program or in-school professional development that is preparing early career teachers for the twentieth century. But apart from that, can readers see that some of these other learning models might be very helpful? They might help by

- diversifying experiences and the daily routine for students,
- diversifying the day for teachers,
- appealing to a variety of unique student and teacher intelligences,
- providing more active learning opportunities,
- diminishing the need for tight teacher controls and student subversive reactions,
- providing opportunities for individualization and less one-size-fits-all instruction, and
- providing teachers with more time to meet with students individually and in small groups.

Certainly, readers can see that these other learning models do have some potential. So now it may be seen that in questioning nearly everything about the assumptions and practices of the traditional school, even classroom instruction may be questioned.

This chapter has taken a close look at the assumptions that underlie our industrial age schools and the practices employed to advance learning in them. In contrast, new assumptions and new models for learning have been considered along with what promise they hold for the future. More and more possibilities for the future will be presented throughout this book. Soon the focus will turn to envisioning new kinds of schools, but before that, there is one additional problem with industrial age schools readers need to consider as a reason to lead change and advance the evolution of teaching.

REFERENCES

Acker-Hocevar, M., Cruz-Janzen, M., Wilson, C., Schoon, P., & Walker, D. (2006). The need to reestablish schools as dynamic positive human energy systems that are non-linear and self-organizing. *International Journal of Learning, 12*(10), 38–52.

Aldrich, C. (2005). *Learning by doing: A comprehensive guide to simulations, computer games, and pedagogy in e-learning and other educational experiences.* San Francisco, CA: Pfeiffer.

Ames, C., & Archer, J. (1988). Achievement goals in the classroom: Students' learning strategies and motivation processes. *Journal of Educational Psychology, 80*(3), 260–267.

Armstrong, T. (2006). *The best schools: How human development research should inform educational practice.* Alexandria, VA: Association for Supervision and Curriculum Development.

Armstrong, T. (2009). *Multiple intelligences in the classroom.* Alexandria, VA: Association for Supervision and Curriculum Development.

Bandura, A. (1997). *Self-efficacy: The exercise of control.* New York, NY: W. H. Freeman and Company.

Bandura, A. (2006). Adolescent development from an agentic perspective. In F. Pajares & T. Urdan (Eds.), *Self-efficacy beliefs of adolescents* (pp. 1–43). Charlotte, NC: Information Age Publishing.

Beaudoin, N. (2005). *Elevating student voice: How to enhance participation, citizenship, and leadership.* Larchmont, NY: Eye on Education.

Beaudoin, N. (2008). *A school for each student: Personalization in a climate of high expectations.* Larchmont, NY: Eye on Education.

Black, P., McCormick, R., James, M., & Pedder, D. (2006). Learning how to learn and assessment for learning: A theoretical inquiry. *Research Papers in Education, 21*(2), 119–132.

Brill, S. (2011). *Class warfare: Inside the fight to fix America's schools.* New York, NY: Simon & Schuster.

Byrnes, R. S. (2005). To improve high schools, listen to the insights of students. *Education Week*, February 23.

Candy, P. (1991). *Self-direction for lifelong learning.* San Francisco: Jossey-Bass.

Capra, F. (1996). *The web of life: A new scientific understanding of living systems.* New York, NY: Random House.

Christensen, C., Horn, M., & Johnson, C. (2008). *Disrupting class: How disruptive innovation will change the way the world learns.* New York, NY: McGraw-Hill.

Christensen, C., & Raynor, M. (2003). *The innovator's solution: Creating and sustaining successful growth.* Cambridge, MA: Harvard Business Review Press.

Cook-Sather, A. (2006). Change based on what students say: Preparing teachers for a paradoxical model of leadership. *International Journal of Leadership in Education, 9*(4), 345–358.

Cushman, K. (2010). *Fires in the mind.* San Francisco, CA: Jossey-Bass.

Damon, W. (2008). *The path to purpose.* New York, NY: Free Press.

Davis, B., & Sumatra, D. (2006). *Complexity and education: Inquiries into learning, teaching, and research.* Mahwah, NJ: Lawrence Erlbaum Associates, Inc.

Deci, E. (1995). *Why we do what we do.* New York, NY: Penguin Books.

Deci, E., & Ryan, R. (1985). *Intrinsic motivation and self determination in human behavior.* New York, NY: Plenum Press.

Deci, E., & Ryan, R. (2008). Self-determination theory: A macro-theory of human motivation, development, and health. *Canadian Psychology, 49*(3), 182–185.

Deci, E., Vallerand, R. J., Pelletier, L. G., & Ryan, R. M. (1991). Motivation in education: The self-determination perspective. *Educational Psychologist, 26*(3-4), 325–346.

Decker, T., & Davidson, K. (2006). *Bloom's and beyond: Higher level questions and activities for the creative classroom.* Marion, IL: Pieces of Learning.

Dewey, J. (1938). *Experience and education.* New York, NY: Kappa Delta Pi.

DiMartino, J., & Clarke, J. (2008). *Personalizing the school experience for each student.* Alexandria, VA: Association for Supervision and Curriculum Development.

Drew, S. (2001). Student perceptions of what helps them learn and develop in higher education. *Teaching in Higher Education, 6(3),* 309–331.

Dweck, C. (2006). *Mindset: The new psychology of success.* New York, NY: Random House.

Dweck, C. S., & Leggett, E. L. (1988). A social cognitive approach to motivation and personality. *Psychological Review, 95* (2), 256–273.

Fried, R. L. (2001). *The passionate teacher: A practical guide.* Boston, MA: Beacon Press.

Fried, R. L. (2005). *The game of school: Why we all play it, how it hurts kids, and what it will take to change it.* San Francisco: Jossey-Bass.

Gardner, H. (1985). *Frames of mind.* New York, NY: Basic Books.

Georghiades, P. (2004). From the general to the situated: Three decades of metacognition. *International Journal of Science Education, 26(3),* 365–383.

Gordon, R., Kane, T. J., & Staiger, D. O. (2008). Identifying effective teachers using performance on the job. In *The Hamilton project: Ideas on income security, education, and taxes.* Furman, J., Bordoff, J. E. (eds.). (pp. 189–226). Washington, DC: The Brookings Institution.

Goyal, N. (2012). *One size does not fit all: A student's assessment of school.* Roslyn Heights, NY: Alternative Education Resource Organization.

Guskey, T., & Anderman, E. (2008). Students at bat. *Educational Leadership, 66(3),* 8–14.

Hanushek, E. (2011). Valuing teachers: How much is a good teacher worth? in *Education Next,* Summer.

Haycock, K. (1998). Good teaching matters . . . a lot. *Thinking K–16,* Publication of Education Trust, vol. 3, mo. 2, Summer.

Hess, F. M., & Manno, B. (Eds.). (2011). *Customized schooling: Beyond whole-school reform.* Cambridge, MA: Harvard University Press.

Holcomb, E. (2007). *Students are stakeholders, too!* Thousand Oaks, CA: Corwin.

Hume, E. (2008). *School of dreams: Making the grade at a top American school.* New York, NY: Harcourt.

Jacobs, H. (2010). *Curriculum 21: Essential education for a changing world.* Alexandria VA: Association for Supervision and Curriculum Development.

James, M., Black, P., McCormick, R., Pedder, D., & William, D. (2006). Learning how to learn, in classrooms, schools and networks: Aims, design and analysis. *Research Papers in Education, 21*(2), 101–118. doi:10.1080/02671520600615547

Jaros, M., & Deakin Crick, R. (2006). Personalizing learning in the post-mechanical age. *Journal of Curriculum Studies, 39*(4), 423–440.

Joselowsky, F. (2007). Youth engagement, school reform, and improved learning outcomes: Building systemic approaches for youth engagement. *NASSP Bulletin, 91*(3), 257–276.

Kelly, F. S., McCain, T., Jukes, I. (2009). *Teaching the digital generation: No more cookie-cutter high schools.* Thousand Oaks, CA: Corwin Press.

Kohn, A. (1993). *Punished by rewards: The trouble with gold stars, incentive plans, A's and other bribes.* New York, NY: Houghton Mifflin Company.

Lave, J., & Wenger, E. (1991). *Situated learning: Legitimate peripheral participation.* Cambridge, UK: Cambridge University Press.

Marzano, R. J. (2009). *Formative assessment and standards-based grading: Classroom strategies that work.* Bloomington, IN: Marzano Research Laboratory.

McNeil, L. (1988). *Contradictions of control: School structure and school knowledge.* New York, NY: Routledge.

Mitra, D. (2008). *Student voice in school reform: Building adult-youth partnerships that strengthen schools and empower youth.* Albany, NY: SUNY Press.

Moe, T., & Chubb, J. (2009). *Liberating learning: Technology, politics, and the future of American education.* San Francisco: Jossey-Bass.

Moller, A. C., Deci, E., & Ryan, R. (2006). Choice and ego depletion: The moderating role of autonomy. *Personality and Social Psychology Bulletin, 32*(8), 1024–1036.

National Association of Secondary School Principals (NASSP). (1996). *Breaking ranks: Changing an American institution*. Reston, VA: NASSP.

National Association of Secondary School Principals (NASSP). (2004). *Breaking ranks II: Strategies for leading school reform*. Providence, RI: The Education Alliance.

National Commission on Teaching and America's Future. (1996). *What matters most: Teaching for America's future*. New York: National Commission on Teaching and America's Future.

National Survey of Student Engagement. (2008). Promoting engagement for all students: The imperative to look within. Retrieved from http://nsse.iub.edu/NSSE_2008_Results/docs/withhold/NSSE2008_Results_revised_11-14-2008.pdf

Paige, R. (2009). Self-directed learning and the mind-set of successful entrepreneurial learning. *ATEA Journal, 37*(1), 16.

Pink, D. H. (2005). *A whole new mind: Why right-brainers will rule the future*. New York, NY: The Berkley Publishing Group.

Pink, D. H. (2009). *Drive: The surprising truth about what motivates us*. New York, NY: Riverhead Books.

Pope, D. C. (2001). *"Doing school": How we are creating a generation of stressed out, materialistic, and miseducated students*. New Haven, CT: Yale University Press.

Rawson, M. (2000). Learning to learn: More than a skill set. *Studies in Higher Education, 25* (2), 225–238.

Richardson, W. (2010). *Blogs, wikis, podcasts, and other powerful Web tools for classrooms*, 3rd ed. Thousand Oaks, CA: Corwin Press.

Ritchhart, R., Church, M., & Morrison, K. (2011). *Making thinking visible: How to promote engagement, understanding, and independence for all learners*. San Francisco: Jossey-Bass.

Rogers, C. Freiberg, H. J. (1994). *Freedom to learn*, 3rd ed. New York: Merrill.

Ryan, R. M., & Deci, E. L. (2000). Self-determination theory and the facilitation of intrinsic motivation, social development, and well being. *American Psychologist, 55*(1), 68–78.

Sanders, W. L., Rivers, J. C. (1996). Cumulative and residual effects of taechers on future student academic achievement. *University of Tennessee Value-Added Assessment Center*. Knoxville, Tennessee.

Scherer, M. (2008). Perspectives/The high school scene. *Educational Leadership, 65*(8), 7.

Senge, P. (1990). *The fifth discipline: The art and practice of the learning organization*. New York: Currency Doubleday.

Senge, P., Cambron-McCabe, N., Lucas, T., Smith, B., Dutton, J., & Kleiner, A. (2000). *Schools that learn: A fifth discipline fieldbook for educators, parents, and everyone who cares about education*. New York, NY: Doubleday.

Thomas, W. T. (2009). *Intrinsic motivation at work: Building energy and commitment* (2nd ed.). San Francisco, CA: Berrett-Koehler Publishers.

Wagner, T. (2008). *The global achievement gap: Why even our best schools don't teach the new survival skills our children need — and what we can do*. New York, NY: Basic Books.

Wagner, T. (2012). *Creating innovators: The making of young people who will change the world*. New York, NY: Scribner.

Wagner, T., Kegan, R., Lahey, L., Lemons, R., Garnier, J., Helsing, D., . . . Rasmussen, H. T. (2006). *Change leadership*. San Francisco, CA: John Wiley & Sons.

Waters, R. (2012). *Secondary students' transitioning from compliance to intentional learning*. (Doctoral Dissertation). Retrieved from UMI ProQuest (Order No: 3504071)

William, D. (2011). *Embedded formative assessment*. Bloomington, IN: Solution Tree.

Yazzie-Mintz, E. (2007). Voices of students on engagement: A report on the 2006 High School Survey of Student Engagement. Retrieved from http://ceep.indiana.edu/hssse/images/HSSSE%20Overview%20Report%20-%202006.pdf

Yazzie-Mintz, E. (2009). Engaging the voices of students: A report on the 2007 & 2008 High School Survey of Student Engagement. Retrieved from http://www.indiana.edu/~ceep/hssse/images/HSSSE_2009_Report.pdf

Zhao, Y. (2009). *Catching up or leading the way: American education in the age of globalization.* Alexandria, VA: Association for Supervision and Curriculum Development.

Zhao, Y. (2012). *World class learners: Educating creative and entrepreneurial students.* Thousand Oaks, CA: Corwin.

THREE

Guiding Step 3: Face Traditional School Culture—The Game of School and Strategic Learning

This chapter looks at a cultural custom shared by all traditional schools, the game of school. In understanding the game of school, readers will see that this cultural custom is inherent in the structures and programs of all traditional schools. That is, the structures and programs of a traditional school actually encourage playing the game of school. In examining this cultural force, this book, again, operates from the common maxim in organizational thinking often attributed to Peter Drucker: "Culture eats strategy for breakfast."

Thus, regardless of a school's stated mission or other goals, the culture of a school will always dominate and be the overriding factor in what happens in the school and the effect the school has on people and learning. As the driver of culture in traditional schools, the game of school will lead to a loss of community and diminished learning for students and teachers. It is a major reason for change.

STAGE 1: TEACHERS AND THE GAME OF SCHOOL

If readers are reading this book as part of an assignment at a college or university, they should consider the assignment for a moment. Which of the following descriptions best captures readers' attitudes toward the assignment? One, readers heard about this book recently, and an eagerness to read it emerged from within. Readers lately have been thinking a lot about the choice to become teachers, so an interest developed to know more about the author's thinking. In effect, readers had personal motives for reading this book.

Or, readers are good students. As good students, when readers receive assignments, they complete them. OK, perhaps reading this book did not come from personal motivation, but because readers wanted to get a good grade, they read it. From a strategic point of view, readers know that reading the book, even if it is a quick read, will be better than not reading it at all. Further, if they did not read the book, their chances of getting a good grade might be damaged, and that would disappoint important people, such as parents, an adviser, and maybe even peers.

Add to this that it is common knowledge that getting good grades would likely lead to other good outcomes, such as a scholarship, choice of teaching positions, on-the-job advancement, or better pay. There are plenty of reasons in the world for readers to get their work done.

What can be seen from readers' responses to these two descriptions is that the game of school has something to do with their motives for doing the work at school. It may be stipulated for now that the game of school has to do with doing assignments not for personal purposes but for getting external things. This usually includes rewards of some kind, such as grades; awards; promotions; or praise from teachers, parents, or peers. In the pursuit of these external rewards, students and teachers tend to lose sight of their personal purposes in learning and fail to make a personal investment in their work.

Please recall that the author made a passing reference earlier to his personal introduction to the game of school. That introduction came in his very first position as a teacher. He described that in adapting to the culture of the school, he learned how to play that school's version of the game of school. So, let's be clear: This author played the game of school, too. This book has been written not from the perspective of an innocent bystander but from that of an aware participant. He has also reflected on his participation. He has recognized that in his career, there were times that he went through the motions of doing the job without making a personal investment in it.

Readers are likely familiar with how to play the game of school because nearly all students and teachers play it. It is not clear, however, whether readers were aware of having played a game. Unfortunately, many of the students and teachers who play the game of school are unaware they are playing it. They think it's just what happens in schools.

Most players also don't recognize how these rules and strategies of the game constrain how they think of learning. In the game of school, the idea of learning becomes something students do to get grades, promotions, and awards or to eventually graduate. More important, as many students and teachers become invested in this definition of learning, they progressively lose sight of how the game of school learning is distinct from and inferior to authentic learning. Many have never even heard of or explored the concept of authentic learning.

Looking back at readers' work in school and college, can they see that in many cases it was just about going through the motions to get the work done and get the rewards, with no personal investment? Surely, readers are aware that the earlier question about motives for reading this book is a lead-in to how one experiences the game. Do readers have a sense of how playing diminishes learning? Can readers see now how the motives with which they might read this book will affect the quality of the learning they get from it? Have readers ever before made a distinction between the game of school learning and authentic learning?

Before proceeding with this discussion and actually defining the game of school, refreshing the context is important. In the introduction, the author explained that this book was going to be personal. It would be personal because this book is about readers thinking about themselves. The author explained that it was going to be about readers as individuals and their deep, intrinsic reasons for wanting to be teachers. It was going to be about readers sorting out their desires to be teachers and whether teaching was going to provide the rewards they sought from it.

The author further explained that this book would be about making choices and asserting leadership that will lead readers to their desired rewards. He speculated that the deepest of their motives for becoming teachers would be satisfied by their caring and personal interactions with students. Readers should keep all of this in mind as they read further.

STAGE 2: SCHOOL CULTURE AND THE GAME OF SCHOOL

Now let's look at the game of school as a cultural phenomenon. Not every organization or school has a gaming culture, but almost all traditional schools do. This can be known because all traditional schools attempt to motivate students and teachers with extrinsic rewards, incentives, and forces from outside themselves. Once this system of extrinsic rewards is set in place, the game of school is inevitable. People start focusing on getting these extrinsic rewards, and they lose sight of their personal motives for learning.

Given what we have considered thus far about the game of school, let's check readers' sensitivity to it as a cultural force. What can readers recall about the cultures of the schools they attended, visited, or worked in? Were people mostly going through the motions of getting things done so they could keep their supervisors off their backs and earn their pay? Was there a lot of complaining? Was there an air of negativity from people being stressed with doing things they didn't want to do? Was there a sense that the work people did was a grind and that they were counting the days to vacation or retirement?

> **A Career Diminished**
> Working in industrial age schools, teachers will become invested in routines and practices inappropriate to the twenty-first century.

Or, could readers sense a cohesion among teachers, that they were working together with enthusiasm toward accomplishing a collective mission? Were there a lot of smiles and laughter? Were teachers enjoying their interactions with students? Could readers see instruction that was vibrant, with kids responding eagerly and actively? Were people deeply focused on work that they clearly enjoyed doing? Might readers have encountered thoughtful discussions among teachers about what drives student progress and the wonderful outcomes they were seeing?

Both of these scenarios are out there in the world. What accounts for the better of these two scenarios is not a mystery. The ingredient that makes the difference is personal commitment. Those organizations that can elicit a personal commitment from their members are more likely to succeed (Deming 1986; Garvin, 2000; Johnson & Chang, 2008; Scott & Dixon, 2009; Senge, 1990; Senge et al., 2000; Song et al., 2009). This leads to the next question. How can schools get people away from gaming and move toward making a personal investment in their work?

Those who have studied organizations have known for a long time that cultures may emerge in organizations that have a negative quality and tend to diminish the productivity of the organization. As a consequence, how students or workers might be prompted to make a personal investment in the work they do has been the subject of considerable research.

Prompting a personal investment in work has been considered from an epistemological perspective (Drew, 2001; Gamache, 2002; Rawson, 2000), a developmental perspective (Armstrong, 2006; Bandura, 2006; Damon, 2008), a learning goal perspective (Ames, 1992; Ames & Archer, 1988; Blackwell et al., 2007; Dweck & Leggett, 1988; Grant & Dweck, 2003; Hong et al., 1999; Mueller & Dweck, 1998), and an instructional perspective (Entwistle, 1977; Fransson, 1977; Gibbs et al., 1982; Martin et al., 2005; Marton & Saljo, 1976; Rossum & Schenk, 1984).

It also has been considered from an organizational perspective (Garvin, 2000; Johnson & Chang, 2008; Scott & Dixon, 2009; Senge, 1990; Senge et al., 2000; Song et al., 2009) and a self-determination perspective (Deci & Ryan, 2008; Deci et al., 1991; Ryan & Deci, 2000, 2002, 2006, 2008).

The point here is that all of this book's focus on the personal has a basis in research. Research verifies that achievement of the core purpose of any organization, including schools, requires that the members of that organization develop a personal commitment to the goals of the organization (Deming, 1986; Garvin, 2000; Johnson & Chang, 2008; Scott &

Dixon, 2009; Senge, 1990; Senge et al., 2000; Song et al., 2009). Hopefully, the reader will be such a teacher.

With knowledge of both gaming and the importance of personal commitment, schools and commercial organizations often go to great lengths to elicit personal commitment from employees and members (Johnson & Chang, 2008; Scott & Dixon, 2009; Senge, 1990; Senge et al., 2000; Song et al., 2009). Those organizations that don't fully grasp the importance of personal commitment or how to get it usually muddle forward, wither, and go out of business.

It is the author's fervent intent that this book will help readers develop such a commitment to working in school. With such a personal commitment, a career as a teacher will not feel like work; instead, it will have the feeling of doing activities and confronting challenges as a chosen mission.

But, there is a problem with readers' or anyone else's achieving such a personal investment in a traditional school. The problem is the game of school. Because the game of school is cultural, readers' adjustment to any traditional school will involve accommodating the pressures of the game. Those pressures will weigh heavily on readers' career satisfaction. To help readers understand these pressures, the author would like to share some recently completed, relevant research.

This research was conducted in a school with the intent of trying to get a better understanding of how students experienced school and how they might be helped to develop a greater personal commitment to their learning. The author became motivated to conduct this research because evidence of low levels of engagement for students in schools had appeared in the academic literature (Yazzie-Mintz, 2007, 2009). He had also observed this in his own work. He had become sensitive to students working really hard but more as an act of competition than as an act of personal interest.

In this research, he discovered studies that confirmed these observations. Other researchers found that many students who worked extremely hard in school and who got high grades did so without making a personal investment in their learning (Demerath, 2009; Fredricks et al., 2004; Humes, 2008; Pope, 2001). Such students were working hard just to get high grades and compare favorably with peers and to keep their parents and teachers happy. There was little personal commitment to the learning.

In light of these troubling reports, the author decided to do research in a school listening to the voices of students as to how they described the experience of high engagement in learning as well as the disconnected learning they often did in school. This research took place over the course of two school years as the author spent a lot of time having reflective discussions with students about learning activities where they felt deeply involved and did not engage in disconnecting behavior as well as situations where they would get bored and felt themselves disconnecting.

STAGE 3: STUDENT DISENGAGEMENT AND THE GAME OF SCHOOL

In one of the author's earliest meetings with students, he attempted to get right to the heart of the issue of their classroom disconnection. He presented to them a list of specific behaviors. The author asked the student participants whether it was true that they spent a lot of time during their classes doing these disconnecting behaviors:

Watching the clock	Writing notes to friends
Daydreaming	Going on Facebook
Looking out of the window	Planning for after school
Doodling	Whispering to a friend
Texting	Doing homework for another class
Thinking about life	Admiring another student

The answer was a unanimous and emphatic yes. In the many discussions with them, students did a lot of complaining about boring teachers. They testified to disengaged behavior in reaction to too much teacher talk, too many school controls, too much routine, and too much sitting around. When faced with a boring situation, it was very hard for students to avoid wanting to do or think about other things. These discussions went on for months. Then one day in a discussion, the expression "game of school" emerged. From that time on, more and more students explained their disconnected behavior as part of the game.

At that time, the author was unaware that the game of school was a concept used in the education literature. His discovery of the game of school as an influence on students' experience of school was an unexpected development in his study. Yes, he had a vague, unexamined notion of how school could be gamelike, but it was a notion on which he had never become focused. In an effort to understand the dynamics of the game of school, he went back to the literature.

His searches in a variety of databases eventually led him to two works by Robert L. Fried, *The Passionate Teacher: A Practical Guide* (2001) and *The Game of School: Why We All Play It, How It Hurts Kids, and What It Will Take to Change It* (2005). Both of these works gave lengthy examinations of the game of school that were consistent with this author's discoveries.

So, what exactly is the game of school? As the students explained it, the basic idea is that when students go to school they don't really go because they want to learn or master what is in all of the textbooks. They experienced going to school as "going because we have to." Students explained that they also knew that they had to behave and get good grades or they would disappoint their parents and friends and other people they cared about.

Students also expressed awareness that if they did not go to school and do the work, they might also be giving up "the good life": getting good grades, going to a good college, and earning good money and all the good things that money would provide. So, as students explained it, they did not go to school because they loved doing schoolwork. They did it because "we have to," and they made no personal investment in most of it.

After much discussion, students were able to clarify for the author and themselves the most critical element of the game of school, deception. Students made it look like they were being good students *by creating the appearance of doing what they were supposed to be doing even when they were not*. Readers probably know how it works. Students provided the following examples of how to game school:

- Instead of reading a book, ask a friend what was the book was about and then make very general comments in class to impress the teacher.
- Write answers on your hand for a short-answer test.
- Instead of taking work home, just do the homework in the morning or copy off another student.
- Students gang up to convince the teacher to change the date of the test with the promise that they will all get an A on the test.
- Instead of reading a book, go to SparkNotes or CliffsNotes.
- Use Google to get book summaries or write reports.
- Ask a friend for answers before the test.
- Have all students say they don't understand when the teacher announces a test.
- Say "I'm sick" on the day of the test or when a paper is due.
- Say to the teacher "I don't get it" or "You didn't teach us this."
- Keep asking the teacher for a lot of help so you really don't have to work yourself.
- For a research paper, copy someone else's paper and paraphrase.
- Always give the impression that you are interested and trying hard.
- Everyone asks the teacher to delay an assignment.
- Make friends with someone who will let you copy homework.
- If you're assigned a research paper and you don't want to do it, put it off for as long as possible or try to get a college student to give you a paper.
- Have somebody else take your SATs for you.

Of course, readers have likely known all of this for a long time. It is, after all, just the way it is in school. Readers should consider that in teaching in a traditional school much of the human interaction is based on sycophantic behavior and deception. In such a place, how will early career teachers get the personal, intrinsic rewards they are seeking?

As this research was pursued and leads were followed, the author was particularly interested in hearing how the students explained the motivation behind playing the game of school. What satisfaction could they get out of the game of school if the end result was low-quality learning? Didn't they see the game of school as self-defeating?

Students responded by describing their experience of school as highly controlled and one they responded to with a sense of resignation. They did what they had to do to get the grades they needed, all with the goal "just to get it over with."

It was the custom of the school for students to create the appearance of compliance with the school's power structure in fulfilling requirements, such as being orderly, listening, taking notes, reading books, writing papers, doing homework, preparing for tests, and passing tests, all with the intent of achieving the grades necessary to get the desired approval from parents and teachers and favorable comparison with peers but without making a personal investment in learning. Students agreed that the resulting quality of learning was regrettable.

But something else emerged. After many discussions, the author began to hear a theme in the students' testimony about their motivation. When students played the game of school, they particularly enjoyed a sense of control when outsmarting their teachers. In such moments students not only felt satisfaction from having protected a certain grade level but also from having protected their autonomy. By playing the game of school, they retained control.

This is a critical point. On the surface many observers may see students' motives in playing the game of school as one of avoiding working, but this study suggested that there was a deeper primary motive. Yes, students did want to avoid work, but they wanted something else even more. Students played the game of school to satisfy their need to be in control, to be the source of their own behavior. In effect, the game of school gave students a sense of control in an institution they perceived to be threatening to their autonomy.

The act of taking control, as facilitated by the game, may be seen as happening in two stages. First, students do not do what they are required to do. Thus, they assert control. Two, students choose to demonstrate certain behaviors that make it look like they have done as required even though that's not the case. This maneuver keeps students in control. Instead of being compliant, students falsify the compliance. The act of learning has now been falsified by copying from a friend, downloading from the Internet, just giving the assignment a thoughtless effort, or any number of other common yet strategic techniques.

Thus, with respect to various class assignments, students' behavior may be revealed for what it is in these expressions: "Yes, I did the homework, but I really copied it from a friend"; "I wrote the paper, but I actually downloaded it from the Internet"; "Yes, I worked hard on the assignment and did an exemplary job, but I did it only to get a high grade, not because I was really personally interested in it."

Students also explained, "I discussed the book we were assigned, but I really read the SparkNotes, not the book"; "I appear to be taking notes from the lesson, but, no, I am actually writing a note to my friend"; "I look studious bringing my laptop to class, but I'm actually playing solitaire"; "I'm looking the teacher in the eyes as if I am listening, but, really, I am daydreaming and planning what I am going to do after school."

Seen in this way, the game of school is all about calculated maneuvers that create the appearances that garner approval without actually giving up control and capitulating to the demands of school. Students interviewed in this study attested to a sense of accomplishment and control when they "got over" on the teacher. The game was all about appearing to do what they are told to do—learn—without really doing what they are told to do—learn. In effect, students falsified their learning; in the words of Scherer (2008), youths "pretend" to be students (p. 7).

Consideration of students' testimonies suggested that logic underlies the game of school. Students pursued the game of school knowing that what the power structure really measures and gives credit for is compliance or the appearance of compliance, not learning. Students knew what they had to do, or appear to do, to earn credits whether or not they were really engaged or learning from what they did.

It was just the doing, going through the motions, and the appearance of doing that really counted. As Machiavelli (1940) explained, "[T]he great majority of mankind are satisfied with appearances, as though they were realities, and are often more influenced by the things that seem than by those that are."

This logic is further confirmed for students because ultimately what they got credit for was the compliance, not the learning. Most students had successfully passed classes wherein they learned very little. They did the assignments up to the point where they knew it would get them the grades they wanted. This often involved many strategic shortcuts that would significantly discount the learning. They also did their work knowing that all would be forgotten when all of the testing was done. They had done this many times over the years and were aware that they could hardly remember anything from many previous classes.

Moreover, students also saw around them other students who had done less and learned even less but managed to pass the class by exercising a variety of compliant and sycophantic behaviors that elicited the sympathies of their teachers and resulted in a passing grade. It should also be reemphasized that the strategic learning described here has been found in other studies involving high-achieving students (Demerath, 2009; Humes, 2008; Pope, 2001).

STAGE 4: TEACHERS ALSO PLAY THE GAME OF SCHOOL

If this testimony from students is disturbing, consider that one of the students' stated reasons for engaging in the game of school was because they perceived teachers as also playing.

This is a student-described scenario: A teacher has a student who is pleasant and compliant and who hands in work that is not satisfactory, but "at least the student tried." The outcome, more often than not, is that this student will pass. Maybe some extra credit will be needed here or there, but the student will pass.

As explained earlier, if the teacher takes a hard line and fails the student, that teacher will face lots of aggravation as a result. Final answer: pass the student, avoid the aggravation, play the game, and move on. The net effect is that students see that compliance is more important than learning, and they see that teachers generally obey this rule of the game.

> **A Career Diminished**
> **In industrial age schools, teachers will become trapped in the game of school culture.**

Over the course of the research, both the author's and the students' understanding of the game of school grew. One aspect of that was observing details of how teachers played the game. Students testified to seeing that teachers focused on creating their own appearance of compliance. They kept their classrooms orderly, they provided instruction and assigned work, and they graded the work and gave students report card grades.

Most students eventually passed their classes. In effect teachers made sure that they kept all of the manifest points of measurement in good order. Is it wrong to do these things? Of course not. But one must ask, do any of these things ensure that students are learning? Does any of it ensure that students are prompted to make a personal investment in their learning?

Or, could a student have a teacher who does all of the right things to create the appearance of compliance and then have a student respond by creating his or her own appearance of learning? The student does this by completing all assignments but only as a rote activity "to get it over with," which will soon be forgotten, even if that forgetting happens after state testing.

The answer is yes, all of this is possible. In fact, it is possible that whole organizations can comprise people who are technically doing what they should be by going through the motions but the organization's goals are not being reached. This should sound familiar because many schools operate in this way. This is where accountability testing came from.

Although this gaming and teachers' complicity in it are never discussed, people in the school and the community know it to be true because they know students with little knowledge and weak skills routinely get promoted. They also know that the grades teachers give cannot be trusted to reflect student learning and this lack of reliability in grading is the basic reason states have resorted to standardized testing to monitor student learning.

School leaders also know that if students who hadn't learned were not promoted, there would be too many students in the school, so many that the school would be unable to accommodate them all. Facing these realities, readers must conclude, as students have, that adults play the game of school, too.

As a early career teachers, the extent to which readers have ever considered this dark side of what happens in schools is uncertain. However, at some point in their careers, most teachers will come to recognize the game and their role in it. When this recognition comes, it will be a red flag signaling low career satisfaction and the deterioration of their personal mission. So, what is the answer? How do teachers find their way out of the game of school and get students to make a personal investment in their learning? The answers to these questions will lead us to new kinds of schools.

REFERENCES

Ames, C. (1992). Classrooms: Goals, structures, and student motivation. *Journal of Educational Psychology, 84*(3), 261–271.

Ames, C., & Archer, J. (1988). Achievement goals in the classroom: Students' learning strategies and motivation processes. *Journal of Educational Psychology, 80*(3), 260–267.

Armstrong, T. (2006). *The best schools: How human development research should inform educational practice.* Alexandria, VA: Association for Supervision and Curriculum Development.

Bandura, A. (2006). Adolescent development from an agentic perspective. In F. Pajares & T. Urdan (Eds.), *Self-efficacy beliefs of adolescents* (pp. 1–43). Charlotte, NC: Information Age Publishing.

Blackwell, L. S., Trzensniewski, K. H., & Dweck, C. S. (2007). Implicit theories of intelligence predict achievement across an adolescent transition: A longitudinal study and an intervention. *Child Development, 78*(1), 246–263.

Damon, W. (2008). *The path to purpose.* New York, NY: Free Press.

Deci, E., Vallerand, R. J., Pelletier, L. G., & Ryan, R. M. (1991). Motivation in education: The self-determination perspective. *Educational Psychologist, 26*(3-4), 325–346.

Deci, E. L., & Ryan, R. M. (2008). Facilitating optimal motivation and psychological well-being across life's domains. *Canadian Psychology, 49*(1), 14–23.

Demerath, P. (2009). *Producing success: The culture of personal advancement in an American high school*. Chicago, IL: University of Chicago Press.
Deming, W. E. (1986). *Out of the crisis*. Cambridge, MA: Massachusetts Institute of Technology.
Drew, S. (2001). Student perceptions of what helps them learn and develop in higher education. *Teaching in Higher Education, 6*(3), 309–331.
Dweck, C. S., & Leggett, E. L. (1988). A social cognitive approach to motivation and personality. *Psychological Review, 95* (2), 256–273.
Entwistle, N. (1977). Strategies of learning and studying: Recent research findings. *British Journal of Educational Studies, 25*(3), 225–238.
Fransson, A. (1977). Qualitative differences in learning: IV. Effects of intrinsic motivation and extrinsic test anxiety on process and outcome. *British Journal of Educational Psychology 47*(3), 244–257.
Fredricks, J. A., Blumenfeld, P. C., Paris, A. H. (2004). School engagementL Potential of the concept, state of the evidence. *Review of Educational Research, 74(1)*, 59–109.
Fried, R. L. (2001). *The passionate teacher: A practical guide*. Boston, MA: Beacon Press.
Fried, R. L. (2005). *The game of school: Why we all play it, how it hurts kids, and what it will take to change it*. San Francisco: Jossey-Bass.
Gamache, P. (2002). University students as creators of personal knowledge: An alternative epistemological view. *Teaching in Higher Education, 7*(3), 277–294.
Garvin, D. (2000). *Learning in action: A guide to putting the learning organization to work*. Boston, MA: Harvard Business School Press.
Gibbs, G., Morgan, A., & Taylor, E. (1982). A review of the research of Ference Marton and the Goteborg Group: A phenomenological research perspective on learning. *Higher Education, 11*(2), 123–145.
Grant, H., & Dweck, C. S. (2003). Clarifying achievement goals and their impact. *Journal of Personality and Social Psychology, 85*(5), 541–553.
Hong, Y., Dweck, C. S., Chiu, C., Lin, D., & Wan, W. (1999). Implicit theories, attributions, and coping: A meaning system approach. *Journal of Personality and Social Psychology, 77*(3), 588–599.
Humes, E. (2008). *School of dreams: Making the grade at a top American high school*. New York, NY: Harcourt.
Johnson, R. E., & Chang, C. (2008). Organizational commitment and its antecedents: Employee self-concept matters. *Journal of Applied Social Psychology, 38*(2), 513–541.
Machiavelli, N. (1940/c. 1517). *The prince and the discourses*. L. Ricci & C. E. Detmold (Trans.). New York, NY: Modern Library.
Martin, F., Hounsell, D., & Entwistle, N. (Eds.). (2005). The experience of learning: Implications for teaching and studying in higher education. (3rd Internet ed.). Edinburgh: University of Edinburgh. Retrieved from http://www.ed.ac.uk/schools-departments/institute-academic-development/learning-teaching/staff/advice/researching/publications/experience-of-learning
Marton, F., & Saljo, R. (1976). On qualitative differences in learning: I. Outcomes and process. *British Journal of Educational Psychology, 46*(1), 4–11.
Mueller, C. M., & Dweck, C. S. (1998). Praise for intelligence can undermine children's motivation and performance. *Journal of Personality and Social Psychology, 75*(1), 33–52.
Pope, D. (2001). *"Doing school": How we are creating a generation of stressed out, materialistic, and miseducated students*. New Haven, CT: Yale University Press.
Rawson, M. (2000). Learning to learn: More than a skill set. *Studies in Higher Education, 25*(2), 225–238.
Rossum, E. J., & Schenk, S. M. (1984). The relationship between learning conception, study strategy, and learning outcome. *British Journal of Educational Psychology, 54*(1), 73–83.
Ryan, R., & Deci, E. (2002). Overview of self-determination theory. In R. R. Ryan & E. L. Deci (Eds.), *Handbook of self-determination theory*. Rochester, NY: The University of Rochester Press.

Ryan, R., & Deci, E. (2006). Self-regulation and the problem of human autonomy: Does psychology need choice, self-determination, and will? *Journal of Personality, 74*(6), 1557–1585.

Ryan, R., & Deci, E. (2008). From ego depletion to vitality: Theory and findings concerning the facilitation of energy available to the self. *Social and Personality Psychology Compass, 2*(2), 702–717.

Ryan, R. M., & Deci, E. L. (2000). Self-determination theory and the facilitation of intrinsic motivation, social development, and well-being. *American Psychologist, 55*(1) 68–78.

Scherer, M. (2008). Perspective/The school scene. *Educational Leadership, 65*(8), 7.

Scott, S., & Dixon, K. (2009). Partners in a learning organization: A student-focused model of professional development. *Educational Forum, 73*(3), 240–255.

Senge, P. (1990). *The fifth discipline: The art and practice of the learning organization*. New York, NY: Doubleday.

Senge, P., Cambron-McCabe, N., Lucas, T., Smith, B., Dutton, J., & Kleiner, A. (2000). *Schools that learn: A fifth discipline fieldbook for educators, parents, and everyone who cares about education*. New York, NY: Doubleday.

Song, H. J., Kim, H. M., & Kolb, J. (2009). The effect of learning organization culture on the relationship of interpersonal trust and organizational commitment. *Human Resource Development Quarterly, 20*(2), 147–167.

Yazzie-Mintz, E. (2007). Voices of students on engagement: A report on the 2006 High School Survey of Student Engagement. Retrieved from http://ceep.indiana.edu/hssse/images/HSSSE%20Overview%20Report%20-%202006.pdf

Yazzie-Mintz, E. (2009). Engaging the voices of students: A report on the 2007 & 2008 School Survey of Student Engagement. Retrieved from http://www.indiana.edu/~ceep/hssse/images/HSSSE_2009_Report.pdf

II

Embrace Positive Forces for Change: Twenty-First-Century Learning Will Be Different

FOUR

Guiding Step 4: Focus on Learning Engagement—A Premise for New Schools

Part II of this book turns from looking at the problems inherent in industrial age schools to positive trends for educational change. One of those trends is a new attention to the concept of learning engagement. Learning engagement is the level of involvement and connection that students experience in doing their schoolwork. In recent years more and more schools, although still a small minority, have taken an interest in understanding the real involvement of students with what they do at school (Farris-Berg, Dirkswager, & Junge, 2012; Fredricks et al., 2004; Yazzie-Mintz, 2007, 2009).

There is a sense in which this chapter might be seen as the centerpiece of this book. Every page that follows in some way will be related to changing schools and what teachers and students do in them based on understanding what invites learning engagement for both groups. Understanding what invites engagement will be the outcome of teachers listening carefully to each other and students' testimonies about how they experience learning and schooling. This focus on listening to the voices of students will be a critical part in developing an ongoing, organizational dialogue about what engages students and its implications for changing schools.

Psychologists and educators have known for a long time that there are conditions in life that invite people to reach out and engage or, conversely, to withdraw, disengage, and assume postures of defense and disconnection (Brown, 2013; Deci & Ryan, 2008; Maslow, 1968). The same is true in schools. Schools need to create the conditions for students and teachers to fully engage and make wholehearted, personal investments in their work.

Understanding this new interest in learning engagement will, then, help in addressing the question of how an organization, particularly a school, can elicit from its members a personal investment in their work. It will explore how school and teacher evolution should be an outcome of their understanding of the factors that enhance engagement for students and themselves. With such an outlook, schools will have a basis for continual improvement, devising better and better ways of getting students engaged. And, teachers will be able to make their careers truly engaging and not something done out of routine while withdrawing into functionary behavior.

The concept of learning engagement is complex and multidimensional (Fredricks et al., 2004). However it may be defined, the idea of measuring students' engagement acknowledges important phenomena. A student may be in a classroom in a school, with eyes focused on the teacher, but in reality that student may be absent emotionally, socially, cognitively, or otherwise. That it has occurred to educators to investigate student engagement is a very good thing.

Checking student engagement shows depth of understanding and awareness that educators may not be attuned to their students on a variety of levels. It recognizes that no matter how good educators may think their schools or classrooms may be, they understand that what teachers are providing may be inadequate. Thus, they wisely try to get a reality check by investigating learning engagement.

Both those institutions that develop surveys of student engagement and those that use them claim the information they provide and the improvements they inspire are of great benefit (Farris-Berg, Dirkswager, & Junge, 2012; McCarthy & Kuh, 2006; Yazzie-Mintz, 2007). Unfortunately, the vast majority of schools do not employ student engagement surveys, nor do they attempt to monitor student engagement in any systematic way. Those schools that do may reap significant insights into how and why students engage. They also help teachers learn a lot about the nature of authentic learning.

GETTING PEOPLE PERSONALLY INVESTED IN WORK AND LEARNING

Chapter 3 deconstructed the game of school. That led to asking a question: How do schools get away from the impersonal and disconnected ways of the game of school and move toward getting students personally invested in learning? Asking this question will lead to the heart of new school thinking: Learning must be personal. As the author invites readers to begin envisioning new schools, the idea of paying attention to students' engagement is an important concept in seeing how new schools will be different.

Getting students to make a personal investment in their learning begins with paying attention to how they experience learning. For example, in the course of this writing the author carefully considered what he might write that would prompt readers to make a personal investment in teaching. As with students, his conclusion was to inquire about readers' engagement, to ask some questions about their personal experiences in teaching.

However, in this context, his inquiry into readers' engagement would be done only because the author wants readers to make such inquiries for themselves. As teachers begin their careers, it is important to first understand the process as they apply it to themselves. So, the author urges readers to try to understand themselves as learners and assess the quality of their experiences and learning as early career teachers.

THE QUALITY OF ENGAGEMENT AND THE QUALITY OF THE LEARNING

Let's start the process with this. Can readers recall a situation where they experienced fun, learning, and deep involvement? It might have been collecting baseball cards, helping a parent refinish the basement, collecting food for the poor, creating a summer retreat for church teens, or going on a family fishing trip. The fact is that it could be nearly any experience at all where readers did some enjoyable learning.

As readers recall this experience, how might it be described? Could it be described as something they really enjoyed, learned a lot from, and had a lot of fun doing? Time flew by, and there were momentary flashes of deep focus. There was never a sense of distraction, and there were no impulses to think about or do something else. The challenge of learning from others and mastering new skills was fully embraced. All the readers' thinking was about advancing the project. Overall, readers had a strong sense of ownership over the project and yearned for its success. If all of this were true, this would be a picture of full learning engagement.

Mihaly Csikszentmihalyi (1990, 1997), a famous psychologist, applied a name to such a condition. He called it "flow," a state of deep engagement, wherein a person is so involved in an experience that there is a sense of a psychological zone of complete focus. Having readers recall their own experiences with such deep engagement will provide a reference point by which they might monitor their own levels of engagement in other experiences.

So, let's take a look at the readers' work as teachers. What questions will help them know and understand their personal engagement in what they are doing as teachers? Let's try these questions:

- Do I regard my work in schools thus far as personally meaningful?
- Do I detect in myself a growing enthusiasm to teach, listen, explain, and interact with students?
- Is the activity of being in a busy classroom full of students one that I enjoy? Do I feel myself getting into the flow zone?
- Do I enjoy teaching and counseling students individually?
- Do I detect in myself a growing satisfaction with the career choice I have made?
- Am I getting those human rewards that caused me to be drawn to teaching?
- Do I feel supported by the people I work with? Do I feel others pulling for me, investing themselves in my success?
- Do I experience my work at school as stressful chores or as the fulfillment of a mission?
- Do I feel and see evidence of my personal investment?

As readers consider these questions, it should be added that in the author's experience, some of the positive signs of a good career choice do not appear immediately. They come as teachers get an increasing sense of control over what they are doing. So, readers should not make hasty judgments. Nevertheless, the main point is to start to monitor their own engagement. Why? Because when teachers monitor their own engagement, particularly learning engagement, they are developing sensitivity to quality levels, learning quality levels.

THE PRODUCT AND THE EXPERIENCE

Understanding that learning has quality levels is very important. Industrial age schools thrive on low-level strategic learning. They prompt kids to work for grades and other rewards. Conversely, new schools will thrive on getting students to make a personal investment in learning.

On that note, let's continue to look at readers' engagement. Now the question is slightly different. How did readers feel to be asked these questions about their engagement? How did they feel knowing the author was interested in their engagement? What did it mean that the author employed words such as "enjoyed," "enthusiasm," "meaningful," "satisfaction," "human rewards," "mission," and "personal investment"? To understand the effect of such questions, consider this example.

Let's imagine for a moment that the author is the supervisor of those reading this book. And, let's say that during a conference, he did *not* give readers technical tips on how to improve their instructional performance. Those tips he did *not* give might be something like the following. During instruction

- employ an illustration along with explanatory remarks;

- walk around the classroom, make eye contact, and check that students are following along; and
- when posing questions, allow for thought time before accepting answers.

These are all good instructional tips, but in this example, the supervisor doesn't focus there. Instead, he focuses on helping readers enhance their personal experience of teaching. For instance, the supervisor suggests that readers do the following:

- Initiate three warm, eye-to-eye interactions with students as they introduce instruction. Example, "Oh, I love the pattern on your shirt." Or, "I see your homework is well prepared." Or, "I know you have been sick. I hope you are feeling better."
- Insert a brief, funny story about themselves as students while they instruct.
- During class, make a sincere confession to their students.

Just to be clear, both lists of tips would be appropriate and helpful for early career teachers. Still, they are different. One set of suggestions is telling readers how to improve instruction. The other set is more focused on how to enjoy the experience of instruction—by deepening a personal connection with students. Again, the author wants to bring readers' attention to the human rewards that all teachers want. And, yes, he is sure readers can observe how the second set has a theme: Make it personal.

> **A Career Diminished**
> Working in industrial age schools, teachers will fail to employ the growing number of twenty-first-century models for learning.

Now let's put readers into a different situation. Students have just completed papers for the teacher, who is now going to have a brief conference with each student. The students think their teacher is going to give them some wholesale, perfunctory statements of praise and then tell them what they did wrong. They are expecting comments such as the following (factory supervisor–type comments):

- You didn't reference that statistic on page 4.
- Your second paragraph is too long.
- Those items in a series are not parallel.

Isn't that how it goes?

But the students' teacher surprises them. Instead, their teacher asks questions that have to do with the quality of their learning experience. They might be questions such as the following:

- Did you enjoy writing this paper?

- Can you think of anything that I could do or you could do to make such an assignment more interesting or enjoyable?
- Did you feel that working on this paper helped you learn something you actually wanted to learn?

The author's interest here is not on how students might answer these questions. He would be more interested in how these students would interpret the fact that their teacher asked such questions at all. What would it mean to them?

The author suggests the following: The students would get the idea that their teacher was interested in the quality of their experience. They would get the idea that enjoyment was an important factor. They would further think that their teacher thinks students have something to offer to help him or her be a better teacher. They would think that their teacher thinks that what they really want to learn is an important factor in learning at school. How would readers feel about students getting these impressions?

Looking back at these two scenarios, one set of questions is about getting a better product—effective instruction. The other set of questions has to do with getting a better experience in making the product—greater personal engagement and an enhanced desire to learn. Readers might ask why it is important how students experience learning as long as they learn what they need to learn. This question is key. Why is the feeling of the learning process so important? The answers to this question lead to new thinking about schools and learning.

EXPERIENCING VALUE IN LEARNING LEADS TO MORE LEARNING

The author offers this analogy. Readers are retailers on Main Street. As with most smart retailers, only high-quality merchandise is offered for sale. Readers know that in the long run, quality will bring people back into the store. But readers also know that selling quality goods is not the only factor. Customers must also feel that their shopping experience is of high quality. When a customer comes in the door, readers provide prompt, courteous service with no pressure. Readers go out of their way to be helpful. There is a commitment to a high-quality shopping experience because this is the experience that brings people back.

The author would submit that one of the most important things teachers should want to accomplish is to give students learning experiences that will bring them back for more and build their desire to learn. Educators often talk of creating lifelong learners. But how can they talk that talk if they do not pay attention to what it is that beckons students back to learning: an enjoyable, meaningful experience. Understanding this, it is possible to see the value of understanding learning engagement but also to lament the infrequency with which it is attempted.

It is not possible to provide high-quality learning experiences unless teachers are paying attention to the experience behind the learning. They have to let kids know that they care about those experiences. Yes, the textbooks are loaded with wonderful things people should know (the product). But, if teachers really want students to be return customers and continue learning after they leave school (an absolute must in the twenty-first century), these students must have in their past many meaningful, happy, and fun experiences with learning. These positive experiences will become a frame of reference for what it means to do all the things that result in learning.

This analogy is worth extending. When a business person decides to open a store on Main Street, part of the process is to develop a business model. A good business model will consider providing a product or service that people want or need in a way that is better than what the competitor down the street provides. In creating this business model, a business person attempts to create an experience for customers. That experience is value.

What is the experience of value? When customers get the products they want in a store, they walk out with a cognitive emotional complex: "I got what I wanted; it was pleasant to buy; I got it at a good price; I'm happy that I have it; I have a nice feeling." Good value is a nice feeling that people seek.

ENTERING THE LEARNING VALUE ZONE

The author now asks readers to consider this question. At school, should teachers pay attention to the concept of value? OK, yes, teachers have knowledge and skills, and the students should want them. There is no debating the importance of the knowledge and skills. At the same time, do students walk out the door with that good-value feeling? Do they have the feeling "I'm coming back for more of this?" Should they? Of course. Certainly readers know that the author believes they should. He is also pretty sure that readers might think he is getting crazy here. Really, how much should teachers honestly expect kids to love their learning?

The author has already expressed that teachers should pay attention to students' experience of learning. Now he is trying to convince readers that when teachers let students know that they are interested in how they experience learning, they are letting them know that they are interested in how students experience value at school. That experience is on the inside of the student. It is personal, and it is what brings students back for more.

There is a wonderful book by Phillip Schlechty that the author always recommends, *Working on the Work: An Action Plan for Teachers, Principals, and Superintendents* (2002). The premise of this book is that teachers should place special focus on creating work for students that is engaging. They should not see their job as just covering material and explaining. Instead, their real job is the creation and facilitation of work that creates learning engagement. If the lesson is not fun, exciting, and engaging, come up with something new. Creating exciting work for students is the real work of teachers.

Imagine that when teachers are preparing work for students, the work could not be used unless it passed a fun, exciting, and meaningful test. Wow, what kind of school would that lead to? Yes, the author is saying let's make the work that we expect kids to do enjoyable, meaningful, and, yes, fun! The author's interpretation of this is that teachers must send their students home with memories of enjoying learning—a sense of value.

The author's sense of what value means for students came as a result of his research and discussion with students. He specifically asked students what conditions would be necessary to get away from the low-value learning in the game of school and toward personally meaningful learning for all students (Waters, 2012, p. 187). Students' answers were used in developing the following list, called the Learning Value Zone. Look at the list below. Are there some other experiences that might be added to it?

1. I feel that the teachers and students around me really care about me and my progress.
2. I know that my individual differences and uniqueness as a learner are appreciated.
3. I know that my teachers and school leaders have an interest in how I experience school.
4. I see my personal strengths, weaknesses, talents, and goals are being clarified.
5. I enjoy the work I do at school and discover the pleasures of learning.
6. I sense that my schoolwork is relevant and has purpose for me now and for my future.
7. I sense my personal growth in knowledge, skills, and social maturity.
8. I feel my power to make choices regarding what and how I learn.

In regard to students' sense of value, it is worth noting the work of authors Hebert, Durham, and Silver (2008), whose book, *High Stakes Teaching: Practices That Improve Student Learning*, argues the detriments of schools focusing on standardized testing because of adverse effects on student perceptions.

These authors cite the research of Lawrence, Jones, and Smith (1999), whose study concluded, "As the stakes continue to be ratcheted up by administrators, education boards, and policy makers, large percentages of students feel less and less cared for" (as cited in Hebert et al., 2008, p. 1). While the current force of standardized testing in American education is likely to ignore such an effect, readers are asked whether they can see how placing a high priority on students' sense of being cared for would enhance their relationships with students and, thereby, their careers?

ORGANIZATIONS AND THE EXPERIENCE OF QUALITY

As readers consider the nature of quality levels in learning and the questions posed, it would again be helpful to refresh the context of this discussion. It should be observed that there is a puzzling phenomenon that has been observed in the study of organizations, particularly schools.

This organizational phenomenon may be described as everybody doing what she or he is supposed to be doing. The teachers are teaching, and most students are passing and graduating, yet the school fails to accomplish its goals. Test scores are falling and employers, colleges, and universities are all complaining about the poor skills of students coming out of schools. Add to that the skill levels of graduates don't compare well with those of other nations. Does this sound familiar?

Back at school, the principal and the supervisors see all the teachers and students doing their work, down to the finest detail, while at the same time the quality and desirability of the organization's product—learning—deteriorates year after year. This phenomenon in schools has existed for decades and in corporations for even longer (Fisher, 1999; Senge et al., 2000). How does this happen? What is missing? Without taking a long trip through organizational history or theory, the missing ingredient has been determined. Of course, the author is referring to personal commitment.

Somehow, some organizations are able to elicit from their members a personal commitment to work while others have members only going through the motions of doing the job with no personal investment. In many schools, teachers' work is mechanical, done with little zeal; in other schools, there is passion and personal mission.

Going back to consider readers' personal experiences of teaching, which of the two supervisors would have elicited from readers a more personal commitment to teaching and learning? Would it have been the supervisor who offered coaching on the techniques of instruction or the supervisor who gave coaching on improving the experience of instruction?

Similarly, when readers were hypothetically conferencing with students about their papers, which set of prompts would most likely have elicited from the students a personal investment? Would it have been those observations about the technical correctness of the paper or those questions about how they experienced their work? Answering these questions will get readers ready to imagine new schools. This is because the twenty-first century is demanding happy learners, people who are happy to learn, unlearn, and learn again, and again, and again. Learning is not a chore. The challenge is enjoyed and there is delight in getting better at many skills.

WHERE DOES PERSONAL COMMITMENT COME FROM?

Research suggests that personal commitment to work comes when it is invited. A personal commitment to work may be thought of as a mind-set. Mind-sets are not stable. They are subject to the influences from around them (Dweck, 2006). When a person enters an environment, that environment is full of stimuli that suggest to her or him how to respond and behave.

Whatever the situation in a school, students will get signals about whether a situation is going to be personal, impersonal, or somewhere in between. The strength of these signals in combination with an individual's personality and his or her unique construction of reality will influence the individual's mind-set and how the individual will respond.

Research in psychology has suggested that such signals may influence how students approach their schoolwork and whether they make a personal investment in learning (Ames & Archer, 1988; Blackwell et al., 2007; Dweck & Leggett, 1988; Grant & Dweck, 2003; Hong et al., 1999; Mueller & Dweck, 1998).

> **A Career Diminished**
> Working in industrial age schools, teachers' collective action will be largely constrained to what works for standardized test preparation.

Shortly, two sets of signals will be presented, to which students would respond either by doing schoolwork strategically and without a personal investment or with a deep personal investment. The previous experiments examining readers' experiences in teaching should have helped them in getting ready to understand and interpret such signals.

THE GAME OF SCHOOL THWARTS THE PERSONAL

Before getting to those specific signals, however, let's return to the game of school for a moment. As the game of school unfolds, it is customary that students and teachers not speak of it. This is a signal. Students and teachers do not have discussions about the game of school and its inherent pitfalls. There is no inquiry into the very obvious, disengaged behavior of students or teachers. Students learn that there is a part of life in school that doesn't get discussed: the experience of doing the work, their engagement.

In this way, the game of school culture is much like alcoholism in a family. The game drives the behavior of the school, yet it is never discussed. Students and teachers do not point out to each other how they appear to be gaming. Although student deception and outright cheating are rampant (Noah & Eckstein, 2001), there is little discussion of it. At the same time, teachers game the system with their grading and rule enforcement, but it is rarely brought up.

In the press of getting all of the things done that must be done in a school, teachers rarely inquire with students about how they personally connect or fail to connect with the work they do. There is never any confession from either group. What does this avoidance of such a crucial topic signal? The signal is that the quality of students' experience in learning is something that is not discuss. It doesn't count. What counts is that an assignment has been completed—productivity. Unless there are obvious indications of cheating, how the assignment was accomplished is not discussed.

What is more interesting about this analogy is that like alcoholism in a family, the subject of engagement has a forbidden quality. Like bringing up alcoholism in an affected family, bringing up issues of engagement in school is perceived as having a catastrophic quality. It could cause a blowup. People will turn on each other. Important structures and habits could be disrupted. As this avoidance unfolds, it is rationalized: Teachers ask, can the school really afford to spend time discussing and reflecting about whether a student finds work "enjoyable," "meaningful," "satisfying," or "relevant"?

To consider the analogy further, let's say school leaders and teachers really did examine student engagement. Where might it lead? If educators did find out that school is not "enjoyable," "meaningful," "satisfying," or "relevant" for many students, where would that take them. One place it might take them would be to think "Gee, maybe we should change the system. Maybe we could do things differently." In effect, paying attention to student engagement could lead to the end of industrial age thinking about schools.

This is a critical point. Schools measure learning by testing for information or skills. It sounds like common sense. Do students know these things? Can they do these things? But the sense of it seems less common if a distinction is made between strategic, game of school learning and authentic learning.

If educators acknowledge that there are different quality levels in learning (Ames & Archer, 1988; Asch, 1952; Ausubel et al., 1978; Hatano & Inagaki, 1986; Hatano & Oura, 2003; Nichols et al., 1989; Nolen & Haladyna, 1990), just as there are in all other human activities, they might have to face the low quality of learning in industrial age schools. They might be forced to think of ways to deepen learning. They might see the need to move away from standardization of learning.

But this would be dangerous for school leaders because pursuing an understanding of quality levels in learning and authentic learning could very well lead to the catastrophic recognition that the industrial age system just doesn't work. That recognition might lead to seeing a reason to replace the system. The traditional school would in a sense be destroyed. This would be catastrophic for the obstructors of change and the protection of their comfort zones. For others this truth might lead to some new ideas about learning.

THERE ARE TWO KINDS OF LEARNING

Authentic Learning

Authentic learning is engaged in because an individual has a personal motive to learn something. The individual enjoys the challenge and the process, desires to do more of it, and likes the confidence that comes when he or she acquires new knowledge and skills. An individual feels like the learning has become a part of him- or herself. When authentic learning is experienced, it makes an individual feel changed, and a desire for more authentic learning ensues.

Game of School, Strategic Learning

This is not learning an individual does out of enjoyment of the subject or the challenge. It is mechanical and done to get the grades, promotions, college acceptances, or the awards needed to keep parents and teachers happy and to look good to friends. It is done because the individual was moved by external pressures to do it. There is no personal investment.

TWO SETS OF SIGNALS: IN WHICH SCHOOL DO TEACHERS WANT TO LEARN?

This digression from the discussion of learning engagement to revisiting the game of school has a point. Personal engagement and the game of school are antithetical. If teachers start paying attention to students' engagement at school and the quality of their learning experiences, that very behavior will begin dismantling the game of school and the institution on which it depends—the traditional industrial age school.

In Table 4.1, two sets of signals are provided that might be sent by a school's culture. Readers should take the time to compare and contrast them and ask which set of signals would invite students to personally invest in their learning. Which set of signals would likely encourage students to resort to the game of school? Why?

Table 4.1.

Learning Culture in a Traditional School	Learning Culture in a Twenty-First-Century School
1. Teachers and school leaders frequently talk about important requirements, government mandates, testing, and fixed schedules.	1. Teachers and students present and discuss many learning choices for the students.
2. Teachers and school leaders emphasize that most learning challenges are requirements, and the school offers few electives. Electives are thought of as less important "fun and games" classes.	2. The school provides many electives and encourages student-initiated and -invented courses along with anytime, anywhere learning opportunities.
3. Teachers and school leaders focus on evaluation outcomes (letter grades or other scaling devices and test scores) over effort or process.	3. Teachers recognize and emphasize effort (hours devoted, start overs, learning from failures, and extraordinary behavior) as key to learning.
4. Teachers and school leaders give much recognition for compliance: Students are appreciated for working hard regardless of whether they experience the work as interesting or meaningful.	4. Teachers look for and facilitate unique and divergent interests to which students show a high level of commitment (the mind-set that a person loves or finds special meaning in certain activities and work).
5. Technology is used to standardize what students learn and how they learn it and are evaluated.	5. Technology is used to individualize, personalize, and customize learning.
6. Teachers and school leaders promote decontextualized learning (students are expected to do work because "it is good for you," without understanding its place in their lives or the world).	6. Teachers and school leaders promote learning in context. Work is an outcome of student interest and is situated in real-world environments of practice: laboratories, courtrooms, fire stations, hospitals, corporate offices, water treatment plants, etc.
7. Teachers and school leaders do not seek student input on how to improve teaching and learning.	7. Teachers seek feedback and input from students about learning and instruction. Students help teachers reflect on their teaching techniques and instructional practices.

8. Teachers and school leaders emphasize memorization, right answers, work completion, and short-answer or multiple-choice testing.	8. Teachers provide demonstrations of and invitations to complete complicated, long-term projects and problem solving. Quizzes and short-answer and multiple-choice testing are rare.
9. Students experience schoolwork as routines of compliance (just getting the work done, with little personal interest, so they don't get in trouble).	9. Students experience work as missions to be accomplished to further personally important learning that helps them get to the next level.
10. Teachers are not interested in student complaints about being bored in school. They give stock responses about the students needing the knowledge and needing to take an interest in their education.	10. Teachers listen to and respond to students' concerns about boring experiences. And, teachers accept students' concerns about boring experiences and explain why some boring experiences may be necessary.
11. Students are almost always listening, never presenting their expertise.	11. Students are provided many opportunities to present and demonstrate knowledge of nuanced information or skills.
12. Students' personal strengths are unrecognized in favor of learning requirements.	12. Students' personal strengths are monitored, and students are often provided opportunities to employ and/or demonstrate personal strengths.
13. There are no formal opportunities for students to employ their strengths to help others.	13. Students are provided opportunities to help others improve.
14. Teachers and school leaders place emphasis on extrinsic motivation: Learn in order to get good grades, keep parents happy, get respect of peers, get into a good college, get a good job, make good money.	14. Students are provided opportunities to express intrinsic motivation.
15. Teachers and school leaders offer few or no opportunities for students to express intrinsic motivation (doing things they want to do just because they enjoy doing them).	15. Teachers and school leaders encourage and provide opportunities for fun, flow, and zoning in on subjects of passion.
16. Students sit alone in single desks and do work primarily by themselves.	16. Students are provided opportunities to network and work in groups.
17. Work assignments require following routines and formulas, not creativity.	17. Students are frequently invited to be creative.
18. Mistakes and setbacks result in lower grades.	18. Adults accept mistakes, setbacks, and dead ends.
19. Course work involves little or no reflection on efforts, goals, and achievement, no putting them in a whole-life context.	19. There is regular reflection on efforts, goals, and achievement, putting them in the whole-life context.

20. There is no reflection on students' emerging sense of purpose in life.	20. There is regular reflection on students' emerging sense of purpose in life.
21. Students have no dedicated individual relationship with one or more adults at school.	21. There are one or two teachers who know a student in a deep way and provide guidance.
22. When teachers prepare lessons, they are primarily focused on exposing students to information or skills as required in the curriculum or state standards.	22. When teachers collaborate on critical lessons, they are primarily focused on making the lesson engaging, novel, fun, exciting, and adventurous.
23. Teachers use assessment tools that do not include models, benchmarks, or student input on assessment or assessment design.	23. Assessment is provided that includes models, benchmarks, and student participation in assessment and assessment design.
24. Assessment is primarily based on short-answer testing and quizzes; compliance assignments, such as homework completion and book reports; and unchallenging projects, such as drawing a map or baking a cake (no portfolios or e-portfolios).	24. Assessment is based primarily on demonstrations and artifacts (performances, presentations, demonstrations, portfolios, and e-portfolios).

This comparison helps clarify the signals students get from their schools. It helps in seeing how students might consciously or unconsciously decide whether to make a personal investment in learning.

One set of signals implicitly invites students to take ownership of their learning, to guide it, and to connect to their schoolwork on a personal level. The other set of signals indicates the influence of powerful, external controls; no interest in the experiences of students; and a threat to individual autonomy. When these signals are considered, it further helps in anticipating how new schools would be different. This contrast clarifies how authentic learning must be personal, and it suggests specific behaviors to convey the invitation to learn authentically.

The fact is that when teachers start to pay attention to student engagement and to encouraging a personal investment in learning, they also will start to see reasons for changing schools as well as getting glimmers of what new schools might look like. When educators look carefully at the issue of engagement, the very concept requires that they look at an array of other concepts that account for why students get engaged. Here are three steps for readers' consideration:

1. Students have very individual reasons for taking an interest in one thing and not another (Silvia, 2006) and getting engaged. If educators are going to pay attention to students' engagement and try to encourage it, they are necessarily going to have to *individualize*

students' work to appeal to and build on each student's unique interests.
2. The implications of making the individual student's person an important consideration in developing work for that student necessarily means that student work will have to be *personalized*. Educators will to have to take the time to know students in a deep way and help the students know themselves and discover their interests. Teachers will have to take time to interview students and to converse and reflect with the students in more personal ways. By virtue of this attention, students will begin to see that teachers do indeed value them as people. Students will see that teachers value understanding how students experience school and that teachers value helping students make a personal connection to their work.
3. Finally, when teachers value knowing students and encouraging a personal connection with the work at school, they will necessarily begin to consider unique programs of learning and ways to *customize* the work that the students do. Each student is, after all, different.

Having considered this, readers may be saying that it all sounds good in theory, but how could schools ever give all students this kind of attention and how could every student having a unique learning program possibly be organized?

These are not unreasonable questions, but for now the author would respond by asking readers this question: "Is this response coming from the mind-set of industrial age schooling?" He would further ask, "Are there not other organizational models that might be used that could provide such individualization? Might not schools experiment with inventing new models the way businesses create and recreate their own business models?"

Now the rationale for new schools for new learning is beginning to emerge. The way of the future in schooling will be individualization of learning. However, before going too far with this, there is still one more traditional school concept that grossly interferes with engagement and that is going to be very hard for educators to shed—the concept of requirements.

REQUIREMENTS AND LEARNING

Very often when speaking with educators about the importance of personalizing learning, one thing that always comes up is the issue of requirements. People rightly sense that there is a conflict between the personalization of learning and requirements. Requirements might be thought of as subjects that some powerful people have decided everyone should know.

Such requirements include familiar subjects such as English, American history, biology, algebra, algebra II, foreign languages, and more. Educators who consider the ideas in this book see that enforcing requirements could interfere with personalization. So they want to know how the author would handle requirements. They ask, "Requirements do make sense, right?"

There is a two-part answer to this question. Part one, like most issues about the structure and programs of a school, the decision to have required subjects should be left to local communities and school stakeholders, not to state and federal governments. Part two, required courses are a bad idea. Consider all of the requirements that schools make students take. Most of these requirements come from decisions made by important people who work in state government offices.

These important people think the schools have to make students know all sorts of things that will help them be better citizens, better workers, or better college students. Requirements are an attempt by powerful people to control what people learn and the outcomes of schooling. It's sort of like quality control in a factory. The truth is that almost everything that these powerful people want students to know is pretty good stuff. It would be good for most people to know it. So what is the problem?

The problem comes from human nature. The reality is that not everybody wants to learn the same thing at the same time in the same way. In fact, very often students won't learn it and nothing can make them. Or, if they are coerced to learn it, the process will be gamed, and the information soon will be forgotten. Everybody is different. One student has certain interests. Her friend has different interests. They both go about learning at different times, at different paces, and in different ways. It's human nature.

This reality of human variation and diversity is a well-established concept in education, but policy makers and school leaders usually choose to ignore it when it comes to the matter of requirements.

Their choice to ignore human variation is primarily because it does not fit the industrial age, assembly-line learning model. In this model, schools will function more efficiently if students are all taking the same subjects, at the same age, and in the same way. The more choices there are, the slower the assembly line will move, the more problems that might develop, and the more uncertainty about outcomes. Complexity is seen as the enemy.

When all students are taking the same subjects, at the same time, in the same places, it will be much easier to create standardized tests that measure what students are learning. If students are following many learning paths, then standardized testing would be much more complicated, maybe impossible.

But still the fact remains. Every person is different. These differences make things complicated and hard to control. So, the policy makers and politicians choose to ignore them and insist that most of what students learn should be standardized and required. These people believe they have a compelling logic because there are so many things that people should know, from learning to read and write to knowing the names of the states or why the Civil War was fought. It is just hard to get away from it. There are many things that people should know.

Of course, the problem comes when students are forced to learn things in which they have little interest. Readers should know by now how students will respond. They will begin to game school. They will undertake learning as a strategic exercise done with the least amount of effort and with no personal investment. Their learning quality becomes low.

In fact, the whole concept of requirements is a further indication of how schools are invested in the product of learning and not in the experience of learning. Policy makers and school leaders are focused on *what* students know instead of *how* students know. As developed in chapter 3, in the industrial age schooling model, there is little attention paid to ensuring that the process of learning is a positive experience as long as students know the answers to questions on a standardized test.

A Career Diminished
Working in industrial age schools, teachers' relationships with students will be filled with gaming and deception.

In this context, another question must be addressed. Is it really true that students could not succeed without studying all of the requirements? Again, the author asks readers to look at their own experiences. Do readers know people who have had less than conventional educations but who have managed to succeed in life? Of course. The same is true in the author's experience. And, because he is older, he has known many such people. Add to that so many students he has known who were poor students in school but who went on to become very successful in life. So, for the author, the answer is no, people do not have to have all of the requirements.

There are obviously many successful people in the world who didn't have a second year of algebra, or didn't have the health unit on communicable diseases, or didn't read *Romeo and Juliet*, or don't know how the Civil War started. There are many successful people in the world whose educations took very unconventional paths, yet they became successful in the real world. Some would say, in fact, that it was the unconventional nature of the learning path that has led many to success (Wagner, 2012; Zhao, 2012).

What complicates matters even more is that there are also many people who have had the most conventional of educations and who have not succeeded in the real world (Damon, 2008; Wagner, 2012; Zhao, 2009). So is it necessary to have a highly regimented, conventional education with all of the important requirements? No. There are just too many exceptions to this strategy to affirm it as being valid.

The good news is that all human beings want to learn, but they do NOT all want to learn the same things at the same time. Each person is unique, and schools should focus on developing that uniqueness. The universe and civilization thrives on and grow from variety and uniqueness in all things (Capra, 1997), including human personalities.

The mind-set that says students should learn all the requirements comes from the industrial age, which prized standardization, compartmentalization, and bureaucracy. This is an old frame of reference that no longer stands up to the understanding of human organizations in the twenty-first century (Charmer, 2009; Garvin, 2000; Schlechty, 2009; Senge, 1990; Senge et al., 2000; Senge et al., 2004).

What *is* absolutely necessary is that students be encouraged to think about what they want to know and how they want to find it out. Students need to learn to make thoughtful decisions and choices about their learning. They need to take ownership of their learning. They can't do that if everything is required and predetermined by other people. Everybody is different, and everybody needs to think about it and create his or her own learning path. Remember these three things:

1. If a school does not systematically check on student engagement by asking questions about how students experience school, then the adults in that school have no idea whether students are learning in a deep way.
2. At the same time, everybody knows that just because students are getting good grades does not mean they are learning. And it certainly doesn't mean students are learning to love learning or to invest in learning personally.
3. Finally, the reason states give big standardized tests at the end of the year to monitor student learning is because they don't trust the grades that teachers give students. They know those grades are often inflated, like much of the other data that come out of schools.

A TRANSITION: TEACHERS BUILDING CULTURES FOCUSED ON ENGAGEMENT

In this chapter a corner was turned. The focus moved from the pitfalls of industrial age schooling to understanding learning engagement as an emerging force for change. Making individualization the driving concept of new schools would serve youths and teachers better because a growing body of research tells us that

- students don't have the desire to learn the same things at the same time in the same ways,
- students have varying degrees of motivation depending on the subject,
- appealing to students' interests enhances the pace and depth of learning,
- personalizing learning enhances the pace and depth of learning,
- individual students learn in different ways and at different paces,
- eliciting students' intrinsic motivation should play a much larger role in schooling, and
- standardized schools have inherent cultural flaws that encourage gaming school and low-level strategic learning.

The textbox below provides a primer list of the professional writing and research that support the idea of individualization in learning.

THE INDIVIDUALIZATION OF LEARNING: A PRIMER REFERENCE LIST

Armstrong, T. (2000). *In their own way: Discovering and encouraging your child's multiple intelligences.* New York, NY: Putnam.

Armstrong, T. (2006). *The best schools: How human development research should inform educational practice.* Alexandria, VA: Association for Supervision and Curriculum Development.

Beaudoin, N. (2008). *A school for each student: Personalization in a climate of high expectations.* Larchmont, NY: Eye on Education.

Cordova, D. I., & Lepper, M. R. (1996). Intrinsic motivation and the process of learning: Beneficial effects of contexualization, personalization, and choice. *Journal of Educational Psychology, 88*(4), 715–730.

Deci, E., & Ryan, R. (2008). Self-determination theory: A macro-theory of human motivation, development, and health. *Canadian Psychology, 49*(3), 182–185.

Deci, E., Vallerand, R. J., Pelletier, L. G., & Ryan, R. M. (1991). Motivation in education: The self-determination perspective. *Educational Psychologist, 26*(3-4), 325–346.

Deci, E. L., & Ryan, R. M. (2008). Facilitating optimal motivation and psychological well-being across life's domains. *Canadian Psychology, 49*(1), 14–23.

Dewey, J. (2012). *Interest and effort in education*. Charleston, SC: Forgotten Books.

DiMartino, J., Clarke, J., & Wolk, D. (2003). *Personalized learning: Preparing high school students to create their futures*. Lanham, MD: Scarecrow Press, Inc.

Gardner, H. (2006). *Multiple intelligences: New horizons in theory and practice*. New York, NY: Basic Books.

Gibbons, M. (2002). *The self-directed learning handbook: Challenging adolescent students to excel*. San Francisco, CA: Jossey-Bass.

Guay, F., & Ratelle, C. F. (2008). Optimal learning in optimal contexts: The role of self-determination in education. *Canadian Psychology, 49*(3), 233–240.

Hess, F. M., & Manno, B. (Eds.). (2011). *Customized schooling: Beyond whole-school reform*. Cambridge, MA: Harvard University Press.

Jaros, M., & Deakin Crick, R. (2006). Personalizing learning in the post-mechanical age. *Journal of Curriculum Studies, 39*(4), 423–440.

Levine, E. (2002). *One kid at a time: Big lessons from a small school*. New York, NY: Teachers College Press.

Littky, D. (2004). *The big picture: Education is everyone's business*. Alexandria, VA: Association for Supervison and Curriculum Development.

Nagel, D. (2009). Students as "free agent learners." Retrieved from http://www.thejournal.com/the/printarticle/?id=24308

Paige, R. (2009). Self-directed learning and the mind-set of successful entrepreneurial learning. Retrieved from http://www.thefreelibrary.com/Self-directed+learning+and+the+mind-set+of+successful+entrepreneurial...-a0213958130

Pink, D. (2009). *Drive: The surprising truth about what motivates us*. New York, NY: Riverhead Books.

Silver, D. (2005). *Drumming to the beat of different marchers: Finding the rhythm for differentiated learning* (rev. ed.). Chicago, IL: Incentive Publications.

> Sousa, D. A., & Tomlinson, C. A. (2010). *Differentiation and the brain: How neuroscience supports the learner-friendly classroom.* Bloomington, IN: Solution Tree Press.
>
> Sulo, B. (2007). *Activating the desire to learn.* Alexandria, VA: Association for Supervision and Curriculum Development.
>
> Turville, J. (2007). *Differentiating by student interest: Strategies and lesson plans.* Larchmont, NY: Eye on Education.

In addition to the works listed in Textbox 4.1, two more stand out for special attention: *Assessing What Really Matters in Schools* (2009) and *Schools of Hope* (1999). These two related works develop how research into student engagement is pointing educators to new, more personalized directions in the reconception of schooling and teaching.

The case for individualization of learning in schools also is served by another fact. Our society now has the capacity to deliver a highly individualized learning experience to all students not by relying primarily on the large-group classroom instructional model but rather by employing a broad variety of instructional models customized to the needs of individual students.

The chapters that follow will clarify that schools that individualize, personalize, and customize are well within the capacity of our society. Everywhere, an elaborate marketplace of educational experiences is growing, which stands to meet the needs of every learner in very personalized ways. For many reasons yet to be explored, this will be the way of new schools for new learning.

REFERENCES

Ames, C., & Archer, J. (1988). Achievement goals in the classroom: Students' learning strategies and motivation processes. *Journal of Educational Psychology, 80*(3), 260–267.

Asch, S. E. (1952). *Social psychology.* New York, NY: Prentice Hall.

Ausubel, D. P., Novak, J. D., & Hanesian, H. (1978). *Educational psychology: A cognitive view.* (2nd ed.). New York, NY: Holt, Rinehart and Winston.

Blackwell, L. S., Trzensniewski, K. H., & Dweck, C. S. (2007). Implicit theories of intelligence predict achievement across an adolescent transition: A longitudinal study and an intervention. *Child Development, 78*(1), 246–263.

Brown, B. (2013). *Daring greatly: How the courage to be vulnerable transforms the way we live, love, parent, and lead.* New York, NY: Gotham Books.

Capra, F. (1997). *The web of life: A new scientific understanding of living systems.* New York, NY: Anchor/Random House.

Charmer, O. (2009). *Theory U: Leading from the future as it emerges.* San Francisco, CA: Berrett-Koehler Publishers.

Csikszentmihalyi, M. (1990). *Flow: The psychology of optimal experience.* New York, NY: Harper Perennial.

Csikszentmihalyi, M. (1997). *Finding flow: The psychology of engagement with everyday life.* New York, NY: Basic Books.

Damon, W. (2008). *The path to purpose.* New York, NY: Free Press.
Deci, E. L., & Ryan, R. (2008). Facilitating optimal motivation and psychological well-being across life's domains. *Canadian Psychology, 49(3),* 14–23.
Dweck, C. S. (2006). *Mind-set: The new psychology of success.* New York, NY: Random House.
Dweck, C. S., & Leggett, E. L. (1988). A social cognitive approach to motivation and personality. *Psychological Review, 95* (2), 256–273.
Entwistle, N. (1977). Strategies of learning and studying: Recent research findings. *British Journal of Educational Studies, 25(3),* 225–238.
Farris-Berg, K., Dirkswager, E., & Junge, A. (2012). *Trusting teachers with school success: What happens when teachers call the shots.* Lanham, MD: Rowman & Littlefield Education.
Fisher, J. (1999). *Six silent killers: Management's greatest challenge.* Boca Raton, FL: St. Lucie Press.
Fransson, A. (1977). Qualitative differences in learning: IV. Effects of intrinsic motivation and extrinsic test anxiety on process and outcome. *British Journal of Educational Psychology, 47(3),* 244–257.
Fredricks, J. A., Blumenfeld, P. C., & Paris, A. H. (2004). School engagement: Potential of the concept: State of the evidence. *Review of Educational Research, 74(1),* 59–109.
Fried, R. L. (2001). *The passionate teacher: A practical guide.* Boston, MA: Beacon Press.
Fried, R. L. (2005). *The game of school: Why we all play it, how it hurts kids, and what it will take to change it.* San Francisco, CA: Jossey-Bass.
Garvin, D. (2000). *Learning in action: A guide to putting the learning organization to work.* Boston, MA: Harvard Business School Press.
Grant, H., & Dweck, C. S. (2003). Clarifying achievement goals and their impact. *Journal of Personality and Social Psychology, 85(5),* 541–553.
Hatano, G., & Inagaki, K. (1986). Two courses of expertise. In H. Stevenson & J. Azuma (Eds.), *Child development and education in Japan* (pp. 335–355). New York, NY: W. H. Freeman & Co.
Hatano, G., & Oura, Y. (2003). Commentary: Reconceptualizing learning using insight from expertise research. *Educational Researcher, 32(8),* 26–29.
Heath, D. H. (1999). *Schools of hope: Developing mind and character in today's youth.* Bryn Mawr, PA: Conrow Publishing House.
Hebert, T., Durham, S., & Silver, D. (2008). *High stakes teaching: Practices that improve student learning.* Lanham, MD: Rowman & Littlefield Education.
Hong, Y., Dweck, C. S., Chiu, C., Lin, D., & Wan, W. (1999). Implicit theories, attributions, and coping: A meaning system approach. *Journal of Personality and Social Psychology, 77(3),* 588–599.
Maslow, A. (1968). *Toward a psychology of being* (2nd ed.). Princeton, NJ: D. Van Nostrand Co.
McCarthy, M., & Kuh, G. (2006). Are students ready for college? What student engagement data say. *Phi Delta Kappan, 87(9),* 664–669.
Meece, J. L., Blumenfeld, P. C., & Hoyle, R. H. (1988). Students' goal orientations and cognitive engagement in classroom activities. *Journal of Educational Psychology, 80,* 514–523.
Mueller, C. M., & Dweck, C. S. (1998). Praise for intelligence can undermine children's motivation and performance. *Journal of Personality and Social Psychology, 75(1),* 33–52.
Newell, R. J., & Van Ryzin, M. J. (2009). *Assessing what really matters in schools: Creating hope for the future.* Lanham, MD: Rowman & Littlefield Education.
Nicholls, J. G., Cheung, P., Lauer, J., & Patashnick, M. (1989). Individual differences in academic motivation: Perceived ability, goals, beliefs, and values. *Learning and Individual Differences, 1,* 63–84.
Noah, H. J., & Eckstein, M. A. (2001). *Fraud and education: The worm in the apple.* Lanham, MD: Rowman & Littlefield Publishers.

Nolen, S. B., & Haladyna, T. M. (1990). Personal and environmental influences on students' beliefs about effective study strategies. *Contemporary Educational Psychology, 15*(2), 116–130.

Schlechty, P. (2002). *Working on the work: An action plan for teachers, principals, and superintendents.* San Francisco, CA: Jossey-Bass.

Schlechty, P. (2009). *Leading for learning: How to transform schools into learning organizations.* San Francisco, CA: Jossey-Bass.

Senge, P. (1990). *The fifth discipline: The art & practice of the learning organization.* New York, NY: Doubleday.

Senge, P., Cambron-McCabe, N., Lucas, T., Smith, B., Dutton, J., & Kleiner, A. (2000). *Schools that learn: A fifth discipline fieldbook for educators, parents, and everyone who cares about education.* New York, NY: Doubleday.

Senge, P., Scharmer, C. O., Jaworski, J., & Flowers, B. S. (2004). *Presence: Exploring profound change in people, organizations, and society.* New York, NY: Currency Doubleday.

Silvia, P. J. (2006). *Exploring the psychology of interest.* New York, NY: Oxford University Press.

Wagner, T. (2012). *Creating innovators: The making of young people who will change the world.* New York, NY: Scribner.

Waters, R. (2012). Secondary students' transitioning from compliance to intentional learning. (Doctoral dissertation). UMI Proquest (Order No. 3504071).

Yazzie-Mintz, E. (2007). Voices of students on engagement: A report on the 2006 *High School Survey of Student Engagement.* Bloomington, IN: Indiana University.

Zhao, Y. (2009). *Catching up or leading the way: American education in the age of globalization.* Alexandria, VA: Association for Supervision and Curriculum Development.

Zhao, Y. (2012). *World class learners: Educating creative and entrepreneurial students.* Thousand Oaks, CA: Corwin.

FIVE
Guiding Step 5: Reconsider the Emerging Marketplace of Educational Experiences

A new reality has emerged outside of schools, the marketplace of educational experiences. In this marketplace, youths and adults go shopping for learning experiences.

Evidence of this marketplace is everywhere: on highway billboards, in Main Street shops, at the mall, at corporate offices, on TV and radio, on smartphones, and especially on personal computers connected to the Internet. It is a reality that is already putting pressure on our traditional schools. This chapter will be devoted to considering what this marketplace is, how it affects schools and teachers, and how both should respond to it. The development of this marketplace will have a natural fit in the conversation about readers' careers and the importance of individualizing, personalizing, and customizing learning for all students.

WHAT IS IN THE MARKETPLACE?

In the space of this chapter, it would be impossible to capture the full scope of the ever-changing, ever-expanding marketplace of educational experiences. It would be very hard even to capture it in a very fat book. Still, it is important to be reminded of what is out there to get perspective on what is offered in our industrial age schools.

For ease and brevity let's approach this marketplace from the standpoint of a catalog. The items about to be presented will represent categories of offerings. Readers must remember that within each category there could be hundreds or thousands of separate educational opportunities. Yes, thousands. Although there is no such catalog (yet), the point here is that any student could look around at the marketplace of educational experiences and build a personal learning program with any combination of the thousands of choices from the category items.

- Following a blog
- Researching and writing a blog
- Participating in a wiki
- Participating in a discussion board
- Watching posted videos, including YouTube's vast collection
- Accessing Khan Academy videos
- Attending an in-person remedial class operated as a business
- Being tutored by a neighbor, peer, or professional
- Attending in person a remedial class or an advanced seminar operated by a local nonprofit organization, such as a church, library, foundation, or government office
- Using a CD-ROM for guided instruction
- Using a smartphone app
- Entering a virtual world, such as Second Life
- Accessing a virtual classroom
- Developing an electronic portfolio
- Employing collaborative software for networking and problem solving
- Viewing webcasts
- Using canned computer-based instructional modules
- Engaging with adaptive learning machines
- Doing programmed learning from a book
- Doing programmed learning from a computer program (or from the Internet)
- Playing and/or creating educational games and simulations
- Learning with a community partner (volunteer teacher of a specialty, such as stamp history)
- Apprenticing with a local tradesman
- Independently researching a topic of interest
- Doing action research to solve a school or community problem
- Preparing for student presentations
- Creating art
- Inventing things
- Starting a business
- Studying someone else who is starting a business
- Joining an in-person discussion group
- Learning through observing or witnessing presentations, such as the playing of music; the discussion of artwork; or the viewing of a TV program, movie, or play
- Tutoring others

- Conversational cross-cultural learning online with people from other parts of the world
- Learning through travel (this is not new but it is increasingly used)
- Visiting collaborative networking websites for defined problem solving
- Engaging in online collaborative learning 2.0, such as on Blogger or Skype
- Mobil-assisted language learning

Let's just summarize for a moment before moving on. The aforementioned list gives an idea of several ways that a student could venture into the marketplace and put together a variety of learning experiences, which could provide much meaningful learning, advance a personal passion, provide a platform for meeting people, present many new political and cultural perspectives, and otherwise keep the learner happy and engaged.

This list again must inspire readers to think that so many learning models would be impossible to organize and manage. But what's even more interesting about this list is that it is only the tip of the iceberg. Notice what was left out?

Online Courses

Certainly, readers are aware of online courses, and the likelihood is great that readers have taken online courses. From its inception in the early 1970s, online education has grown enormously as an enterprise undertaken not only by for-profit and not-for-profit online schools but also by educational service companies, corporations, foundations, philanthropies, museums, libraries, government offices, and trade associations. More recently, brick-and-mortar schools also are offering many classes online. Overall, these entities provide online learning for millions, ranging from fully accredited elementary school programs to PhDs.

The Open Source Movement: Software and Courseware

Another contributor to the huge marketplace of educational experiences is the open source movement. Simply stated, the open source movement refers to the creation and sharing of computer codes and other knowledge usually by a network of collaborators. These collaborators have a strong interest in democratizing and advancing the spread of knowledge, so they post their work online to make their computer-coding creations and other knowledge open to the public.

Others may then access these codes or knowledge over the Internet for a variety of uses, including education. They may also modify and improve these codes while networking with the original creators or within a new network. Thus, even more knowledge is created. It is the collaborators' intent that through a kind of worldwide network of open source contributors, knowledge and know-how will be rapidly advanced and shared unencumbered by profits, patents, or other issues of intellectual property.

The open source movement has, in fact, resulted in many of the intended outcomes, as it has perfected a great deal of computer code, educated many with it and about it, and shared the benefits of all of this learning with millions. Some examples are the Mozilla browser and the Wikipedia encyclopedia.

> **A Career Diminished**
> **Working in industrial age schools, teachers' professional learning will continue to be constrained by central planners focused on standardized test preparation.**

The open software movement also has led to another concept in knowledge sharing called open courseware. Open courseware includes lectures and complete courses, including materials, that have been put on the Web for access by the general population of the world, usually for free. The number of colleges and universities placing their courses on the Web is growing by the day.

A driving concept is that just like food and water, everyone should have access to knowledge. Often these courses may be taken for credit, without entrance requirements and for minimal fees. In effect, knowledge is no longer being treated like an exclusive commodity but something that should be made available to all people. The term MOOC, massive open online course, has emerged to name many of the lectures and lessons offered on the Web.

Private Money, Public School Funding: Foundations

Another big change in the marketplace is the funding of public schools by private foundations. While this has been happening for decades, it is happening more often recently in light of the perception by many that our public schools are failing. In almost every case, foundations choose to fund public education to either advance their own goals or to promote social change by, for example, reducing racial prejudice or improving literacy. Schools are sometimes sought out by foundations to provide support.

In other cases, schools actively court foundations by instituting programs to which the foundation would be sympathetic. In almost all cases, this relationship has translated into much experimenting on the part of schools trying to provide a better service. An example of this is the Harlem Children's Zone. Here is a list of foundations and their gifts, as reported in *Education Week* (November 14, 2012), all of which have expressed interest in school change.

Bill and Melinda Gates Foundation	$208,525,418.00
Walton Family Foundation, Inc.	$109,540,986.00
W. K. Kellogg Foundation, Inc.	$ 58,116,096.00
Michael and Susan Dell Foundation	$ 54,855,756.00
Silicon Valley Community Foundation	$ 35,280,476.00
Robertson Foundation	$ 32,444,850.00
Carnegie Corporation of New York	$ 30,906,200.00
William and Flora Hewlett Foundation	$ 30,263,571.00
Eli and Edythe Broad Foundation	$ 26,521,643.00
GE Foundation	$ 25,830,277.00
James Irvine Foundation	$ 24,188,000.00
Doris & Donald Fisher Fund	$ 17,496,500.00
Communities Foundation of Texas	$ 14,213,682.00
Daniels Fund	$ 12,420,635.00
Ford Foundation	$ 12,211,966.00
Oberkotter Foundation	$ 12,135,131.00
Conrad N. Hilton Foundation	$ 11,875,000.00
Ewing Marion Kauffman Foundation	$ 10,866,155.00
Helen Bader Foundation, Inc.	$ 10,435,000.00
New York Community Trust	$ 9,885,526.00

Such support by foundations for public schools is an important part of the marketplace because it is a source of experimentation and continues to expand the choices for learning for both students and parents.

Private Money, Public School Funding: Wall Street

Like many foundations are doing, a number of big corporations are actually creating and funding their own public schools. Consistent with their goals, these corporations have created schools that prepare youths for work in particular industries, especially high tech. Examples of these technology companies that will provide unique curricula aimed at nurturing the skills needed in their industry's marketplace are IBM, Cisco, Microsoft Corporation, Motorola Solutions, and Verizon Wireless.

Most of these schools have their own school model and look to support teens in unique ways by providing certificates and some early college experience (Khadaroo, 2013). Remember, this author does not present this information as an endorsement of any of these schools. It is presented to readers to demonstrate that there is a growing marketplace of educational experiences. There are individuals, along with private and public companies, who are experimenting with new models for learning outside of our public schools. In fact, many such companies are already inside many of our schools providing unique, commercially relevant programs.

Data Analytics

Data analytics is a process whereby student data are collected and analyzed with the purpose of seeing patterns, clarifying student preferences, developing student strengths, answering questions of suitability, or drawing valuable conclusions about what to study and where to go to college. Some students are already getting this kind of support in their schools, but most are getting it from private vendors in the marketplace.

How does it work? Think of it this way. Throughout a student's schooling, elementary and secondary, much data could be collected about a student. These data might include a record of a student's in-and-out-of-school behavior and in-and-out-of-school choices, as well as performance around school, in classrooms, and online. Eventually, this accumulated data provide students with objective feedback on their behavior. Such feedback could include where their passions lie, what their strengths are, where they need help, and which higher education options will likely be best suited to their personal advancement.

The collection and interpretation of such data is assisted by an ever-growing array of data analytic commercial products, such as Knewton, Learning Catalytics, edMatch, Naviance, ConnectEDU, eAdvisor, Degree Compass, and others.

These analytic programs can help students in school by assisting the learning process or guiding their study options. It can help them after school by guiding some good choices and avoiding some bad choices. In both cases students are making choices on the basis of data collected over years. They are not making the choices because they are following the crowd, saw exciting pictures in college catalogs, are feeling peer pressure, saw beautiful buildings on a campus, or want to go to the school where Uncle Harry graduated.

Being provided with such data can improve a student's reflection on what careers and higher education choices fit the student's personality and why they are a good fit, as well as indicate specific training schools, colleges, or universities that would be a logical choice for the student. When students get such help, they are likely to get a much greater feeling of support and value than they would from getting just general counseling from a guidance counselor, who doesn't have data to support recommendations.

Electronic Portfolios

Electronic portfolios are software or websites for the electronic storage of artifacts of learning. An electronic portfolio might include many of the things ordinarily contained in a traditional paper portfolio, such as transcripts and academic records as well as papers, photographs, and essays written by a student. However, electronic portfolios have additional capacities for the inclusion of digital photography and videos with sound along with Internet links, which thereby offers students opportunities for the creative management and presentation of their work in preparation for college or workplace applications.

Because electronic portfolios are under the management of the students, they are often seen as supporting students in taking ownership of their learning and personal development. Creation of a portfolio facilitates students' making the connection between what is done as youths and how it will translate into achieving an academic or professional goal. In so doing, it helps them be more reflective about the future and the learning needed to support that future. Readers should take a moment to think about whether this marketplace of educational experiences has anything good to offer students or schools.

STUDENTS AS SHOPPERS OF EDUCATIONAL EXPERIENCES

Although not widely discussed in schools, student behavior as shoppers of educational experience has already been recognized in the academic and professional literature. Students live in a world that is awash in educational sales, digital customization (Cronin, 2010; Kamenetz, 2009, 2010; Martinez, 2010; Pink, 2009), and customer choice (Anderson, 2006). Moreover, this disruptive notion of twenty-first-century students as voluntary consumers has already advanced to a basis for discussing change in schools (Christensen et al., 2009; Kelly et al., 2009; Schlechty, 2009).

The idea that textbook-based curricula, along with state and national standards, all of which have been developed by experts in what our youths should know, will be replaced by a marketplace of learning experiences shopped for by savvy young consumers must, at first, seem farfetched, maybe ridiculous. It is so far from the linear hallways and classrooms, the desks in rows and the bells, and the textbooks and teachers' manuals, so much that constitutes what we think of as school. But this new world of learning is not so far away.

Think of all the ads for supplemental or remedial learning support on billboards and TV. Think of the proliferation of private schools, charter schools, and online schools, not to mention informal networking. Think of the developing industry of electronic games and how these games are increasingly seen as valid mental exercises and learning experiences.

Add to these developments all of the games that are branded "educational" and have a dedicated agenda to assist learning. Think of the urgent efforts to market our public schools to communities. Think of the increase in homeschooling and homeschooling networks. Consider Google's digitization of 7 million books and the advent of MOOCs, MIT OpenCourseWare, the OpenCourseWare Consortium, Wikipedia, YouTube EDU, iTunes U, and Peer 2 Peer University.

Consider that in 2009, 2011, and 2013, the first of their kind, Venture Capital in Education Summits were held to consider an array of proposals involving multimedia social-learning platforms, live video teaching, online multiplayer instructional games, and adaptive learning engines that promise "to customize content for each student, down to the concept level, with integrated assessment tools" (Kamenetz, 2009).

An important part of accepting the reality of the marketplace is recognizing how it is conducive to and inviting independent learning. Martinez (2010) has detailed important evolutionary developments that include educational entities away from a student's school, such as Sylvan Learning Services. Such services, which previously offered "to help students with learning challenges," are now being marketed as entities that "can accelerate learning" in a variety of other areas (Martinez, 2010, p. 74).

Demonstrating the breadth of this expansion of learning choices, Martinez (2010) further cited Rai, 2005, who documented the outsourcing of homework assistance from tutors in India to American children. Referring to these developments as a new "learning economy," she explained:

> Open source courseware, shared curriculum repositories, home-school community networks, and many other bottom-up activities are unbundling education from the traditional system and providing children and families with new ways to experience learning. A growing system of free and easily accessible online learning is supporting students, educators, and parents. (Martinez, 2010, p. 74)

Christensen et al. (2009) anticipated continual reinforcement of this trend toward independent learning, and they projected that by 2019, half of all school courses will be delivered online and favored by students for their convenience. As evidence of this emerging marketplace of new educational options, they have cited the State of Florida's Virtual School, which already has the motto "any time, any place, any path, any pace" (p. 98).

Students surely will be impressed with the fact that they won't even have to go to school, with all of its related hassles and expenses. They will notice that the number of courses available to choose from will be greater and greater, and moreover, the courses they can take will be much more individualized and even personalized. In fact, Christensen et al. (2009) suggested that even more than convenience, students' desires for more individualization, personalization, and customization will drive the growth of the emerging marketplace of educational experiences (p. 121).

As part of this emerging marketplace of educational experiences, there will be many other "student-centric" ways to learn that are highly individualized and customized and for these reasons, will be more appealing than classroom instruction is. Recently the Los Angeles Public Library announced it would start offering 850 continuing education courses online and awarding high school diplomas, also using online instruction (Ferguson, 2014).

Other options will be formal and informal learning opportunities derived from an increasingly large array of neighborhood, community-based, or regional networks wherein students can learn the basics along with special interest content that has high personal appeal, anything from automobile mechanics to astronomy.

One area of particular appeal to youths and a growing number of learning scholars is the area of gaming, in person and particularly electronic. Aldrich (2005, 2009), Davidson (2013), Kapp (2012), and Salin (2007) argued for the important role of computer games and simulations as superior learning modes because of their active and interactive learning format with emphasis on performance skills and getting to the next level as opposed to the passive information processing done by most students in most schools.

Also compelling about these authors' work is that they tie the educational value of gaming to research-based theories in psychology and learning. (Can test-focused industrial age schools do that?) An example of the work of foundations and the emergence of gaming as a viable learning model can be found in the collaboration of The John D. and Catherine T. MacArthur Foundation with Salin (2007) in the creation of Quest2Learn, a public middle school in New York City that promotes learning through gaming practices.

> **A Career Diminished**
> Working in industrial age schools, teachers will not experience the satisfaction of working in small, caring learning communities.

When considering the emergence of the marketplace of educational experiences, even in this brief way, readers cannot avoid beginning to think that all of these choices are bound to influence youths to feel less dependent on formal schooling for learning. Our youths, consciously or unconsciously, are developing an ever-greater sense of independence in their learning paths.

FROM THE MARKETPLACE TO FREE AGENT LEARNING

This observation on how youths become increasingly independent is, of course, timeless. That their sense of independence is enhanced by knowing of the marketplace of educational experiences (much of it free) should not come as a surprise. Evans, 2009, cited in Nagel, (2009) has invoked the term "free agent learner" to describe the phenomenon. The noted developmental psychologist, Albert Bandura (2006), has developed the concept in this way:

> [N]ew realities ushered in by the transition to the information era are placing a premium on the role of personal efficacy in educational self-development. . . . Students now exercise substantial control over their own learning. . . . Students now have the best libraries, museums, and multimedia instruction at their fingertips through the global Internet. They can educate themselves independently of time and place. This shift in locus of initiative involves a major reorientation in students' conception of education. They are agents of their own learning, not just recipients of information. (p. 10)

This change in students is going to affect readers' careers. In the face of this student independence, how should schools react? Should educators reconsider who students are and what they want from school?

As one respondent to this question, Richardson (2008) pointed to the opportunity to change the way school leaders think of knowledge to accommodate students who are becoming agents of their own learning. He has suggested that the changes in society demand that educators move their concept of learning from a "supply-push" model of "building up an inventory of knowledge in the students' heads" (p. 30) to a "demand-pull" approach, which requires students to own their learning processes (pp. 18–19) as they attempt to meet the demands of employers in a new economy.

Other respondents see the increasing student ownership of their learning as changing their concept of learning itself (Kelly et al., 2009; Rennie & Mason, 2004). Students are moving away from seeing learning as school based and teacher dominated. They are moving away from seeing learning as compliance behavior and right-answer outcomes. They are moving the "locus of initiative" to themselves and toward active, self-directed learning, whereby learning is seen as more of a personal process. If these observations are true, what does it suggest for readers' careers and for how schools should accommodate their customers?

NEW SCHOOLS WILL ACCOMMODATE STUDENTS AND TEACHERS AS INDEPENDENT LEARNERS

Earlier in this book, the author presented a frame of reference from which he viewed the career of teaching. He explained that per this frame of reference, people want control over their own lives. They want to make choices and freely pursue what they believe will make them happy and allow them to actualize their potential. He explained that he believed that teachers overwhelmingly came into the profession because they wanted to help youths and enjoy the deeply personal rewards that came from doing that.

Unfortunately, the author has also observed that teachers were losing their control over their profession and their professional learning. He anticipated that losing this control would result in teachers not getting the rewards they sought. It was this loss of control that moved him to write this book about change and leadership. This chapter on the marketplace of educational experiences clarifies that, like teachers, students will increasingly want the freedom to pursue learning that will make them happy and afford them the opportunity to actualize their potential.

Thus, the emergence of the marketplace of educational experiences calls for leadership. The conditions described by Bandura (2006) raised the question of how schools should respond to our youths' new independence in learning.

Is it a good thing that youths are feeling more empowered to control their learning? Should schools in any way help or discourage students in their independent efforts to learn? What if students go astray or make bad choices? Is it really clear that self-directed learning in the vast marketplace of educational experiences is good preparation for the twenty-first century? How should teachers respond to students becoming independent, voluntary customers? What does all of this imply for the career of teaching?

REFERENCES

Aldrich, C. (2005). *Learning by doing: A comprehensive guide to simulations, computer games, and pedagogy in e-learning and other educational experiences.* San Francisco, CA: Pfeiffer.

Aldrich, C. (2009). *The complete guide to simulations and serious games: How the most valuable content will be created in the age beyond Gutenberg to Google.* San Francisco, CA: Pfeiffer.

Anderson, C. (2006). *The long tail: Why the future of business is selling less of more.* New York: Hyperion.

Ash, K. (2012). George Lucas' promise to invest in education prompts speculation. *Education Week* (November 14).

Bandura, A. (2006). Adolescent development from an agentic perspective. In F. Pajares & T. Urdan (Eds.), *Self-efficacy beliefs of adolescents* (pp. 1–43). Charlotte, NC: Information Age Publishing.

Christensen, C., Horn, M., & Johnson, C. (2009). *Disrupting class: How disruptive innovation will change the way the world learns.* New York, NY: McGraw-Hill.

Cronin, J. M. (2010). The education world in 2020: How the decade of 2010 turned out. *Education Week, 29*(16) (January 6, 2010).

Davidson, C. N. (2013). *Now you see it: How technology and brain science will transform schools and business for the 21st century.* New York, NY: Penguin Books.

Ferguson, K. (2014). The L.A. Public Library expanding its services with a high school diploma program. Retrieved from http://thelosangelestribune.com/l-public-library-expanding-services-high-school-diploma-program/

Kamenetz, A. (2009). Who needs Harvard: How Web-savvy edupunks are transforming American higher education. Retrieved from http://www.fastcompany.com/1325728/how-web-savvy-edupunks-are-transforming-american-higher-education

Kamenetz, A. (2010). *Edupunks, edupreneurs, and the coming transformation of higher education.* White River Junction, VT: Chelsea Green Publishing.

Kapp, K. M. (2012). *The gamification of learning and instruction: Game-based methods and strategies for training and education.* New York, NY: Pfeiffer.

Kelly, F., McCain, T., & Jukes, I. (2009). *Teaching the digital generation: No more cookie-cutter schools.* Thousand Oaks, CA: Corwin Press.

Khadaroo, S. T. (2013). In Texas, Obama lauds "new tech" school. Model for the future? *The Christian Science Monitor,* May 9. Retrieved from http://www.csmonitor.com/USA/Education/2013/0509/In-Texas-Obama-lauds-New-Tech-high-school.-Model-for-the-future-video

Martinez, M. (2010). The learning economy. *Phi Delta Kappan, 91*(6), 9.

Nagel, D. (2009). Students as "free agent learners." Retrieved from http://www.thejournal.com/the/printarticle/?id=24308

Pink, D. H. (2009). *Drive: The surprising truth about what motivates us.* New York, NY: Riverhead Books.

Prensky, M. (2008). Turning on the lights. *Educational Leadership, 65*(6), 40–45.

Rennie, F., & Mason, R. (2004). *The connecticon: Learning for the connected generation.* Charlotte, NC: Information Age Publishing.

Richardson, W. (2008). *Blogs, wikis, podcasts and other powerful web tools for classrooms.* Thousand Oaks, CA: Corwin.

Salin, K. (2007). *The ecology of games: Connecting youth, games, and learning.* Cambridge, MA: MIT Press.

Schlechty, P. (2009). *Leading for learning: How to transform schools into learning organizations.* San Francisco, CA: Jossey-Bass.

Tapscott, D. (2009). *Grown up digital: How the net generation is changing the world.* New York, NY: McGraw-Hill.

SIX
Guiding Step 6: Start Seeing Students as Independent, Voluntary Customers

Having acknowledged the marketplace of educational experiences, the purpose of this chapter is to consider how educators should think about the emergence of students as independent learners and voluntary customers (Bandura, 2006; Christensen et al., 2009; Schlechty, 2009).

This chapter advances questions such as these: How should schools relate to the external marketplace of educational experiences? Should that marketplace be viewed as an enemy of public education, as some kind of competitor, or possibly as an ally? How should public school teachers react to entities in the marketplace that provide students with better services, experiences, and outcomes than schools do?

Should teachers attempt to change their schools to be able to compete in the marketplace of educational experiences? Should schools consider a service model that respects students as customers in a marketplace? In the most general terms, what can society and schools do to provide the best educational outcomes for youths? How these questions are answered will have a significant impact on teaching as a career.

In response to all of these questions, an uncertainty about the marketplace of educational experiences must be acknowledged. It is not clear how that marketplace will evolve in years to come. What is more certain, however, is that it will keep evolving. It will not go away. The many choices it offers will continue to get the attention of youths, and they will increasingly factor those choices into their educational plans.

Even now many students turn to the marketplace even when a similar offering is made within their schools. It is in light of this trend that this author would propose that the best choice for schools and teachers is to help students become educated consumers of educational experience.

Let's educate students about the nature of real learning so they can make informed decisions about what will best suit their personal development.

In 2002 the *Harvard Business Review* published an article titled "Customers as Innovators: A New Way to Create Value," by Thomke and von Hippel. They explained that many corporations have come to see the wisdom of not only doing consumer research but also actually involving customers, hands on, in the innovation of new products.

How do these manufacturers not only save money but also increase value by getting customers to create designs that might otherwise require the expensive input of engineers and other experts? They do it by providing customers with well-designed tools. Customers are then expected to use these "tool kits" to carefully think through what it is that they actually need and then, with help design what it is they want. Thomke and von Hippel (2002) have reported that this innovation on how to innovate has grown to account for a multibillion dollar market selling products to customers designed by the customers themselves.

The emergence of the marketplace of educational experiences and this author's interest in providing students with learning that is individualized, personalized, and customized suggest that schools that help young people understand and design what they need to steward their own personal growth represent the emerging future of education. To better understand this emerging future, it is right to question whether it would make sense for schools to involve students, as customers, in the design of their own learning experiences. Would it really increase educational value for them?

A careful look at the potential benefits of such an approach suggests an emphatic yes. But before detailing how the benefits would be derived, it is important to note that the value of thinking of our students as customers of educational experiences is not just about borrowing from economic or marketing theory. It is about responding properly as educators to a reality, a reality that bears on human development and the concept of knowledge itself.

REFLECTION ON LEARNING AND PERSONAL DEVELOPMENT

While the emergence of students as voluntary customers must certainly be an unsettling idea, it may also be a good thing. If students are increasingly inclined to active, self-directed learning, they will certainly need guidance on how to make good choices. This empowerment as consumers, if properly engaged by educators, could encourage students to be much more reflective on the value of the learning experiences they choose for themselves. It could incline them to focus on their unique needs as learners and how those needs can best be met.

Properly engaged, supporting students as independent learners could invite creativity, as it encourages students to think of themselves as their own personal development planners who seek and create an education that is not standardized but properly individualized, personalized, and customized.

The question of how schools will be reconfigured then hinges on the decision of whether to engage students as the customers they have become. Ignoring this choice likely will perpetuate schools that rely on tactics of control and standardization to garner their clientele, which leads to the gaming of school and students' increasing sense of school's irrelevance.

Or, schools could engage students as the shoppers they have become, help them become educated consumers of educational experience, and serve them as unique, valued stakeholders who are practiced in self-advocacy and the ways of the free market democracy we want them to uphold.

CAN STUDENTS HELP IN DESIGNING NEW KINDS OF SCHOOLS?

So let's consider how schools might do as industries have done and engage their customers in creating the innovation schools desperately need. In doing this, let's also approach head on the most likely question: "How are kids going to design learning experiences that are realistically good for them when they know little about the nature of learning or what they will need to know for college and/or their adult lives?" It's a good question. To answer it, consider a common scenario wherein students are asked to design new ways of learning or a new kind of school where they would enjoy and commit to learning. What positive suggestions could they make?

Skepticism is not unreasonable here. Would schools end up not much different from what they are now but with longer lunch periods and no homework? In fact, such a result was reported by Scherer (2008) in *Educational Leadership*. When students were asked how to improve school, they predictably responded with mostly complaints. While one student did presciently suggest that schools should get rid of the desks, few suggestions emerged for changing school processes or structure that were in any way transformative. So questioning what students have to offer would seem a strong and thoughtful point.

But there is another way to look at this. Students' inability to imagine and design more engaging schools might be very much the fault of educators. Industry, as reported by Thomke and von Hippel (2002), might be telling us that we haven't given students the tools that empower them to see education in a new way. But what would those tools be? The answer to this question is that students need to be engaged in a process that they have already started on their own while education shopping. They need to be helped to become educated consumers of educational experiences.

Helping students become educated consumers of educational experiences means educators have to engage students in learning about learning itself. It is a metacognitive process, the absence of which in our schools is a common complaint (Damon, 2008; Givens, 2002; Mezirow, 2005). And though learning about learning should be formalized, for now it means that educators and students need to put the curriculum aside from time to time to reflect on and have frank conversations about the nature of learning and some of its in-school "realities."

Such conversations should deal with many of the messy and unspeakable topics that support the deep structure of industrial age schools. These topics would include boredom, student passivity, subject irrelevance, cheating, the real emptiness of grades, and how students game their schools by compliantly going through the motions of learning without really learning.

Such conversations likely should include some confessions from educators, who often feel trapped in school structures or curricula they don't believe in and who also find themselves just going through the motions and gaming school. In the course of this frankness, students should be helped to understand the difference between superficial, strategic learning and deep, authentic learning.

As these ideas for change are offered, the author is aware that the colleges that readers are now attending or the schools where they are now teaching have probably not invited them into such conversations. That, of course, is all part of the game of school, where raising such topics is taboo. Knowing that they have never been invited to have such a conversation in their schools should tell readers much about why our society should want to get away from the industrial age schooling model. It should suggest the need for frank conversation.

Having honest conversations with students will do a lot to start the change process, and it will also do a great deal to enhance their learning. As part of these conversations, students should be advised about the core skills they should be getting as preparation for living and working in the twenty-first century. These skills would include creativity; critical thinking; and analyzing, synthesizing, and applying these skills in communicating and solving problems.

There should also be talk about why these core skills are often neglected in favor of memorizing information for short-answer tests. Students also will be helped by knowing that these core skills are not exclusive to fancy academic subjects but are necessary and usable in all subjects, from athletics to physics. The topic of twenty-first-century skills will be developed further in chapter 7.

In the context of these core skills, educators should help students reflect on their own unique talents as learners and the important role these unique qualities play in being a happy, committed learner. Schools will want to engage students in learning about their own special learning strengths, weaknesses, and styles. They will need to help students explore all the possible ways learning happens.

There should be some affirmation to those who don't like school and get little from it but who are loaded with potential. More important, the help provided should include a stipulation that students have a right to expect from their teachers well-designed and highly engaging strategies for learning and that it is not unreasonable for students to make suggestions and expect to be part of the designing process.

In addition to helping students with understanding themselves in relation to the learning process, they also should be helped to become market-wise, strategic shoppers of educational experience. Just as in any marketplace, students should be taught "let the buyer beware." They should be taught that when they shop for an education, they need to get past the course titles—honors, advanced placement, college prep—and all the other packaging and think about things such as the depth of the experience, fact or opinion, personal relevance, inspiration, reliability, and customer service.

Students should be prompted to think about whether they are buying (taking courses) because they have to; they are impulsively getting on a bandwagon, intoxicated by either brand, status, or ease; or they find the experience is right for them and right for their future.

> **A Career Diminished**
> Working in industrial age schools, teachers will not be respected by local communities as the primary planners and stewards of youths' development.

Students need some facts of life about the learning marketplace. First of all, it's so much bigger than going to school. In learning, the world is their oyster! Second, students can learn anywhere if they have the intention. Third, and just as with shopping, students have to know what they are doing, or they could waste their time, buy something shoddy, get cheated, or end up buying things that will eventually be useless. Finally, vendors should be expected to take an interest in students, their ideas and special needs.

Much of this might sound like platitudinal fluff, but if readers are agreeing with any of this, caution is advised, because if students had a greater understanding of the nature of learning and their entitlement as consumers, they would not tolerate schools as they currently exist.

Don't think so? Go back to the scenario in which educators were asking students to design their own schools, and imagine that a group of students who have been given the tools to innovate have been assembled.

These are students who have been engaged in reflecting on their learning, learning about learning itself, and learning about their own unique qualities as learners. Because of this, they will have considerable understanding of effective and ineffective learning designs and instructional techniques.

Students with these experiences will be far less susceptible to status names and educational packaging because they have more clarity about their purpose in life, their personal learning agenda, and their personal learning endowments and how all of these will help them achieve their personal learning ambitions.

These students may very well know why they want to learn. They will have divested themselves of compliance learning strategies and invested in intrinsically motivated, intentional learning. Moreover, these students will be confident and recognize themselves as having something special to bring to the planning table. Because of this, they will feel entitled to make imaginative suggestions to educators on how to create learning experiences that are personally satisfying and that actually address a newly discovered personal learning agenda.

These students are informed that they may suggest *any* possibility for learning. Given this scenario, are these students going to suggest reconstituting traditional schools? "Oh, please, please, please, can we have sit-and-listen classes four to six hours a day? Oh, please, please, please, can we have schools that are dominated by standardized testing? Oh, please, please, please, can we have schools and all the other stuff that de-selves us with passivity, stress, and boredom?" No, they won't!

THE VOICES OF STUDENTS WILL HELP CHANGE SCHOOLS

Following are some suggestions from the students who have the tools to innovate and who have spent some time thinking about learning, from which they have developed a fuller sense of learning's possibilities and become educated consumers of educational experience:

- Let's have learning that is more active.
- Let's have learning that is more personally inspired and relevant.
- Let's have learning that happens in the real world.
- Let's learn in more ways than reading, writing, and listening.
- Let's let students learn in the ways that suit their unique intelligences.
- Let's have more community and world service learning.
- Let's have learning where *students* talk and present.
- Let's have learning that is really individualized.
- Let's have learning that involves more adults than just the teachers.
- Let's have learning where every student has a mentor.
- Let's have learning where students are mentors.

- Let's have learning places all over town, not just at the school.
- Let's get lots of businesses to offer courses so students have lots of choices.

Having expressed these general ideals about learning, what specific suggestions might such educated consumers of educational experience make?

- I have some friends and we are all very interested in video games. We would like to form our own class to study them.
- I really love computer-assisted, mechanical drawing, and I would like to be an apprentice to Mrs. Smith for a couple of periods a day.
- I'm interested in ecology, and my friend Dave's father owns a junkyard. I would like to do an independent project on recycling metals at his junkyard.
- A few of my friends and I would like to make a documentary movie about going to the prom.
- I have written several stories about children, and I would like to present my stories to some children in the elementary schools and then teach them about writing stories.
- We would like to form a reading group to read three biographies of young Hispanic women growing up in America.
- We would like to host a weekend workshop to dialogue with local nurses about the realities of being a nurse and the various ways to enter the profession.
- I would like to do an independent project on American automobiles in the 1950s, especially how they got so big.
- A group of us would like to do a Civil War project hiking the Appalachian Trail this summer.
- We would like to set up a series of mini-courses on leadership roles for athletes in society.
- We would like to be teachers, so we would like to set it up so we could apprentice with various teachers and possibly teach classes.
- I am networking with a group of students from four other countries, and we would like to write a curriculum for teaching about global networking.
- My mother is a bookkeeper for Raferty's, a local restaurant. I would like to go into accounting, so I would like to do a project with her during the second semester.
- We would like to take Chinese as an online course and teach English online to Chinese college students.
- I would like to take a county college course for credit here at the school.
- I would like to take a course offered by a historical society on the Web.

- I would like to take the course on the Holocaust being offered at the school in the next town.

And on and on and on into ecstasy (Leonard, 1968).

There are many questions that must come up at this point. First, who would even want a school or learning in general to be this spontaneous, this creative? Second, would that much choice even be good for our young people? Third, again, how could it ever be structured?

None of these are bad questions. Educators need to think carefully about them. But there is a sense in which these questions also miss the point. The point is whether educators think it is a good idea to get young people thinking about the nature of learning itself, whether educators really want students reflecting on the value of their educational experiences and *imagining* how learning might be improved.

Do current educators really want students to be that involved, that enfranchised? Senge (1990) posited that a concept fundamental to effective learning organizations is that all of its members understand themselves to be agents, agents enfranchised to act upon the structures and processes that make up the system so that they may continually participate in its creation and recreation. But should that apply to students? What kind of readiness for the twenty-first century would that produce?

There is a danger. The danger is that such participation and reflection on the value of educational experiences will inevitably lead students to think of themselves as having the entitlement of a consumer and a real stakeholder. Asking students to reflect on and evaluate the quality of their learning experiences will truly open a can of worms. Students will come to understand that they have something to contribute to how learning might be improved. They will want to be heard and to make suggestions. They may even make demands. Are the educators who all of these years have failed to see past their old mental models and who have resisted changing the structure of their industrial age schools ready for that? Are readers ready for that?

If educators start looking at their students as customers and educating them to be effective consumers and creators of educational experience, the likelihood is that schools are going to change and will likely evolve into something educators cannot yet envision.

When asked, students who are educated consumers of educational experience will not say, "Let's just keep doing what we have done before," no matter how much the master scheduler; the teachers' contract; the ambitions of administrators; the pension plan; the law; or local, state and federal governments wish they would. They won't. Engaging our students as educated consumers of educational experience will lead to a new national conversation about learning and to the real change that professionals have not been able to bring about since 1983.

STUDENTS AS EDUCATED CONSUMERS WILL LEAD TO CHANGE

How are schools going to innovate to deal with that new reality and accommodate students and help them become educated consumers of educational experience? In the New York metropolitan area there is a discount clothing retailer called Syms. The founder of the company, Sy Syms, who recently died, had a slogan: "An educated consumer is our best customer." In many of the company's TV ads, the consumer is offered a tip about buying quality clothing. The idea is that the more knowledgeable the consumer is about buying clothing, the more he or she will realize why Syms is a good place to shop.

This is a marketing model worth heeding. The way of the future is that students will go to the schools not because they "have to" but because they have been invited to be stakeholders. They will not go because they passively accept that the local school is the only game in town. Students will be better, more committed learners if as detailed here, they are engaged to learn about learning and confirmed in their entitlement to own and influence the designs for learning. It is thereby that learning will be pushed out of the box and cause the change in schools that educators have not been able to create for thirty years now.

REFERENCES

Argyris, C. (2012). *Organizational traps: Leadership, culture, and organizational design.* New York, NY: Oxford University Press.

Bandura, A. (2006). Adolescent development from an agentic perspective. In F. Pajares & T. Urdan (Eds.), *Self-efficacy beliefs of adolescents* (pp. 1–43). Charlotte, NC: Information Age Publishing.

Christensen, C., Horn, M., & Johnson, C. (2009). *Disrupting class: How disruptive innovation will change the way the world learns.* New York, NY: McGraw-Hill.

Garvin, D. (2000). *Learning in action: A guide to putting the learning organization to work.* Boston, MA: Harvard Business School Press.

Givens, B. (2002). *Teaching to the brain's natural learning systems.* Alexandria, VA: Association for Supervision and Curriculum Development.

Leonard, G. (1968). *Education and ecstasy.* New York, NY: Delacorte Press.

Mezirow, J., & Associates. (2005). *Learning as transformation: Critical perspectives on a theory in progress.* San Francisco, CA: Jossey-Bass.

Scherer, M. (2008). Perspective/The school scene. *Educational Leadership, 65*(8), 7.

Schlecty, P. C. (2009). *Leading for learning: How to transform schools into learning organizations.* San Francisco: Jossey-Bass.

Senge, P. (1990). *The fifth discipline: The art and practice of the learning organization.* New York, NY: Doubleday.

Senge, P., Cambron-McCabe, N., Lucas, T., Smith, B., Dutton, J., & Kleiner, A. (2000). *Schools that learn: A fifth discipline fieldbook for educators, parents, and everyone who cares about education.* New York, NY: Doubleday.

Senge, P., Scharmer, C. O., Jaworski, J., & Flowers, B. S. (2004). *Presence: Exploring profound change in people, organizations, and society.* New York, NY: Currency Doubleday.

Thomas, W. T. (2002). *Intrinsic motivation at work: Building energy and commitment.* San Francisco, CA: Berrett-Koehler Publishers.

Thomke, S., & von Hippel, E. (2002). Customers as innovators: A new way to create value. *Harvard Business Review, 80*(4), 74–81.

SEVEN

Guiding Step 7: Understand Two Related Concepts—Twenty-First-Century Skills and the Learning Organization

Up to this point Part II of this book has been devoted to examining positive forces for change in education. These forces have included the importance of understanding students' learning engagement, the emerging marketplace of educational experiences, and the evolution of students into independent learners and voluntary customers. The goal of Part II has been to help the reader consider the impact and implications of these changes for schools and how these forces stand to enhance a career in teaching. The final force for change to be considered in Part II is the advent of two related concepts, twenty-first-century skills and the learning organization.

Early career teachers have probably heard a lot about twenty-first-century skills in the course of their preparation for teaching. It is a concept to which education leaders give much lip service. Consider, however, that as education leaders speak of twenty-first-century skills, they have steadfastly maintained nineteenth-century schools as places for students and teachers to learn them. It is one more example of how education leaders refuse to abandon their mental models of what happens in schools.

This chapter develops a contrast to the industrial age view of schooling by going into detail about the nature of twenty-first-century skills, why they really are important, and how they do prepare students and teachers for working and living in the twenty-first century. In doing this, it will also introduce the concept of the learning organization, a place where twenty-first-century skills are practiced.

WHAT ARE TWENTY-FIRST-CENTURY SKILLS?

The concept of twenty-first-century skills has come from a number of quarters, but perhaps the most powerful expression of interest has come from the commercial sector. A broad array of business leaders have complained that many of their young employees do not have the skills necessary to contribute to the success of their organizations. This assessment eventually sparked enough concern among business leaders, educators, academics, and politicians that they were moved to specifically identify the skills they believed were missing but necessary in the twenty-first century.

A seminal contributor to this effort was the Partnership for 21st-Century Skills (Partnership, 2007). The Partnership published a list that proffered a set of skills it believed necessary for success in college and the workplace in the twenty-first century. The list has been endorsed by the National Governors Association (2005) and the Council of Chief State School Officers (2009). While also confirming the importance of traditional content knowledge, the Partnership's list presented something new. The skills it identified were personal effectiveness skills that had more to do with attitudes and behavior than with mastery of information.

The following behavioral skills were listed in the Partnership's (2007) document, "21st-century Skills, Education & Competitiveness: A Resource and Policy Guide":

- Flexibility and adaptability
- Initiative and self-direction
- Social and cross-cultural skills
- Productivity and accountability
- Leadership and responsibility
- Creativity and innovation skills
- Critical thinking and problem-solving skills
- Communication and collaboration skills (p. 13)

At first glance, readers might reasonably ask, why is this list even necessary? Haven't educators always thought that these skills were important? Of course, the answer is yes. But it is this very focus on attitudes and behavior that is something new. The newness is in the stipulation that these personal effectiveness skills must be present along with content knowledge. The two must be integrated.

The idea that content knowledge and personal effectiveness must be integrated suggests a transition in the concept of knowledge itself. In the twentieth century, mastery of content and sets of fixed compliance skills was deemed adequate to enter college and the workplace (Thomas, 2002). Students were prepared to apply a narrow set of skills when told how and when to do so. A lot of thinking was not necessary.

By contrast, in the twenty-first century it is now seen as necessary to integrate content knowledge with personal effectiveness. Workers are expected to be thoughtful and have the ability to creatively apply knowledge to complex real-life situations in a variety of domains, without company-provided scripts or supervision (Partnership, 2007; Sternberg, 2008; Wagner, 2008).

In light of this emphasis on personal effectiveness, readers should again consider the current practices of our industrial age schools and how they might or might not encourage development of these personal effectiveness skills. In this consideration, certainly factor in the focus schools place on standardized test preparation. Think for a moment about how standardized testing presents opportunities to demonstrate skills such as initiative, self-direction, and critical thinking.

Readers should also think of how standardized tests measure these social skills and how they are translated into effective communication, collaboration, problem solving, creativity, and innovation. If these are priorities in schools, it must be possible to see opportunities to demonstrate them on standardized tests, right? It should be apparent that teachers are focused on these skills as they prepare students for the tests, right?

Unfortunately, the fact is that these skills continue to be neglected because they cannot be easily measured on standardized tests. Be mindful that it is not adequate to respond that students learn these things implicitly from doing what they have to do in school. Remember, the whole concept of twenty-first-century skills developed because employers told educators that their employees lacked these skills. Students were coming out of school without them. So, again, is it possible to see in our schools specific, in-the-curriculum efforts to encourage these skills? Rarely.

TWENTY-FIRST-CENTURY SKILLS FOCUS ON PERSONAL DEVELOPMENT

As readers consider the advent of twenty-first-century skills as a force for change in society, what should become apparent is that these skills do, in fact, highlight the need to change schools. Twenty-first-century schools will have a strong focus on development of the person, along with the development of knowledge and skills. This focus on the person was accented in chapter 4 on learning engagement and is again renewed in this discussion of twenty-first-century skills, the development of which requires educators to gain an understanding of the inner condition of students and help students access and address that inner condition.

> **A Career Diminished**
> Working in industrial age schools, teachers will have a greatly diminished sense of their importance to students.

Getting students to make progress on their personal effectiveness will require that students be guided in reflecting on how the strengths and weaknesses of their personalities contribute to their ability to learn and assert twenty-first-century skills. This will require teachers to focus more on the students' experience of learning, and that focus will have to become more personalized.

Moreover, such an inquiry into how students experience learning will inevitably lead to individualization because the personality of each student will make him or her more or less capable of applying these skills. Students will need highly individualized and personalized programs to advance their personality strengths and remediate their weaknesses.

TWENTY-FIRST-CENTURY SCHOOLS WILL FACILITATE SELF-MASTERY

Let's look closely at how schools might facilitate the integration of content knowledge with the person who is doing the learning and responsible for its application. It has been previously stipulated that twenty-first-century learning will pay a great deal of attention to the experience of learning. It will encourage students to examine their efforts to learn from the standpoint of pleasure, relevance, and meaning.

When readers consider how acquisition of twenty-first-century skills might be facilitated by schools, then, it should be immediately clear that it would entail a reflective process, one that not only exercises the skills but examines the process from which the skills bloom. The importance of this reflective process is strongly supported in the academic and professional literature (Damon, 2008a, 2008b; Given, 2002; Senge, 1990; Senge et al., 2000; Senge et al., 2004; Thomas, 2002).

But such a process is not now a big part of what is done in schools (Damon, 2008a; Wiggins, 2008). The literature of the twenty-first-century organization confirms the importance of such reflection, of questioning basic assumptions about self, learning, and organizations (Garvin, 2000; Senge, 1990; Senge et al., 2004; Thomas, 2002). Knowing the importance of integrating knowledge with the person, educators must be clear that acquisition of personal effectiveness skills can be realistically undertaken only when students are prompted to look inward to examine and question their own motives for living and learning.

As students proceed through the thoughtful and creative activities of social learning, they must be simultaneously attentive to what is happening on the inside. Following are only a sample of the questions students might be prompted to ask themselves:

- How do I feel and respond when I get a creative assignment without a lot of step-by-step directions?
- How do I feel and respond when there is strong disagreement in my collaborative group?
- How do I feel and respond when there is unequal effort in the collaborative group?
- What am I learning when collaboration is so much fun and so exciting that I don't want to stop?
- What am I learning about the personal strengths that I bring to collaborative groups?
- What am I learning about where I want to direct my personal endowments in this world?

Helping students address these questions and others like them will help them initiate a habit of reflection. It will confirm that school is not just about processing information but a place where learners question themselves. Such examination helps students clarify their personal purposes, which in turn helps them achieve those purposes. There is integration of the person with knowledge because that knowledge will advance a plan for personal development. This self-endorsed purpose is the most fundamentally authentic motive for learning (Damon, 2008a; Thomas, 2002).

TWENTY-FIRST-CENTURY SKILLS COME FROM TWENTY-FIRST-CENTURY LEARNING ORGANIZATIONS

This book is about reflection. From the earliest pages, readers have been asked questions that require reflection. Some of the things that readers were asked to reflect on were the assumptions and practices employed by traditional schools. In the course of that reflection, readers likely came to agree that some of the assumptions and practices of schools might need to be reconsidered, maybe changed. This kind of reflection leads to improvement.

When individuals reflect on themselves, they are helped to avoid previous mistakes and chart paths for a better life. When organization members reflect collectively, they are helped to avoid previous mistakes and to innovate for the future. What's more, reflective organizations produce reflective people.

Yet, there is an astounding reality. Traditional schools don't do much reflecting. There are no meetings wherein the members of the school are asked to reconsider assumptions and practices so they may be changed for the next year. No one asks, should we think about changing the structure of the school year or the school day? No one asks, should we rethink grading, certification of learning, or the role of classroom instruction? The hard-to-believe truth is that it rarely occurs to the leaders of most schools to even raise these questions or reflect with the intention of creating real change.

So now an obvious question must be raised. Can schools—the ones that don't reflect on their own assumptions and practices—do a good job of helping youths to develop a habit of reflection? This is highly unlikely. First of all, the author has made it clear that because traditional schools are so bound up in the game of school, reflection is practically prohibited.

Second, it is the nature of industrial age schools to focus on what is easy to measure and control, such as short-answer tests. School leaders will not want to venture into the uncertainty of reflection whereby knowledge is seen as conditional and tentative. There is nothing inherent in the cultures of traditional schools whereby all of the people who make up the school try, collectively, to better understand what is happening in the school, how the school relates to its environment, or how it needs to change.

SCHOOLS NEED TO BE LEARNING ORGANIZATIONS

Let's begin with a proposition. Reflection must be an important part of school culture for students to develop the habit of reflection. This is why schools need to become learning organizations. So what is a learning organization and how is it different from a traditional school?

Many kinds of organizations can be learning organizations: corporations, foundations, small companies, churches, civic groups, and schools. What distinguishes a learning organization from a traditional organization is that *it learns and changes because of the learning*. If, for example, as a result of action research and reflection, a faculty was to decide that the time limitations on schools needed to be changed, then the school would start a process to change them. The faculty's collective effort in action research and reflection led to learning, which led to collective actions to change a school's time limitations.

Learning organizations make an explicit effort at collective learning, whereby all the members of the organization reflect, examine, investigate, imagine, create, and innovate, all with the purpose of continual improvement of the school. Theoretically, this is what professional learning communities are supposed to do by involving all teachers. This is what professional learning communities could do if their influence had not been limited to a focus on standardized testing.

Considering these conditions, it should be clear to readers that if they want to be part of an organization that encourages thinking, reflection, and judgment, they will need to seek out a position in a reflective school—a learning organization—not a traditional school. Or, it should be clear that readers need to lead change to achieve reflective schools, wherein teachers' voices have real influence.

THE LEGACY OF THE INDUSTRIAL AGE

A learning organization stands in contrast to an industrial age organization. Once it has been established, an industrial age organization keeps doing what it started doing on day one, like our traditional schools do. A traditional organization is machinelike. It just keeps doing what it does. The clock is a common example. It was engineered to operate in a certain way. The clock never stops to think about what it does or to consider new ways of keeping time. It just keeps doing what it has always done.

In the industrial age when people had an ever-growing respect for well-made machines, there was a strong inclination to create human organizations that were like machines, organizations that had the precision of a machine. In these industrial age organizations, people were compartmentalized into many departments and given very precise jobs in the office or on the assembly line. Each employee simply had to do the job assigned, and the organization would run well, like a machine runs. Not much thinking was required of people if they just did their well-defined jobs.

When organizations were structured in this way, they didn't change from year to year. Employees did not question the structure and practices of the organization because that kind of thinking was not part of the job. Many successful companies went on for decades with this kind of organization. So what could be the problem?

The problem with such an organizational structure was that it did not encourage change and innovation. If employees were being paid just to do narrowly defined jobs and not think, the idea of possibly doing things differently in the office or on the assembly line rarely came up. The problem with not facing such issues was that when conditions were changing outside of the organization, people often did not pay attention. The organization was running smoothly, like a machine, so why start reflecting, thinking, or changing?

When people began to study companies, they eventually learned something important about this failure to make changes. Those companies that were successful and long lasting were organizations that paid attention to change. When change in society was apparent, the organization thought about what it should do to deal with that change.

For example, if a company built carriages for horses to pull and it then became aware of the popularity of the recent invention of the automobile, it might consider building carriages powered by mechanical engines. If such an organization had done this, it would likely not have gone out of business and would have grown with the popularity of automobiles. If it did not, it likely would have gone out of business because its product was no longer needed.

The conclusion drawn by most people from this example is that companies cannot just continue doing what they have always done. They need to monitor the conditions in their environment and consider when change is necessary for their company to remain relevant. There are thousands of examples of companies that failed because they didn't recognize the need for change. Some of the most obvious examples are manufacturers of horse-drawn buggies, candles, oil lamps, tube-based radios and televisions, pocket calculators, typewriters, and on and on.

Understanding this need for change and how companies should deal with it has led to the idea of the learning organization. Under this concept, companies should be structured in ways that encourage members of the organization to be alert to the environment and to be constantly thinking and learning in such ways that the company would never be caught off guard and lose the lead in an industry.

Many theorists have introduced a variety of concepts of what constitutes a learning organization and the behaviors necessary within them (Deming, 1986, 1993; Drucker, 1988; Garvin, 2000; Senge, 1990). Many of these concepts also have been applied to schools (Fullan, 2006; Schlechty, 2009; Senge et al., 2000).

One of the most influential of these organizational theorists is Peter Senge (1990), who proposed some concepts that are important to our discussion on reflection and developing twenty-first-century skills. Briefly put, Senge believed learning organizations should:

- have a vision for the organization's success that is shared by all of its members;
- advance toward that shared vision by helping members (through reflection) get away from their old mental models;
- help members move away from thinking of organizations as being like machines and toward thinking about organizations as being organic systems that grow and create change to sustain and develop the organization's capacity; and
- provide for individual learning, reflection, and personal mastery as a way of creating change and increasing an organization's capacity to fulfill its goals. (p. 156)

TWENTY-FIRST-CENTURY SKILLS REQUIRE SELF-UNDERSTANDING AND SELF-MASTERY

It is the last item in this list that is critical to the discussion of twenty-first-century skills and readers' careers. If learning organizations are going to be successful, they must be full of individuals who are also trying to become better, more effective people. Senge (1990) applied the term "personal mastery" to this individual effort.

Primary in this personal learning process of personal mastery is for the person to get to know herself or himself, to acknowledge what is intrinsic to the self. Within this intrinsic domain, Senge believed that a person needed to develop a sense of personal purpose that is about more than accomplishing secondary goals, such as having a nice house or car or living in a nice neighborhood. At some point the individual must find within a purpose that is at once personal but also greater than the person. This purpose must be captured in a vision of how that person wishes the world and life to be.

As readers consider the concept of twenty-first-century skills, they might also consider their vision for their careers. The author asks them to consider how that vision drives their behavior. According to Senge (1990) this vision should not be a static picture in an individual's mind. The vision, too, is part of a learning process.

Given such a vision, an individual will experience a creative tension between what is and what might be, and this tension is what drives the creative process. A person will enter into a process of continually refining the vision and how it might be approached. It is what Senge referred to as generative learning, learning that increases the capacity to learn and, thereby, fulfills the vision for self and the organization. Senge cited Robert Fritz, who explained, "It's not what the vision is. It's what the vision does" (Senge, 1990, p. 142). All of this should prompt readers to consider a personal vision and the role it plays in their careers.

Senge's point was for a person to gain a level of perspective whereby she or he can suspend her or his personal attitudes and beliefs to see in a new way. An individual must be willing to examine the basic assumptions of his or her personal life and culture and eventually see how they might be impeding progress. The vision pushes the core operation, learning. It moves the person forward to new levels. An individual's ability to tolerate the tension between reality and vision is key to sustaining movement toward the vision.

This line of thinking should suggest to readers that working in such an organization promises a genuine focus on personal growth and professional development as thinkers who contribute to a collective advancement of the organization.

While such thoughtfulness suggests intellectual rigor, Senge (1990) would add to such intellectual resources an openness to the nonrational, the intuitive. He quotes Einstein: "I never discovered anything with my rational mind" (p. 158). As systems thinking is about focusing on wholes, Senge sees the learning process as bringing to bear a wholeness of person in the learning process. Senge explained: "[T]he systems perspective also illuminates subtler aspects of personal mastery—especially: integrating reason and intuition; continually seeing more of our connectedness to the world; compassion; and commitment to the whole" (p. 156).

Now what Senge described here is not easily digested, so let's look at it in terms of teaching careers, readers' careers. There has already been a detailed examination of what teachers do in a given day. In that detailed analysis, it was not noted that teachers took time to sit with other teachers to reflect on what they did and how they might want to change their school. Nor was it observed that teachers spent time reflecting on their personal effectiveness as individuals or as a collective. This reflective process is just not something that schools make part of teachers' days. The consequence of this is no change, no evolution.

In the context of readers' careers, is this absence of reflection the desired professional life? Or, would readers want to be in a learning organization that encourages individual and collective reflection on the conditions of the school and its vision? Do readers want to be in a school that encourages reflection on intrinsic purposes, personal goals, or a vision for personal growth? This is not just a theoretical choice. This is a real choice. Readers are going to be much happier people and have much more fulfilling careers if the right choice is made.

TWENTY-FIRST-CENTURY SKILLS MEAN A DIFFERENT KIND OF PERSON

A premise of this book is that the profession of teaching is in hard times, and it needs readers' attention and leadership. The message has been one of encouraging a deeply reflective process so early career teachers will be ready to answer some very difficult questions about the education of our youths as well as their own professional development.

In effect, this text has been explaining that a new generation of teachers needs to be different from the teachers of the past. That difference will be derived from their reflection and the fact that they have personally confronted the hard questions now emerging in education circles. As a result of such deep reflection, early career teachers will be ready to ask hard questions of their own and have some hard conversations with people who they know don't want to change.

This book and the concept of twenty-first-century skills are, in effect, saying that the twenty-first century is beckoning a new kind of organizational citizen, a new kind of teacher, and a new kind of student. That citizen is not the compliant follower of directions, the seeker of right answers, and the doer of narrowly defined tasks, all of which were key to the twentieth-century organization. Rather, the twenty-first-century organization is looking for imaginative thinkers and problem solvers who operate from a sense of purpose and seek meaning in their work (Fisher,

1997; Pink, 2006; Zuboff & Maxmin, 2004). These people understand the importance of twenty-first-century skills:

- Flexibility and adaptability
- Initiative and self-direction
- Social and cross-cultural skills
- Productivity and accountability
- Leadership and responsibility
- Creativity and innovation skills
- Critical thinking and problem-solving skills
- Communication and collaboration skills (p. 13)

They understand that it is by virtue of their engagement with themselves in reflection, examination, imagination, and visioning that these personal capacities will bloom. They understand that twenty-first-century organizations need people who have these skills because change is so rapid and fluid that only individuals with these capacities stand to contribute what organizations need.

THE NEGLECT OF REFLECTION

In spite of the powerful case many have made for the importance of a reflective process in twenty-first-century organizations, this practice continues to be overlooked in schooling (Damon, 2008a; Senge et al., 2000; Wiggins, 2008). It is clearly not what schools do. More urgent, the publication of research by Damon (2008a, 2008b) explains that the majority of students who graduate from secondary schools have little clarity about their mission in life and consequently flounder for years, some for a lifetime.

Perhaps what is even more alarming is that often students who have been highly successful in school never connect their efforts to a reflective self that clarifies personal endowments, intrinsic motivation, or a meaningful purpose. These students were just compliant doers in school and later learned the emptiness of such compliance in an undeveloped self. Encountering so many young adults who were adrift prompted Damon (2008a) to ask these questions:

> But where in our educational system do we introduce this crucial concept to our students? And when do we spend the time and effort to help our students match their abilities and interests with particular job choices (or even, in economic language, with the demands of the labor marketplace)? Too many young people are left to their own devices with respect to some of life's largest questions: What is my calling? What do I have to contribute to the world? What am I here for? It is as if we are running away from these questions, apprehensive about facing them, either for ourselves or for our children. (p. 47)

The concept of twenty-first-century skills should move educators toward getting this kind of reflection into schools. It points to a new kind of school with new ideas about the meaning of learning.

SELF-DIRECTION: A TWENTY-FIRST-CENTURY SKILL

Specifically cited in the Partnership's list of twenty-first-century skills is the skill of self-direction. The previous examination of the emerging marketplace of educational experiences also highlighted the role the marketplace is playing in encouraging our youths toward self-direction in learning. There is a sense in which the concept of self-direction is foundational within the overall list of twenty-first-century skills. It is through self-direction that individuals are able to assert the personal effectiveness needed in twenty-first-century organizations.

In this context, it is reasonable to ask about a school's capacity to enable the skill of self-direction. Is self-direction something that can be taught? Most people think of self-direction as a personality trait, but in fact, there are numerous programs in schools and research with the specific intention of enabling the skill of self-direction (Candy, 1991; Case & Gunstone, 2006; Chew, 2009; Cleary & Zimmerman, 2004; Cornwall, 2010; Covey, 1989; Goleman, 2000). The outcomes of these programs suggest that it is not only possible to teach self-direction, but it is possible to facilitate learning all of the twenty-first-century skills.

Do such programs exist in most schools? Mostly, they do not, but it is notable that programs of emotional intelligence and self-regulation are proliferating (Cleary & Zimmerman, 2004; Cornwall, 2010; Goleman, 2000). There is also a strand of research that demonstrates the capacity of teachers to manage and direct their own schools independent of state and administrative oversight (Farris-Berg, Dirkswager, & Junge, 2012).

Unfortunately the assumption of a self-directed mind-set and thereby the ability to apply twenty-first-century skills is greatly complicated by the fact that teachers and students must try to develop these skills while working in or attending industrial age schools, which are by their very nature compliance cultures that reinforce compliance learning (Schlechty, 2009; Senge et al., 2000) and the game of school.

This reality should be of great concern to early career teachers. They will not be provided opportunities to develop self-direction or the other twenty-first-century capacities to the proper extent in industrial age schools because schools are now being increasingly controlled by forces that are distant from them. In asserting these controls, governments encourage compliance to central authorities, not the self-direction that is the outcome of thinking and reflecting on a school's work.

In effect, central authorities remove the need for collective learning and thinking because what they reward is compliance. Do readers of this book look forward to careers whereby they simply follow directives from central authorities, or would they like to participate in a community of learners who focus on continual improvement of the self and the organization through thinking and reflecting?

If central authorities had a true interest in twenty-first-century skills, they would encourage collective learning in professional learning communities. They would encourage a thorough examination of all aspects of schools. This would entail teachers and students working together thinking and reflecting on how to improve the school community and how teachers and students learn. Learning would not be restricted to achieving success on standardized tests. On the basis of their collective learning, students and teachers would take action to improve schools. They would be employing concepts and procedures, such as those outlined by Senge and many other theorists, to get everybody involved in creating better schools.

Self-direction is not enabled by coerced compliance to central authorities. It is encouraged in cultures in which individuals think, reflect, learn, and then take action.

LEARNING HOW TO LEARN

A concept related to self-direction is learning how to learn. Students who know how to learn will not be dependent on formal structures to be effective learners. With this understanding, schools of the future will focus much less on students mastering bodies of information and much more on learning how to learn.

Because the nature of a twenty-first-century organization will be that it learns and improves how it learns, so a primary purpose of a twenty-first-century school will be to facilitate students' learning about how to learn. The field of learning how to learn has, in fact, developed into a specific area of educational research (Bellanca & Brandt, 2010; Black et al., 2006; Hopkins, 2010; Kamenetz, 2010; Rawson, 2000).

The driving premise of learning how to learn is analogous to the famous saying "If you give a man a fish, you feed him for a day. If you teach him how to fish, you feed him for a lifetime." In effect, when individuals learn how to learn, they can direct and facilitate their own learning as needed. They can get knowledge and develop skills independent of formal schooling. And there is evidence that more and more individuals rely on self-driven, informal learning as a way to advance their personal lives and careers (Paige, 2007).

> **A Career Diminished**
> Working in industrial age schools, teachers will contribute to the inappropriate preparation of youths for the twenty-first century.

Supportive of the concept of learning how to learn is the previously discussed notion that knowledge is an individual construct that is the outcome of a socially based process derived from participation (Brown & Adler, 2008; Gamache, 2002; Polanyi, 1969; Rawson, 2000). Again, it is about individuals asserting a process whereby they learn together. The process is central. Knowledge is not thought of as a static body of information that can be acquired by students only from an expert teacher in a formal school setting.

Thus, in conceiving of knowledge as a socially based process, individuals are at greater freedom to facilitate their own learning in the workplace, in community-based collaborative groups, and in online networking. Participation in any of these is a demonstration of learning how to learn.

The previously cited (see chapter 6) open source movement is a twenty-first-century example of self-direction in learning how to learn. The success of the Mozilla browser and Wikipedia encyclopedia has come in the course of people interacting with others, often informally, and thereby coming to know and contribute to the gradual perfection of outcomes. It is through familiarity with and confidence in the collaborative process that people really learn. By asserting self-direction and placing themselves in these collaborative efforts, people can facilitate their own learning. It is in recognition of this social foundation that twenty-first-century skills become most meaningful.

By contrast, consider what happens in traditional schools. Students are commonly put in individual desks, in rows, for listening to one person talk or to individually read textbooks to complete assignments individually. Learning is not a social process. Most students spend most of their time in school listening individually, reading individually, and working individually. These activities confirm schools' adherence to the antiquated assumption that knowledge is a substance that can be conveyed from teachers or books to the minds of students.

This understanding of knowledge is further confirmed by how schools assess student learning. Students are given individual tests to find out what individual students remember. Whether about information or skills, the emphasis is on what individual students remember. Do these activities or the testing encourage the development of twenty-first-century skills? No. That is why twenty-first-century personal effectiveness skills have become an issue and a force for change. Twenty-first-century skills are not promoted by what is done in industrial age schools, and neither students nor teachers are developing these skills.

This theoretical look at the value of the concept of twenty-first-century skills begs a vision of how schools would encourage the development of such skills. So, now it is time to take a look at a twenty-first-century school. There will be a stark contrast. In doing this, readers should think back to the introduction, which began and ended with an education fantasy.

REFERENCES

Bellanca, J., & Brandt, J. (Eds.). (2010). *21st century skills: Rethinking how students learn.* Bloomington, IN: Solution Tree.

Black, P., McCormick, R., James, M., & Pedder, D. (2006). Learning how to learn and assessment for learning: A theoretical inquiry. *Research Papers in Education, 21*(2), 119–132.

Brown, J. S., & Adler, R. P. (2008). Minds on fire: Open education, the long tail and learning 2.0. *Education Review,* January/February.

Candy, P. (1991). *Self-direction for lifelong learning.* San Francisco: Jossey-Bass.

Case, J., & Gunstone, R. (2006). Metacognitive development: A view beyond cognition. *Research in Science Education, 36*(½), 51–67.

Chew, J. (2009). Engaging MBA students in problem-based learning to foster self-directed learning. *The International Journal of Learning, 16*(6), 37–49.

Cleary, T. J., & Zimmerman, B. J. (2004). Self-regulation empowerment program: A school-based program to enhance self-regulated and self-motivated cycles of student learning. *Psychology in Schools, 41*(5), 537–550.

Cornwall, M. (2010). *Go suck a lemon: Strategies for improving your emotional intelligence.* Shelbyville, KY: Michael Cornwall.

Council of Chief State School Officers. (2009). ESEA reauthorization principles and recommendations: A policy statement of the Council of Chief State School Officers. Retrieved from http://www.ccsso.org/Documents/2009/ESEA_Task_Force_Policy_Statement_2010.pdf

Covey, S. (1989). *The seven habits of highly effective people.* New York, NY: Rosetta Books.

Damon, W. (2008a). The moral north star. *Educational Leadership, 66,* 2.

Damon, W. (2008b). *The path to purpose.* New York, NY: Free Press.

Deci, E. (1995). *Why we do what we do.* New York, NY: Penguin Books.

Deci, R. L., & Ryan, R. M. (2008). Facilitating optimal motivation and psychological well-being across life's domains. *Canadian Psychology, 49*(1), 14–23.

Deming, W. E. (1986). *Out of the crisis.* Cambridge, MA: Massachusetts Institute of Technology.

Deming, W. E. (1993). *The new economics.* Cambridge, MA: Massachusetts Institute of Technology.

Drucker, P. F. (1988). The coming of the new organization. In *Classic Drucker: From the pages of the Harvard Business Review,* 2008. Boston, MA: Harvard Business Review Press.

Drucker, P. F. (2005). Managing oneself. *Harvard Business Review, 83* (1), 15–30.

Farris-Berg, K., Dirkswager, E., & Junge, A. (2012). *Trusting teachers with school success: What happens when teachers call the shots.* Lanham, MD: Rowman & Littlefield Education.

Fisher, J. (1997). *Six silent killers: Management's greatest challenge.* Boca Raton, FL: St. Lucie Press.

Fullan, M. (2006). *Leadership and sustainability.* Thousand Oaks, CA: Corwin.

Gamache, P. (2002). University students as creators of personal knowledge: An alternative epitemological view. *Teaching in Higher Education, 7*(3), 277–294.

Garvin, D. (2000). *Learning in action: A guide to putting the learning organization to work.* Boston, MA: Harvard Business Review Press.

Given, B. (2002). *Teaching to the brain's natural learning systems.* Alexandria, VA: Association for Supervision and Curriculum Development.

Goleman, D. (2000). *Working with emotional intelligence.* New York, NY: Bantam.

Hopkins, K. R. (2010). *Teaching how to learn in a what-to-learn culture.* San Francisco: Jossey-Bass.

Kamenetz, A. (2010). *Edupunks, edupreneurs, and the coming transformation of higher education.* White River Junction, VT: Chelsea Green Publishing.

Mezirow, J., & Associates. (2000). *Learning as transformation: Critical perspectives on a theory in progress.* San Francisco, CA: Jossey-Bass.

National Governors Association. (2005). Retrieved from http://www.nga.org

Paige, R. (2007). Self-directed learning and the mind-set of successful entrepreneurial learning. *ATEA Journal, 37*(1), 16.

Partnership for 21st-century Skills. (2007). 21st-century skills, education & competitiveness: A resource and policy guide. Retrieved from http://www.p21.org/storage/documents/21st_century_skills_education_and_competitiveness_guide.pdf

Pink, D. H. (2006). *A whole new mind: Why right-brainers will rule the future.* New York, NY: The Berkley Publishing Group.

Polanyi, M. (1969). *Knowing and being.* Chicago: University of Chicago Press.

Rawson, M. (2000). Learning to learn: More than a skill set. *Studies in Higher Education, 25*(2), 225–238.

Ryan, R., & Deci, E. (2006). Self-regulation and the problem of human autonomy: Does psychology need choice, self-determination, and will? *Journal of Personality, 74*(6), 1557–1585.

Ryan, R., & Deci, E. (2008). From ego depletion to vitality: Theory and findings concerning the facilitation of energy available to the self. *Social and Personality Psychology Compass, 2*(2), 702–717.

Schlechty, P. (2009). *Leading for learning: How to transform schools into learning organizations.* San Francisco, CA: Jossey-Bass.

Senge, P. (1990). *The fifth discipline: The art and practice of the learning organization.* New York, NY: Doubleday.

Senge, P., Cambron-McCabe, N., Lucas, T., Smith, B., Dutton, J., & Kleiner, A. (2000). *Schools that learn: A fifth discipline fieldbook for educators, parents, and everyone who cares about education.* New York, NY: Doubleday.

Senge, P., Scharmer, C. O., Jaworski, J., & Flowers, B. S. (2004). *Presence: Exploring profound change in people, organizations, and society.* New York, NY: Currency Doubleday.

Sternberg, R. J. (2008). Excellence for all. *Educational Leadership, 66,* 2.

Thomas, W. T. (2002). *Intrinsic motivation at work: Building energy and commitment.* San Francisco, CA: Berrett-Koehler Publishers.

Wagner, T. (2008). Rigor redefined. *Educational Leadership, 66,* 2.

Wiggins, G. (2008). Grant Wiggins on school reform. Presentation given at Kean University, New Jersey, for New Jersey Department of Education, October 24, 2008.

Zuboff, S., & Maxmin, J. (2004). *The support economy: Why corporations are failing individuals and the next episode of capitalism.* London: Penguin Books.

III

New Schools for New Learning

EIGHT

Guiding Step 8: Envision a New Kind of School

A newly conceived school will employ new assumptions about schooling and be designed based on the principle of providing all students highly individualized, personalized, and customized programs of learning. The focus of Part III of this book is on seeing such a new school—and then getting one. With that in mind, most of this chapter and chapter 9 will be presented as narrative description in an effort to *show* a school. It will be a continuation of the fantasy at the end of the introduction.

This narrative description has a goal: to facilitate a vision. Without a vision of a new school, it will be hard to let go of old mental models and achieve one. It is important to remember, however, that what is being shared here is imagined. The author is unaware of an actual school that is specifically like the one described here. But that is not so important. What is important is to remember that in the future not all schools will be structured alike nor will they all be driven by the same goals.

The creation of all new schools will depend on the imaginations of their stakeholders. These stakeholders will include parents, students, teachers, school leaders, and those in the community who care. All stakeholders will be enfranchised to continually think, imagine, reflect, revise, renovate, and innovate as a natural part of schooling. No more letting distant entities think for school stakeholders. No more doing the same things over and over, year after year.

Readers are thus challenged to let go of industrial age thinking, with its premise of standardized schooling and learning in big schools for large groups. Instead, readers are encouraged to embrace a compound of thinking, imagination, and experimentation whose outcomes are not yet fully formed and that portends new kinds of schools that engage teachers and students as full participants in asserting a new premise of individualization within small, caring communities of learners.

Again, readers are asked to please be attentive to their reactions in reading the upcoming description. They may find themselves saying "Oh, that will never happen" or "Oh, that is so unrealistic." The author hears many such remarks from people. He is used to it, and he expects it. While it is not clear how readers will respond, the author wants to make it clear that he has also heard something else, too.

When offered various descriptions of new kinds of schools, some people who had previously been resistant start making suggestions and proposing their own ideas and designs. Perhaps they are not conscious of it, but they start saying things such as "Well, could such a school have . . . ?" or "What if students were encouraged to . . . ?" or "What if we tried this . . . ?" or "How about adding that . . . ?" "Why couldn't we do this . . . ?"

Hearing people respond in this way, the author believes he is witnessing a transition. These people have started to loosen their psychological grip on industrial age thinking. They are starting to consider new possibilities. They are starting the process of imagining a new way forward. For the author, then, such suggestions indicate a new openness to change, a willingness to become entrepreneurial and experimental in the world of twenty-first-century learning. The author's intent is that after finishing this book, readers might find ideas for new kinds of schools bubbling up in them, too.

Remember, the quality of readers' careers depends on such new ideas and taking a new direction in transforming schools and what teachers do. As a matter of introduction to the narrative, readers may find it helpful to note the basic conceptual differences between an industrial age school and a newly conceived school. Table 8.1 provides such a clarification.

A final note before the narrative: Shortly before finishing this book the author discovered a couple of new sources that would help readers envision new kinds of school structures and cultures. As it turns out these sources present visions that are thematically similar to what is to be presented. One of these sources is called the Independent Project. It is captured in a couple of videos on YouTube: http://www.youtube.com/watch?v=RElUmGI5gLc and http://www.youtube.com/watch?v=MTmH1wS2NJY. Another source comes from EdVisions Schools, which has also posted inspiring videos on YouTube: http://www.youtube.com/watch?v=F_gDVGH0qlM&list=PLCEAD525807BD5A7D&feature=c4-overview-vl.

The author congratulates both of these sources on their important work and strongly recommends that readers watch the videos. Besides aiding readers in envisioning a newly conceived school, the videos convey how participation in these projects results in a richer experience for both students and their teachers. Very compelling!

Table 8.1. A Contrast in Concepts of Schooling

From the Industrial Age Perspective	From the Twenty-First-Century Perspective
Schooling is about anonymous local and central authorities coercing students to acquire knowledge and skills deemed important to society as they are conveyed in a one-size-fits-all, mass-production, large-group setting through teacher-centered, teacher-talk classroom instruction, all in preparation for high-stakes, standardized testing.	Schooling is about facilitating students' participation in a caring, student-centered community of learners that employs many learning models in many places and at many times to develop students' desire to learn and facilitate individualized, personalized, and customized experiences judged by the students as customers to be personally relevant, meaningful, and enjoyable.

THE NARRATIVE

Readers are reminded of the fantasy story from the introduction, in which Rena Watson, a learning development coordinator (LDC) at the Arts in the Sciences Learning Community, after having interviewed a candidate for a position as a learning and development specialist (LDS), invites the candidate back for a tour of the community's facilities. Rena has been on staff for fifteen years and is part of the group of people who originally spearheaded the transition from traditional schools to the formation of small learning communities. Rena makes the first stop on the tour a room called the Matrix. She and the candidate are accompanied by two students.

As they all enter the room, Rena explains, "OK, we're going to start with an overview." The candidate looks around to see more than forty flat screen monitors arranged around three sides of the room. On every monitor he sees groups of students working together, most of whom, but not all, have adults working with them.

Rena begins by telling the candidate, "We loved your question during the interview about how we keep expanding our learning opportunities for students and teachers. Our school, Arts in the Sciences Learning Community, sometimes called A&S, has a little fewer than three hundred students, but we share resources with the other five small learning communities of a similar size here in our city and in some contiguous cities.

"Just about everything that is happening in all of our city's learning communities is being videoed for monitoring, supervision, and documentation. That includes everything in this building and every other building where our students meet with LDSs or community partners for sessions, even within private homes.

"We apply the term 'session' to every meeting among members of one of our learning communities. We don't think the word 'instruction' applies nowadays as well as it once did. Not that the term 'instruction' is irrelevant, but we generally do not use it to describe what people do with each other. It applies more to when students are working with software and machines.

"In any case, what you see on each of these screens is our students in session with adults working on projects facilitated by the adults or sometimes other students. Here is an example of a student's schedule that we provide for our visitors. I'll give you a paper copy, and it can also be seen here on the big monitor over the door on the back wall. I will bring it up with my device."

- 8:30 a.m. Home: Check into online course in Japanese and Skype with Japanese students who are home completing homework assignments for an English class at their school in Japan.
- 10:30 a.m. City Hall (Basement): Meet with city service project group on pure water sustainability. There is a discussion of two articles projecting worldwide water shortages. The course is taught by a water utility employee. She is referred to as a community partner teacher.
- 12:00 p.m. 140 Main Street: Working lunch at school satellite meeting room in downtown office building with teacher and project crew to explore a downtown park and pond as an ecosystem. The teacher is a county employee and also a community partner teacher from the county task force on environmental care. She lives in the community and created and volunteered to teach this course.
- 1:30 p.m. School, Room 308: Poetry Class: Hip Hop/Slam/Tumble/Break Out. This class was created and marketed by a traditional English teacher on staff at the old school before change started. To increase staff and student ownership of teaching and learning, he and other teachers have started to invent and market their own classes in cooperation with students. If students don't sign up for the classes, they are no longer offered.
- 2:30 p.m. School Writing Center: Group critique of dialogue being developed for documentary film about the senior prom.
- 3:15 p.m. Individual meeting with college applications adviser/writing instructor.
- 4:00 p.m. America's Field: Track practice with team. Along with the school coach a man and woman from the community who have deep backgrounds in track are assisting students.
- 5:30 p.m. Home: Dinner with family.
- 6:30 p.m. Home: Film crew and community partner film teacher meet in home basement to plan film locations. This teacher is also a community resident whose profession involves doing short films and commercials for ad agencies. He was recruited by students to help with this film project. It has become customary for students to

invent their own courses and recruit teachers from inside the faculty or from the regional community.

8:30 p.m. Home: Check into online course, Culture, Politics, and DNA. This course is provided by a corporation that provides online courses to school districts around the world. This student found the course relevant to his interest in how local community decisions contribute to better use of natural resources.

Independent reading, *Harry Potter and* . . .

Saturday elective: Six-hour communication competency workshop, The Role of Males in a More Feminine World.

"Note that in our A&S Community during the time that this student was here, courses were offered on-site by the police department (two courses), the fire department (two courses), the local hospital (three courses), the city manager's office (one course), the mayor's office (one course), the Office of Animal Control (two courses), and the chamber of commerce (two courses).

"In addition, courses were offered by professionals who lived in the city and came to students' homes to facilitate courses in law, veterinary medicine, stocks and bonds, antiques, child guidance, government, local history, local geology, beach ecology, microbiology, professional music recording, gardening, small business start-up, writing professionally, ballooning, kite art, home construction, cabinetmaking, and Victorian home restoration.

"This is a real student's schedule who has already gone Next Level. Let me point out some unique features of his curriculum. This student also completed some short-term courses that were offered on weekends, evenings, and during the summer. These courses included two workshops, 'Quadratic Equations and Video Games' (three hours on both Friday night and Saturday night and the writing of a combined personal essay/equation demonstration) and 'Athletes as Community Leaders,' which met on Monday nights for five weeks and required initiating and writing about a small but helpful community project.

"Over the summer, he developed competencies and received credit for completing and keeping records on a running/training routine, taking three online math courses (over three summers) and writing a short play based on his discovery that a close friend and teammate was gay. In the final year of school, this student completed a course in the personal essay with a private tutor with whom he met once a week. He declared the completion of his work in three years and went Next Level, which in his case was off to college."

STUDENT LEARNING PROGRAMS ARE AN OUTCOME OF A DELIBERATE NEW DESIGN

"Let me elaborate on how the design of our school translates into individual students' schedules similar to this one. Based on the design of this school, the staff's facilitation makes sure that

- students have a tremendous number of choices from which to build a learning program that is satisfying and supporting their personal goals;
- all of the learning does not have to take place in one building called the school;
- important learning does not have to happen just between the hours of 8:00 a.m. and 3:00 p.m.;
- earning credit for learning can happen on weekends, evenings, and during the summer;
- credit can be earned by working with people other than the adults at school;
- student learning programs involve a combination of quiet reflection and meditation along with social activity and working collaboratively to solve problems and answer difficult personal and social questions;
- student learning programs involve significant use of technology and networking with distant collaborators on the Internet;
- student learning programs reflect the individual interests of one student who chooses to work sometimes alone and sometimes with other people with similar interests;
- student learning programs may have unusual class topics, but they are related to traditional subjects, such as science, math, art, history, English, and social studies, and provide opportunities to advance in all of these traditional areas;
- students may advance through their programs based on demonstrating abilities and competencies, not fixed seat time or course completion;
- students have significant influence over the operations of our learning community along with the creation and execution of their learning plans; and
- students provide concrete and detailed feedback to adults clarifying that they find their learning programs 'meaningful, fun, and exciting.'

"I should explain that our school community stopped what we used to call graduation and all that bogus stuff back in 2024 when we went completely to competency certification, master endorsements, and electronic portfolios. When our students declare completion of their work and their intention to go Next Level, they have learned what they believe they needed to learn to move forward. If they have the certified competencies and master endorsements that they need (all evident in their portfolios) and the staff can see they are ready for the next level, they are out of here.

"We are happy to move students forward as fast as they want to go. We have found that when students are aware that they can move through their programs at their chosen speed, many really accelerate their work. They like the idea of moving at their own pace and not being held back by seat-time requirements, the pace of other students, or any other time constraints. We find it a big motivator.

"And, by the way, we use the term 'Next Level' instead of graduation because for us it clarifies that not every student leaves this step in his or her learning with the same background. There is no standardization of background. Colleges, universities, and prospective employers can find out what they need to know about our students by looking carefully at their electronic portfolios. And, yes, we have very tight security measures to protect the security and authenticity of the portfolios. We'll take a look at one in a moment.

"In our work with students in the A&S Community, we do our best to help them clarify a purpose for learning and living. It is in the context of that purpose that students, in consultation with a variety of adults in and outside of the A&S Community, create programs for themselves that will take them to the next level.

"Such programs could entail preparation for starting a business, joining the armed forces, going to a two- or four-year college, or going off to work. When students create their programs, they, along with their consultants, do a careful assessment of which competencies are needed to be effective at the next level. Believe me, it isn't easy for anyone, but everyone is given maximum support along with lots of reality checks.

"The thing is, as small community schools go, ours is considered somewhat advanced because it involves increasing levels of self-regulation and independence. We like that reputation. Mind you that we give students a lot of help in coming to grips with what self-regulation and independence mean and how every person has to build these qualities over time.

"Nevertheless, when students apply to this school, we ask them to make a hard assessment about how much freedom and responsibility they can handle. We tell them that this is a high-effort, high-responsibility environment. Some back away because they understand that they need more structure and direction. One of our communities is quite highly structured so those students have a place to go. At the same time, many students come to us because they want the status, and they know that they need to work hard and become more self-regulated and independent.

"There are still others who believe they just need more freedom, and that group has brought us a remarkable cross section of students, including some of the most difficult kids who were constantly in conflict with highly structured environments. They have come into our community and done exceptionally well when left to their own devices. Honestly, many of these kids seem to have something to prove.

"Then, there are the academic types, headed off to fancy higher education, and the blue-collar types, headed off to start businesses with pickup trucks. Regardless of their destinations, their preparation in this community is advertised as advanced because of the self-regulation and independence component. We do a lot of thinking here about emotional intelligence and real-world intelligence. We are critical of too much 'book learnin'.'

"Now let me pull up this student's electronic portfolio, which, by the way we have his permission to use, to just give you some examples of his competency certifications and the related demos. OK, here we see the front cover with a picture and a few artistic touches; then there is a brief introduction (we suggest one hundred words, sort of like an abstract); and now, we see a kind of table of contents, some of which are certified competencies and some of which are just deep experiences.

"About 'deep experiences,' sometimes students will declare a competency and no matter what we do, we have no way of certifying it because we cannot bring in an 'expert' to certify it. In that case we call it a deep experience, which is documented in the portfolio with a video or some other demonstration. Students have the option of getting the certification at a later date should they encounter such an expert. We have certified postdeparture a few times before. We think the portfolio should be thought of as a lifelong tool.

"This student has many competencies, so we will look at just a few. One standard competency he has is textual analysis. Several LDSs here have endorsed his text analysis skills, and he has included a demo in a paper on 'Jabberwocky.' Here is another common competency on public speaking, and here is one on complicated explanations. Both are endorsed with demos. Let's look for an unusual competency. OK, here's one. This student knows how to do visual and tactile examination of metals to determine composition. That means he knows how to roughly determine their composition and purity without doing lab tests.

"I think it is an important skill in the recycling biz. He was certified by a man from the county recovery center who advises on recycling. I'm not sure how that fits into his life's plan, but I'm sure he does. Now here is another student's schedule. She has also gone Next Level and given us permission to use her schedule and e-portfolio."

> 8:30 a.m. The Literature and the Psychology of Social Skills, which meets in the basement of a local church. The class was the creation of a teacher, a local clergyman, and several students working together. To date they have read literature as diverse as Pope's *The*

Rape of the Lock, Swift's *Gulliver's Travels*, and Dale Carnegie's *How to Win Friends and Influence People*. Because real-world problem solving is a primary goal of the class, on this date the student met with the other eleven members of the class to create a social-orientation program for incoming freshmen at their school for the next school year.

10:30 a.m. All Politics Is Local, which meets in the home of a former city mayor. The class was the creation of the mayor and his wife, and it has been a popular choice with students for five years. The mayor and his wife have developed a curriculum that focuses on the various influences in the development of good policy and the political implications of good policy.

12:00 p.m. Student returns home for a quick lunch and then takes an online class on surveys and statistical measurements. Students in the group often chat online before the course, then watch a video and work with a teacher on some guided assignments. On this date, students were working in pairs and critiquing each other's survey and measurement proposals. This class was also working online in coordination with a similar school group at a technical school in India.

1:30 p.m. Independent study in school research center. Like all other students, this student earned credits via independent study on student-chosen topics and regularly met with a teacher for guidance and support in preparation for a presentation of her research and outcomes to staff and students. The topic addressed a question important to the student: What is the value of art to society?

2:30 p.m. I Hate Math. This class still meets in the main building and is a combination of working with a teaching machine, watching YouTube videos, and doing programmed study, with occasional individual and group conferences with a teacher. The course is a student–staff creation—an outcome of trial and error.

3:30 p.m. Individual meeting with vocations adviser/art instructor.

4:00 p.m. Writing and Acting for Stage Performance. This class still meets in a conference room at a local theater downtown. The class is a collaboration among the school drama teacher, several drama devotees in the community, and students. Students will write and workshop plays as well as learn techniques for finding various characters in themselves and expressing them on stage.

5:00 p.m. Musical Theater. This class meets at the school. As this student is a musician, for this class she placed special focus on the creative interpretation of musical arrangements in play production.

6:00 p.m. Dinner at home.

7:00 p.m. Online course, The Language of Ballet. As a third-year student in French the student worked with a group online completing and discussing readings about the history and techniques of ballet. As a final project each student submitted a video of a personally choreographed dance routine that is narrated in French and demonstrates important concepts learned during the class. This class works in collaboration with a teenage group of dancers in France that completed a similar class in The Language of Jazz and Modern Dance.

"Note that this student also completed some short-term courses, which were offered on weekends, evenings, and during the summer. This included two workshops, 'What to Expect When Working in a Group' (three hours on both Friday night and Saturday night and the writing of a combined personal essay/group-work analysis), and 'Taking Charge: Becoming Your Own Agent,' which met on Tuesday nights for five weeks and required initiating and writing about a small but helpful 'moment of leadership' doing a community project.

"During the summer, this student developed competencies and received credit for completing a summer camp mentorship, taking three online literature courses (over three summers) and writing a short piece for piano. Another course on staging art was also completed with one other student sharing a personal tutor once a week for seventy-five minutes. This student would begin taking courses at a local community college at the age of sixteen and complete work in the A&S Community in three and a half years.

"I should point out that our LDSs or community partners rarely meet with students for learning in groups larger than eight unless having more is deemed an advantage. As you look at the screens around the room, you will see that most of the groups are at least that small. The ability to keep our groups so small is largely an outcome of our use of resources. We make a specific point of making room in every students' schedules for regular one-on-one meetings with various staff. That is what personalization really means. It's about making room for person-to-person time.

"At any one time our school could have one half to three quarters of our students working with online courses or otherwise involved with learning machines or software, projects, or community partners, so LDSs have plenty of time for individual and small-group work with students. We make sure that every student has at least ten individual or small-group experiences per week.

"By involving the entire city in the education of our young people, we are able to spread our facilitation needs around and give students a much more personalized experience. Our use of LDSs and community partners changes every year depending on our students' needs and interests. But our repertoire of possible community partners keeps on growing.

"So, at any time of day up until 10 o'clock at night, someone can visit the Matrix and see what is going on in our A&S Community. Let's take a look at some specifics. The students you see on all of these screens are working here in this building with various adults usually on some kind of group project, although individuals often run their own projects. Most sessions with an adult run from twenty minutes to half an hour. If the adult wants to give some kind of big demonstration, what we used to call a lesson, that gets put online so students can view it as many times as they want or need.

"We find that the students like this because they can first ask each other questions and then either e-mail in some tough questions to the LDS, wait until the next session with the LDS, or call the LDS on the phone. So most demonstrations are online, and when students come to sessions they talk about the reading, the online materials, and especially how they are experiencing their projects and the whole learning routine.

"We consider understanding the students' experience of what we give them to do as critical to improving our work here in the A&S Community. Students know this and are very up front about what they like and don't like. If we give them something we know they are not going to like, then we make a big effort to explain why it is necessary.

"Still, we listen to students as much as possible. And, students know that the adults they work with are very sensitive to gaming. We still talk about the old game of school routine that used to control schools back in the day. Students know we want their experiences to be high quality, so we ask them a lot of questions about what they think the quality is. At the same time, we ask them what they believe they can do to improve the quality of their learning experiences. It's not just on us.

"On this row of screens we see what is happening in some venues outside of this building. Here is one from the hospital. Here's one in the plumbing equipment store downtown. Here's one with Vera Jenkins, who is a historian who lives here in town. She is working with students on the history of the house where the mayor now lives. She is eighty-four years old, and every course she teaches gets rave reviews from the students. She actually gets kids to help her dig through the city archives. There is a waiting list for her course, but she wants to teach only one per quarter. She is, after all, retired. Our community partners have so much to offer and are so economical.

"One of your responsibilities as an LDS will be to work with our community partners on pedagogical and developmental considerations in their work with our teens. Our LDSs can go to the sites for visits if they have time or come to this room to see what is going on in the groups they coordinate.

"Over on this screen is a group volunteering at the emergency management office, where students are working on the preparation of kits for families affected by fire or storm damage. We have had our share of such emergencies in this city, and we put a lot of emphasis on being ready. Recently, however, our city had to donate all of its kits to another community, so now we have to build more. The students are a big help. They learn a lot about large-scale community projects.

"Over on this screen we see an empty room, but soon it will be filling up with students from around the county. It is a nine-week seminar being facilitated by a couple of chemists who work for the Safra Pharmaceutical Group on the outskirts of town. They typically provide a lot of learning opportunities for students throughout the year, and they pick the kids up in a van, which is really great.

"I should also tell you that even though our A&S Community gives guidelines for facilitating for students, we realize that some of the big groups, such as the chamber of commerce or a number of corporations, such as Safra, like to do things the way they want to do them. We don't mind. We like to see a large variety of learning models out there and a lot of experimenting. Bottom line, our students will let them know in clear terms whether what they are doing is working or not. Our students learn to think of themselves as having a lot to offer in terms of understanding what works in learning and instruction."

THE HISTORY OF THE ARTS IN THE SCIENCES LEARNING COMMUNITY

Rena goes on, "Now that you see evidence of our community's development, let me give you a little background. The Arts in the Sciences Learning Community was formed in 2020. I don't know whether you remember, but around that time there was a kind of breakthrough period for schools, and more and more communities decided to drop the traditional school model.

"Here in our city, we initially formed three small community schools, and over the years that eventually became five small schools. The formation of every school was always an effort to provide students with a more personal experience and to meet the needs of various stakeholders. We regarded it as our mission to make learning personal.

"We eventually dropped the term 'school' and started using the term 'learning community.' Although we were one of the first secondary, small community schools to be formed in our city, we have actually gone through a number of changes and transformations ourselves. It is, in fact, part of the design of our learning community that we change from year to year and sometimes within the year. So, what I am showing you today is the outcome of a new and deliberate design, a design our stakeholders review and critique every year."

As Rena speaks, the candidate looks at all of the screens. On nearly everyone, there was a small group of students talking to each other or putting things together. Rena continues, "With this perspective of our school's broad involvement with the community, one might think of our school as a Wikipedia-type project. It is a democratic collaboration that just keeps creating new relationships this way and that way, up and down.

"Every scene you see on one of these screens is an outcome of incremental growth whereby students and adults have come together to refine the learning process. The I Hate Math course over on this screen is an example. The opportunities for learning just keep growing with each new student, staff member, or community partner who contributes.

"When our school started we were experimenting with five community partners. Now we have more than a hundred partners, thirty interactive teaching machines, and loads of special software and gameware. Soon we will start sharing resources with the county, and that will push us close to a thousand community partners and even more hardware and software. We are always a work in progress, expanding the possibilities for learning.

"One of the projects that the staff has on the front burner is to help the State of New Jersey develop a resource guide of community partners so we can accommodate the learning desires of any student. That will bring us well into the thousands of community partners that our students might work with here in the northeast region.

"One of my favorite stories is about the fact that we found several people who are hubcap experts. Yes, hubcaps. And we stumbled on to these people when we were looking to help an art student who was interested in 1950s automobiles. When we were able to hook this student up with those two guys, who lived in different states, his project and study took off like a rocket.

"That is just one of many stories. At A&S we keep expanding the number of opportunities to learn. Every person who comes into the school, student or staff, gets to make his or her mark on the school by opening new pathways. We all leave something behind that we believe advances the cause of learning. Everyone comes here to create and refine; invent and revise; learn, unlearn, and learn again."

SEEING THE COMMUNITY IN ACTION

"OK, now, let's do a little more walking around. Look in here. We have several rooms like this one where students are given work or laboratory space to work on their projects. This room is three thousand square feet, and there is one adult in the room, whom we call a concierge. So the job is not just supervision. Students have high regard for all of our concierges because when they are asked for help, the concierges really help or show students how to get what they need to move forward. Right now there are likely only one hundred students in this room, but there could be twice that number.

"By the way every cubicle area is monitored by video. Even though all of the cubicles are open, other students are expected to respect the space and stay out of them. You notice that some of the projects are covered either for secrecy, security, or surprise unveiling later.

"I especially want to show you this room. In here we see in action a course that was created by the teacher, and he teaches it in five or six community schools although not always in the same quarter. It's basically a course about the Internet—history and developments—and strategies for effective use. We have no required courses here, but if we did, this and computer programming, also very popular, would be two we would seriously consider. Many of our LDSs routinely sit in on the Internet course for themselves.

"Here in the hallway, we have what the students call our 'mirror mirror on the wall.' Notice the question about the mirror: Who is responsible for your learning, your happiness? This mirror is a big part of our students' orientation. It gives them something to think about before joining the community.

"In this room we have to just look through the window in the door because what is going on in this circle of students is an advisory session. In advisory sessions, students may talk about very personal issues in their lives. They may be seeking support or advice or just need to be listened to, and we try to provide it all. Everyone agrees not to discuss advisory issues out in the world of gossip. It's the very real part of everybody caring about everybody else in our community.

"Every student attends an advisory session at least once a week with about eight to twelve other students, wherein each student is encouraged to share important events in his or her life. If a student has had a big victory, then we might try to arrange a celebration. If there has been trauma, then we take the necessary steps to support the individual, including professional help. We make a big effort to make sure nobody falls through the cracks here.

"Here is a room with our latest teaching machines. Many of our students say they enjoy the teaching machine experience and prefer to use them for certain competencies instead of going to a class or taking a class online. These newest machines, which are connected to all student data collected through the years, provide structured, adaptive learning experiences on a gaming platform so everything is fun. Some of this can be done at home on a computer, but some of our most advanced machines require being hooked into our community data network for maximum adaptivity, so, for now, use of the machine has to be in this building.

"If you were to sit in front of this machine, it would know if you were a student, an adult, or a stranger. If you are part of the community, it will know your name and a lot of your learning background. It will ask you questions, and when you give an answer, it may even probe for a more thinly sliced answer. It will keep doing this until it senses it is ready to start helping you understand something.

"The makers of these machines really know what makes you learn and remember things, and when you sit down to work on a skill, they pull out all of the stops and you learn that skill. The kids love the machines. They can get certain competencies behind them very quickly. Their only complaint is that they can't take them home.

"Over in this room is a group of students who created their own course to study the feasibility of a business start-up idea that they had, something to do with a new model for USPS paper mail delivery. They have gotten all kinds of professional people, including a patent attorney, to come and consult with them." (An aside from the author: You have to remember that almost everybody wants to help kids advance. I mean really, when a teenager calls you and asks for your help, what are you going to say?)

"The funny thing about this project is that it is all very top secret. The adults who come into the room to consult actually have to sign nondisclosure agreements. The A&S Community even had to agree not to monitor the discussions in the room. We went along with it. We trust the students and parents, and we're pragmatic.

"We have another five student-created courses this year. One has to do with electronics of TV broadcasting, another with doll collecting, and another with the consumption of cactus plants. There is one focused on dark energy research, and one with solar panel siding for residential housing. In almost every case, the students pulled together their own consulting group. What's wonderful is that when students reach out in such a way, people reach back and try to help. These kids could not get someone to be the regular LDS, but they have so many consultants coming and going that they are with an adult most of the time.

"If you look in this room, you see a student presentation under way. I don't know what project these students worked on, but it is part of the routine of the school that students make presentations after their projects. Attendance is usually by invitation only, but students can advertise their presentations and open them up to whomever. We usually do whatever works.

"Also, notice that there are refreshments set up on the side tables. All student presentations must include a social period and refreshments facilitated by the presenter after the formal presentation. We believe learning is social. A video of a student presentation is a common item to find in a student's portfolio. Because of so much presenting, getting a competency in public speaking and complicated explanations is a no-brainer around here.

"One of the things I can't show you now is our out-of-network learning experiences. Students can be given certification for the learning they do in remote parts of the world where there is no video connection and no member of our community would be available for assessment or input. Still, we give students credit for their experiences if they can demonstrate competency when they return.

"We did this for a student who did oil rigging as part of a fracking project in Idaho over the summer. He brought video and did a demonstration with plastic straws. One of our favorite ways of verifying competence is by getting some kind of demonstration in front of an expert and also attaching a personal essay to the experience, one that explains the importance of the experience in terms of the students' learning goals. All of that goes into the portfolio somehow.

"In most cases it works out pretty well. We have given credit for all kinds of travel experiences, unique adventure experiences, community volunteering, tutoring, big sister and big brother work, and mentoring new entrants here at school. Some of the most exotic experiences were bungee jumping with a self-made bungee cord, a disappearing act in a magic show, and climbing into the steel rafters of the gym without anything but ropes. The father signed off on it. The kid now works in a unique position for the FBI.

"We have also given credit for building a tree house, a first-time small plane flying experience, and a videotaped high-diving demonstration. Students in our community are also given certification for having a job in the commercial sector. These students do have to participate in seminars and write papers, but they will get credit for going out and getting and keeping a job. Then the follow-up seminars and paper writing add a lot to the experience.

"We like real-world experience, and we make a concerted effort to make students aware of and take seriously what employers want from employees. And we always emphasize how many of our graduates are now running businesses."

TECHNOLOGY HAS A SPECIAL ROLE IN TWENTY-FIRST-CENTURY LEARNING

Rena goes to great lengths to emphasize that the A&S Community puts great stock in the use of technology. "Every student in the community has a school-issued tablet that has all required reading loaded or linked to it; an array of reference apps; and other educational apps from Google, Apple, and others as well as special links for dedicated chat rooms and collaboration sites specific to the projects in this school. Students do a great deal of research and paper writing on these tablets. And it's funny to hear our students laugh about how we old timers used to carry those gigantic textbooks. Remember them? And students read about 10% of them!

"I should add that when students come into this community, they are given orientation on how to create a course. So, when a student gets an idea for a course, there is a protocol to follow for how to get student partners and develop the materials and experiences for the course. Part of the protocol is to check the Internet.

"When the desire is expressed, we get together with a tech super and start exploring what is on the Internet in terms of open software, courseware, blogs, and what not. We encourage students to take the Internet course I mentioned earlier, and it is built into nearly every course that students should participate in some kind of networking project online and some kind of crowd sourcing process online.

"This room is a technology resource room, a room always in transition. Students come here to consult with a tech supervisor or just to do work on a computer. Because every student now has a school-issued tablet, the number of computers available is shrinking every year as demand declines and equipment breaks down. We are beginning to question the value of this room at all, but even now you can see that it is half full. Many students have expressed a preference for doing some work on a larger screen.

"I should also explain that just about all of our students take some courses online. And just about every course taken by students in our community will have at least one online component, usually more. We see technology as a huge facilitator of learning. We are part of the Northeast Regional Network, so our students have literally thousands of courses to choose from. The NRN is very sensitive to students' interests and learning styles, so the selection for students is very good, and our students have given the NRN high grades.

"We look forward to a time when local schools will be supported by a kind of Amazon of education, whereby a student could access a line of study among many thousands and be provided with online guided work, readings sent electronically, videos, suggested activities, experts to communicate with, local peer contacts and groups to meet with, and a learning concierge to check on student satisfaction/problems with the learning module."

A RESEARCHED-BASED RATIONALE

"Again, I want to emphasize that all of the adult stakeholders in our community made a point of making sure the school we created had a strong basis in research, not like in the old days when everybody just accepted the industrial age ways of schooling. In the early days of convincing people to go the route of small learning communities, we did a lot of reading and consulted with many scholars.

"We determined a primary goal of helping students move toward a self-directed, intentional learning mind-set. This goal is supported by research and theory from a variety of disciplines. Primary among these is the work of Edward L. Deci, Richard Ryan, and others who have contributed to a field known as self-determination theory" (Deci & Flaste, 1995; Deci & Ryan, 2008a, 2008b; Deci et al., 1991; McInerney & Van Etten, 2004).

"The self-determination theory maintains that people are motivated by three primary needs: autonomy, competence, and relatedness. This foundation in clinical psychological research was, however, convergent with other important and timely research, all of which suggested to us the importance of developing a self-directed, intentional learning mind-set in our students. Prominent in this regard is transformational learning theory (Mezirow et al., 1990, 2000; Mezirow & Taylor, 2009), which had bearing on the design of our transition period, during which we carefully questioned all of the assumptions and practices we employed in the traditional school.

"A group within our transition team was also heavily influenced by the work of Glasser (1998), who while making personal freedom the centerpiece of his choice theory, contended that people have much more control over their lives and their emotions than most people realize. Contrary to common belief about the overwhelming force of life's determining factors, Glasser made the case that it is not life's extrinsic imposing forces but rather individuals who decide what they do and how they feel about it.

"We were also heavily influenced by the works of Tony Wagner (2010, 2012) and Yong Zhao (2009, 2012). Both of these scholars were sounding the alarm about how inadequate our traditional schools were back in the early 2000s. Not many people were listening then because of the accountability craze, but these authors figured significantly in helping us design a school that was really different and that encouraged entrepreneurial learning. Oh, and I'll mention one more book that was very important to us early on. It's called *Schools That Learn: A Fifth Discipline Fieldbook for Educators, Parents, and Everyone Who Cares About Education* (Senge et al., 2000). That book helped us see that we were not alone in trying to make changes."

With this discussion of the community's basis in research, Rena concludes this part of the candidate's tour, and they break for lunch. This tour provides a visual experience of a newly conceived school. It allows readers to see how a school became smaller yet encompassed more space and resources. In spite of its reduction in population, learning in this school now took place not in just one large building but throughout a city, including within private homes.

In all of these places, student learning was facilitated in small groups by caring adults eager to contribute to helping students understand various fields of specialty. All of this learning was also supported by county, state, and national resources along with the support of private groups and large corporations.

These new circumstances in education also clarify new roles for the primary constituents of schools—students and teachers. Those new roles are the subject of chapter 9.

REFERENCES

Deci, E., & Flaste, R. (1995). *Why we do what we do*. New York: Penguin Books.

Deci, E., & Ryan, R. (2008a). Self-determination theory: A macro-theory of human motivation, development, and health. *Canadian Psychology, 49*(1), 182–185.

Deci, E., Vallerand, R. J., Pelletier, L. G., & Ryan, R. M. (1991). Motivation in education: The self-determination perspective. *Educational Psychologist, 26*(3-4), 325–346.

Deci, E. L., & Ryan, R. M. (2008b). Facilitating optimal motivation and psychological well-being across life's domains. *Canadian Psychology, 49*(1), 14–23.

Glasser, W. (1998). *Choice theory: A new psychology of personal freedom*. New York, NY: Harper Perennial.

McInerney, D. M., & Van Etten, S. (Eds.). (2004). *Big theories revisited: Volume 4 in research on sociocultural influences on motivation and learning* (p. 47). Greenwich, CT: Information Age Publishing.

Mezirow, J., & Associates. (1990). *Fostering critical reflection in adulthood: A guide to transformative and emancipatory learning*. San Francisco, CA: Jossey-Bass.

Mezirow, J., & Associates. (2000). *Learning as transformation: Critical perspectives on a theory in progress*. San Francisco, CA: Jossey-Bass.

Mezirow, J., & Taylor, E. (Eds.). (2009). *Transformative learning in practice: Insights from community, workplace, and higher education*. San Francisco, CA: John Wiley and Sons.

Ryan, R., & Deci, E. (2002). Overview of self-determination theory. In R. R. Ryan & E. L. Deci (Eds.), *Handbook of self-determination theory*. Rochester, NY: The University of Rochester Press.

Ryan, R., & Deci, E., (2008a). A self-determination theory approach to psychotherapy: The motivational basis for effective change. *Canadian Psychology, 49*(3), 186–193.

Ryan, R., & Deci, E. (2008b). From ego depletion to vitality: Theory and findings concerning the facilitation of energy available to the self. *Social and Personality Psychology Compass, 2*(2), 702–717.

Senge, P., Cambron-McCabe, N., Lucas, T., Smith, B., Dutton, J., & Kleiner, A. (2000). *Schools that learn: A fifth discipline fieldbook for educators, parents, and everyone who cares about education*. New York, NY: Doubleday.

Wagner, T. (2010). The global achievement gap. Why even our best schools don't teach the new survival skills our children need—and what we can do about it. New York, NY: Basic Books.

Wagner, T. (2012). *Creating innovators: The making of young people who will change the world*. New York, NY: Scribner.

Zhao, Y. (2009). *Catching up or leading the way: American education in the age of globalization*. Alexandria, VA: Association for Supervision and Curriculum Development.

Zhao, Y. (2012). *World class learners: Educating creative and entrepreneurial students*. Thousand Oaks, CA: Corwin.

NINE

Guiding Step 9: Envision New Roles for Youths and Adults in a New Kind of School

Part of rethinking the design of schools will be rethinking what people do in them. Thinking about it in this way will be driven by a basic principle in learning theory: People will learn what they do (Dewey, 1938; Lave & Wenger, 1991; Polanyi, 1969).

In this regard, a primary consideration should be that stakeholders are designing a learning environment for two groups of learners, school students and adult learning specialists. What should these two groups do that will maximize learning and development for both? In reading the following description, readers should insert their own imaginations and envision their careers and the kind of personal and professional growth that will leave them satisfied.

What follows is a continuation of the descriptive narrative from chapter 8. It provides images of students and the adults they work with doing the things they want to learn. As readers read the narrative and see the descriptions, they should be mindful of both the new assumptions of a new school, the practices that invite a personal investment in learning, and the effort of the adults to provide a highly individualized, personalized, and customized learning experience for all.

FULL STAKEHOLDERS: STUDENTS' LEARNING PARTICIPATION AND PERSONAL EFFECTIVENESS

After lunch Rena's tour takes on a different theme, and she goes to great lengths to make it clear that in the A&S Community the roles of students are very different from those of the past. As a demonstration of these new roles, she asks two students, Barry and Lisa, to join them to take over the tour. Lisa has an eager look on her face and quickly begins by saying, "In this school students are major stakeholders. They have power."

She explains that in the view of everyone, including students, "some of the most important preparation students are getting for living and working in the twenty-first century comes from our participation as stakeholders in and managers of the A&S Community. Knowledge," she says, "is really about participation, and as students participate they get it in their blood what it is about full involvement that makes an organization effective" [Deming, 1986; Lave & Wenger, 1991; Polanyi, 1969; Senge et al., 2000].

"Our fellow students are going to go out into the world expecting to be participants in whatever organizations or communities they join. They will expect to be regarded as thinkers with important perspectives to share. This is a school where everyone is truly involved and learning is something we accomplish together."

As the group walks down the hall, Lisa continues to talk about the importance of student involvement. She invokes some familiar words about learning organizations and a greater role for students in them (Dale, 1997; Holcomb, 2007; Schlechty, 2009; Senge et al., 2000). She also insists that students contribute greatly to the learning of learning development specialists [LDSs] (Cook-Sather, 2002, 2006; Cushman, 2010; Fielding, 2003; Holcomb, 2007; Joselowsky, 2007; Mitra, 2004; Rudduck, 2002; Rudduck & McIntyre, 2007).

She explains that it is by virtue of all of this participation that students see the importance of twenty-first-century skills and the need to improve their own personal effectiveness in working with others. With this background, Barry adds that the meaningful participation of students falls into three categories: as community facilitators, students learning, and partners in learning facilitation.

STUDENTS AS COMMUNITY FACILITATORS: BUILDING CONNECTION, ACTING COLLECTIVELY

As an illustration, Barry directs the candidate to a room where students are receiving special leadership training from adults, whom he describes as "fervent student advocates," who give the training to students throughout the state. In these training sessions it is made very clear to students why their input to the community is not only important but crucial. As the group stands outside the room, a student stands in the middle of a circle of other students seated at desks, making an argument about why students should be part of the certification of the learning process.

Lisa then points out that what they are seeing now is practice, but that she soon expects to see this presentation for real in a Community Congress session. She explains that their community is enmeshed in a controversy about student involvement in the final certification of the learning process.

She further explains that in such venues as this, students learn their entitlement to speak up and to negotiate for what they believe in or want. When students participate in meetings about the general operations of the school, they feel fully enfranchised to say what they want to say and to disagree with adults who think differently. At the same time, this student influence is also balanced with a high level of responsibility.

Every year students are involved in the review and revision of the code of conduct for members of the A&S Community. Although this code is affirmative—suggesting positive behaviors—not prohibitive, it sets a high bar for how students should support a caring learning community.

"This school is all about character development," Lisa explains. "As students experience all of the difficult situations that come from full participation in our community, they are always prompted to ask, what is the right thing to do? That question becomes a lot harder when students can't just default to pretending obedience to authority but instead have to think through why they choose to do what they do and then are asked to explain their answer."

As Barry directs the candidate to a small stadium-style auditorium, he explains that this is where the Community Congress meets. He also explains that students have representatives on the A&S Community Congress, which makes important decisions about the operation of the school, including budget decisions. There are often heated debates, and students always have an adult at the meeting who is dedicated to supporting students in such a debate should they be needed. The adults rarely are needed because of the kind of training student representatives receive to be members of the Community Congress.

In a nearby room the group finds students who don't want them to enter because they are planning a special LDS appreciation day. Although the day would not be a surprise, the activities would, and these students do not want any of the surprise spoiled. Lisa says that both students and staff are very aware of their responsibilities to steward a positive community. One outgrowth of this is the institution of Spirit Days, when students and staff just do fun stuff, such as watch movies together, come to school in costume, paint their faces, wear crazy hats, play music or sing together, or do what students like to call "weird acts of kindness."

As they continue walking, they come upon a group of students in the hallway receiving their school orientation from two older A&S students, who are trying to set a serious tone. No adults are present. One of the student leaders is heard talking about the need for the younger students to figure out what their purpose is for going to school at all and in particular for going to the A&S Community School.

One of the younger students asks whether it is true that this school is a lot of fun. An older student responds by asking the younger student a question: "Are you good at having fun?" The younger student seems puzzled for a moment and then responds, "Sure, I'm great at having fun." The older student responds back, "That's good because this school will not entertain you, but it will require you to make things a lot of fun. And, in this school, we love games." The younger student seems quite happy to have this point clarified.

Soon the tour group comes to another room where students are doing their initial pitch of a course they want to create to a panel of adults and students. Barry explains that when students come into this learning community, one of the first things they learn is the protocol for creating a course. This pitch to a panel is the first stage. If students show that they have thought through the objectives of the course, then they can begin to test the water to see whether they can get eight students. Then they have to start looking for advisory personnel. Sometimes an on-staff LDS is available, sometimes not. In that case, students would have to find a community partner.

In reaction to this panel scenario, Lisa immediately points out that the school has a panel of students who review educational games for entry into the curriculum. Some of these games are brought to school by students, some by LDSs, and some from education vendors who promote the use of games in learning.

As the candidate listens to all of this, he notices on a nearby wall a poster announcing the possibility of a new student-created course, which is described as "A New Departure in Nano Code Development." Another poster announces an acting class for nine weeks with a student who has returned from college eager to pitch in at his old school. The sign reads "It's Me, Jeremy. I'm BAAACK!"

As the candidate absorbs what he is hearing and seeing about students' facilitation of the community, Barry points out that many students are actually employees of the school itself. In fact, as part of the school's constitution, positions for work at the school have to be offered to students first before they can be posted or advertised for adults from outside of the A&S Community.

These jobs usually involve less than 15 hours a week, and pay is just above minimum wage, but students are eager to get them. Walking about the building, the candidate sees students assisting LDSs in classrooms, serving in office clerical positions, working in the cafeteria kitchen, cleaning the building, and demonstrating in the computer lab.

LEARNING ABOUT LEARNING, LEARNING INFORMATION AND SKILLS, AND LEARNING ABOUT SELF

As they pass several more posters inviting students on travel adventures, Lisa goes on to explain how students are encouraged to think of their learning as not only mastery of information and skills but also as mastery of the self. She explains, "We often tell students that it is good to know things, but it is even better to know how to make things happen. That kind of personal effectiveness comes from an intentional focus on self development."

Lisa explains, "In this community we look to develop our minds and our personal effectiveness. That can come about only through participation in a learning organization where students have opportunities to assert themselves by making choices, making changes, and creating new opportunities to learn. We want a lot of metacognitive activity for our students, learning and thinking about learning and thinking about one's own learning and how it can be done in better ways. This focus on personal development can be advanced only if students play more consequential roles in helping to guide the operations of their learning community."

When Rena, Lisa, Barry, and the candidate stop at one room, a circle of students and one adult are in discussion, and the term "emotional intelligence" is being used. Barry reacts by explaining that because of the community's full-participation philosophy, the community takes the idea of twenty-first-century skills very seriously and makes it clear to students that learning in the community is about preparing for the outer world and mastering their inner world.

Two popular e-books that all students, staff, and community partners are encouraged to read are *Emotional Intelligence: Why It Can Matter More than IQ*, by Daniel Goleman (2012), and *Social: Why Our Brains Are Wired to Connect*, by Matthew Lieberman (2013). Members of the staff often run brief courses using each of these works. Many drama activities also give students opportunities to explore inner territories to discover new capacities. And, as work is presented to students, they are often asked by staff to identify the emotional and social intelligence needed to do it well.

In another room students are preparing yet another argument to be presented to the adult staff about some problems they are having with the use of rubrics in the assessment process. Lisa, somewhat apologetically, explains that the whole evaluation process always creates a little tension between the students and staff. In this case, there is some debate about the wording of a rubric, and students are demanding some clarification.

Staff members are actually quite pleased with these student arguments because they like for students to develop their argument skills, and they want students deeply involved in thinking about the quality of work. Rena emphasizes, "The quality of the learning is an ongoing discussion here. We don't just use the buzz term 'high standards'; we have big discussions about what makes work high quality."

They briefly stop at the next room, where eight students sit in a semicircle as one student puts geometric shapes on a white board and challenges the seated students to put them into meaningful groups. Lisa believes it is part of a research project. Toward the rear of the room, an LDS is videotaping the presentation. Barry guesses that it is probably something the presenting student intends to include in his e-portfolio as an outcome of individual research.

On that note, Rena takes the occasion of this brief visit to reemphasize by saying, "In this school, we like big projects. The reason we like them is because we have come to know big projects as the places of wholeheartedness, of full engagement. When we see that we have gotten a kid or a group of kids deeply involved in some project, then we believe this school has reached a benchmark in serving that kid, and the student has reached an educational benchmark.

"We want our kids to leave this school with a history of all-in commitment to some project where they experienced both success and failure. That experience of being all in on some effort is what we believe will be the foundation for students' success in the real world. As part of students' electronic portfolios we ask them to identify and present their all-in projects as part of the presentation to describe the all-in experience for the viewer."

PARTNERS IN LEARNING FACILITATION: LEARNING ABOUT LEARNING BY HELPING ADULTS LEARN

The final part of the tour is meant to demonstrate that students really are important partners in learning facilitation. Students help each other learn, and they help LDSs learn about learning. The candidate, Rena, Barry, and Lisa then walk past one area where all the students seem to be involved in quiet study. In fact a sign reads "Quiet Study Room."

Lisa explains that if groups want to get together for talking, they would go to the cafeteria commons. She points out to the candidate that the primary helpers in the room are other students. These students walk around with tablets attached to lanyards, which hang around their necks. The tablet has a feature for receiving help calls from students situated within a certain radius. The helpers often use their tablets to demonstrate something to students. More interesting to the candidate is that these helpers are taking a class in learning facilitation in which they participate in seminar discussions and write papers on their efforts helping others learn.

Barry then takes the candidate to a room that seems to be running an old-fashioned class with up-front LDS instruction. But, as you might expect, an LDS is not up front but rather a student is presenting the outcomes of a model-building project that he and a partner had worked on.

Barry proudly emphasizes, "In our community, students do a lot of presenting. We discourage LDSs from doing too much talking, especially from the front of the room, but being a confident presenter is such an important skill that we make it a big part of what students do here. And we also like to get students thinking about the pitfalls of talking too much and thinking about innovative alternatives to explaining." As they are about to depart, the candidate hears the presenting student ask all of the listening students to come up and touch the model. Lisa explains that the presenting student is making a deliberate effort at participatory presenting.

They then walk up some steps to another floor, and Lisa indicates that what they will see next will relate to what is likely the most important part of students' participation. Students play an important role in the evaluation and development of effective learning models. As they walk on, she tells the candidate that students regularly participate in evaluating their learning experiences.

Then from a folder she pulls a notice to all LDSs and community partners explaining how students will evaluate their courses. She emphasizes that most LDSs actually evaluate each component of their courses separately as students complete them. They think of this as a kind of formative assessment for the LDS so improvements might be made in future components of a course. Still, so everybody is on the same page, this explanation is provided to all. The notice reads as follows:

At the end of your course, students will provide feedback. They will be asked the following questions:

- Did you learn a lot in the course? Explain.
- Did you enjoy the course? Explain.
- Did the course require a high level of effort? Explain.
- Did the LDS or community partner appreciate your learning level and help you get to the next level? Explain.
- Did the course provide opportunities for you to apply your personal strengths as a learner? Explain.
- Were you able to influence what you learned in the course? Explain.
- Were you given all the help you needed? Explain.
- Did this course spur you to want to learn more about this or other fields? Explain.
- Would you recommend that other students take this course? Explain.

- What constructive suggestions for improvement would you offer the LDS or community partner?

Rena then turns to look the candidate squarely in the face. "To let you know exactly how far we go with this, our orientation for community partners is often done by students. You should see the look on community partners' faces when students sit down with them and start talking about adolescent psychology, learning theory, good pedagogy, and facilitation. But the students do it well, and it sends a message we want sent. We are all working together to understand learning and what kinds of facilitation work best."

When the group reaches the media research center, Rena is delighted to see that a learning focus group is under way and being led by a student from a university. She explains that the learning focus groups are part of the function of the school as a professional development school. The A&S Community conducts all sorts of induction activities for prospective LDSs, and among them are learning focus groups.

In these focus groups, students are seated in a circle of about 10 students, with a facilitator. Today, the facilitator is a graduate student. The facilitator presents one guiding question: *What do the adults you work with do that makes you want to learn?* The rules are that there is to be no complaining and no naming of adults. Students are to keep it positive and tell what the adults do that makes them want to learn. They step in to listen briefly.

It seems the students take the whole matter very seriously, and if they are asked to speak, they take the time to think carefully about their answers. Students are mentioning all sorts of adult behavior, from smiling and joking to admitting mistakes. As they do, the facilitator writes notes on a pad she has in her lap. When they feel the impulse, other students jump into the conversation to piggyback on what another student is saying.

Occasionally, the facilitator says things such as "Can you give me an example of that from your personal experience?" or "Can you explain to us why you find it so motivating when the adults act that way?" It is apparent that the students feel they are being taken very seriously, and they take their time to respond to questions in a very thoughtful manner.

Interesting enough, around the students is another ring of young people who are candidates from the university and part of the professional development school induction program. They are going to fishbowl the discussion. Rena says that listening to school students in this way is often a big wakeup call for the interns because they hear students say things that they would not read in their college books. The A&S Community conducts these focus groups on a weekly basis for the university and for the edification of its own staff.

Rena also explains that graduate students at the university do all sorts of research in their school, and she believes that some of the attendees that day are students from the university who are going to interview the community students later about how it feels to be part of the focus group. She emphasizes, "We like the students seeing adults conducting research. Action research is a big part of our focus on project learning here in the community."

As they leave the center, Lisa goes on to explain that along with working with LDSs to improve learning, students also play a big role in the assessment of their own work. She describes how a large part of student assessment is the use of models and rubrics, which are used for the purposes of establishing a competency level. With such measures, students know beforehand to what level they have to perform to be certified as competent and are guided while their work is being done so they know where they stand in terms of achieving success on a given project.

As part of this process, students get together with adults and explain why they believe their work is successful. If the adult and the student do not agree, the student can have his or her work reviewed by a panel of anonymous students, which would lead to some negotiations and usually to some student revisions and a successful project. Rena insists, "Although complicated, we love the process because it makes our students very quality conscious, and we like that."

FROM TEACHERS TO LEARNING AND DEVELOPMENT EXPERTS

After Lisa and Barry complete their presentation of the new role for students, Rena puts the focus on new roles for teachers, who in the community are called learning and development specialists. She begins her explanation by going back to the early days when municipalities began to let go of the industrial age school model and started to look for something new. She notes that in her school, it was students who started the 21st Century School Club and that she first realized change was happening when she and some parents had been invited to one of their meetings.

Lena attributes her receptivity and that of the parents to the negative effects of focusing on standardized testing. She recounts, "People had become fed up. Teachers, students, and parents were ready to rethink their roles in school." As the tour unfolds, she explains that the new roles for LDSs could be best captured in three categories similar to those of students: learning facilitation, community facilitation, and professional learning.

LEARNING FACILITATION: HELPING LEARNERS ACHIEVE THEIR GOALS

Rena explains that the driving concept of most but not all of the new small learning communities in her city is to provide students with highly individualized, personalized, and customized learning experiences. And even those that have a narrow focus on developing technology service skills are much more personalized. This is, in effect, is a rejection of the standardization, one-size-fits-all approach from the old days.

With this driving concept in mind, original staff members decided to go beyond standard large-class instruction and employed as many learning models as possible so the learning styles and intelligences of as many students as possible could be accommodated. To make these accommodations, LDSs knew that they would have to reconsider their roles and shape them to provide the best possible services for students.

In that context, Rena also explains that "the charter for the Arts in the Sciences Learning Community is the result of a simple contract between the community's faculty and stakeholders. The A&S Community exists by virtue of this contract. It has been quite a few years now that we have operated independently of many of the old state regulations or applied state standards for grades or graduation. This is a copy of the contract."

The Stakeholders' Contract

The faculty of the Arts in the Sciences Learning Community promises all stakeholders that this community of learners will facilitate the acquisition of all of the competencies students and their parents desire and that are needed to go to the Next Level in achieving students' personal and career goals.

All stakeholders promise to make a significant investment in the community's efforts to facilitate learning. It is understood that because evaluation of student work will be competency based, the A&S faculty will maintain high standards, and failure to meet those standards will ultimately be the students' responsibility.

Fulfillment of this contract will be subject to the judgment of the students, parents, and other community stakeholders in consultation with this faculty. It is understood that the A&S Community is flexible and will respond to expressions of dissatisfaction by making changes expeditiously.

If the A&S Community of learners is judged at the end of this contract's term to have done an inadequate job in facilitating student competencies and preparing youths for the future, it is understood that the stakeholders may dissolve the community and form another school with different staff, different leadership, and a different approach to learning.

"With this simple, good-faith agreement, our adult staff tries to employ as many learning models as possible. Having as many as we do means that students will be involved in many other learning activities that do not require direct adult supervision or direct LDS instruction." Remember these learning models include all of the following:

- Online learning
- Blended learning: Part teacher instruction, part guided learning online
- Adaptive learning machines
- Nings
- Learning from videos
- e-Game learning and simulations learning
- Community partner learning
- Independent research
- Action research
- Voice threads
- Student presentations
- Art creation learning (other than in art class)
- Tinkering and invention and innovation learning
- Cultural learning whereby students observe or witness the playing of music; look at artwork; or watch a TV program, movie, play, or novel presentation and discuss it
- Tutorial learning
- Conversational learning
- Travel learning
- On-the-job learning
- Apprenticeship learning
- Model-building learning
- Community project learning
- Creating and conducting survey learning
- Interview learning

"We are particularly proud of our use of this broad array of learning models. All of these models, plus the individual attention we provide, allow us to address the needs of a great variety of students, including students functioning well below grade level. I should point out that students in this city could develop a very traditional schedule with all kinds of old-fashioned requirements, such as physics, world literature, algebra II, and all of that, if they wanted.

"We have one community that is still very traditional and some students go that direction, but more and more students are seeking specialized variations that meet their special needs and interests. As one student put it, 'Why take general physics if your real interest is the physics of flight or the physics of weather? One way or the other, you learn physics.'

I would add that when learning what you want to learn, your learning is more authentic.

"It was the more traditional learning community that was popular at first, but little by little students are choosing greater freedom to pursue intrinsic interests. That's when they come to us or one of the other learning communities. Students are also aware that more and more colleges are seeking students who are motivated by special purpose and intrinsic interests, not students who have just jumped through the highest academic hoops.

"At the same time, you may have noted that the A&S Community offers students opportunities to take college courses, a special year-long Transition to College program, or a direct matriculation into college when appropriate. Students make these decisions in consultation with their parents, A&S staff consultants, and our partner university advisers."

As they walk about the building, the candidate never sees LDSs standing in front of classrooms giving direct instruction. Mostly he sees small groups in circles or groups on their feet making things at a table.

Rena elaborates, "Having students involved with all of these other models for learning accomplishes several educational goals. First, it allows students a greater range of choices for learning. Second, it allows them more independence in pursuing their learning goals. Third, students learn that they could be less reliant on LDSs for learning.

"All of this also frees up adult staff to meet with individuals and small groups on a regular basis. During these individual and small-group sessions, staff have time to get to know students in a deeper way and thereby be better able to facilitate in ways that address their individual needs, strengths, talents, and ambitions. Moreover, it gets kids away from thinking that learning is just a school-based concept and dependent on getting classroom instruction. We want our kids to learn how to learn and to become independent learners, knowing that they have many choices inside and outside of school."

As it was in the Matrix during the earlier tour, today's focus is on seeing individual and small-group work with adult staff. Rena points out that when all that is happening in this building is added to all that is happening outside of it with around one hundred community partners, students are being provided with a bounty of choices and lots of individual attention. Everywhere, people are meeting in small groups, usually in circles, working with each other and LDSs on projects, getting counseling, reflecting on accomplishments, and planning for the future. Rena insists that the individual and small-group sessions are what make learning in the A&S Community a very personal experience. The staff really gets to know each student in a deep way, and that is above and beyond the fact that every student has a dedicated adult mentor, and all new students have a dedicated student mentor *and* an adult mentor. It is part of the culture of this community that everyone is known and cared for in a deep way.

COMMUNITY FACILITATION: ACTING EFFECTIVELY COLLECTIVELY

As part of this focus on personalizing the schooling experience, Rena emphasizes that both the adult staff and the students are encouraged to think of themselves as facilitators of a community and a learning organization. Every member of the community is challenged to continually step back and look at how people are working with each other, supporting each other, learning together, and taking collective action to make the community even better. If things are not right, they have to be talked about and addressed quickly.

Rena is emphatic that being a learning organization means more than occasionally invoking some lofty language about the school's vision, mission, and goals. She is well aware of how that always failed in big schools. But the A&S Community is deliberately small so incorporating the community's vision, mission, and goals into everyday life is truly feasible.

In this community there is a thorough orientation of all members into the community so people understand that this community of learners operates with purpose. They are not just going through the motions and coating it with lofty language. Then Rena turns and looks at the candidate. "The time I'm spending with you is a case in point." She then points to a posting on the wall.

> **Vision:** A caring community learning together.
>
> **Mission:** To provide highly individualized, personalized, and customized learning for students and LDSs.
>
> **Goal:** To send every student and LDS to the next level of learning well prepared as an independent learner who knows how to learn.

Rena continues, "As a learning organization, we know that our school must have the full participation of all of its members. Individually, each of these members is committed to developing her or his twenty-first-century personal effectiveness skills and to improving the organization to accommodate changes in its members' needs, the needs of the local community, or the needs of the world.

"So, in our school, our LDSs assemble or chat online as a community and talk about the need for change all of the time. We expect the adult staff, in particular, to be knowledgeable and sensitive to any community problems or dysfunction. Every year we ask the question, what have we learned as a community? We even still talk about the game of school although it's not the cancer it used to be." At this point Rena takes out her device and shows the candidate some chat that LDSs are engaged in at that moment.

The chat involves some excitement about a student project involving cockroaches and mice. Rena goes on, "All of our staff and community partners are provided professional learning in small-group dynamics, and in that setting we encourage trust and the building of a personal commitment to learning. We encourage our LDSs to become learning and development experts."

PROFESSIONAL LEARNING FACILITATION: CREATING CONTINUAL PROFESSIONAL GROWTH

"When we started our A&S Community, we started with the premise that we had to serve two groups of learners, students and adult staff. For the adults who come here every day, our community has specific design features to facilitate ongoing adult learning and professional development." Rena insists, "We are quite serious here about providing LDSs with opportunities for collective and individual learning, both aimed at greater professional fulfillment.

"And, as part of our community's interest in fulfillment, this year the staff is reading the book *Happier: Learn the Secrets of Daily Joy and Lasting Fulfillment* [Ben-Shahar, 2007]. We, of course, want a happy community, and we are deliberate about it. Sometimes on Fridays, the staff gives itself and students homework assignments to 'create happiness.' We want everyone to understand that he or she is responsible for creating his or her own happiness and that it involves taking action. This school is an example of that action. Later, people give reports, and we reflect on the happiness we create here and around us.

"Our partnership with two local universities means we frequently have professors come to our community for various presentations, seminars, research, and coaching." Rena then shows the candidate a room where one of the universities has an office. At 5:00 there is going to be a group counseling session there for staff considering a certain degree path.

She then goes on, "Most of our staff pursues advanced degrees by doing research here in our school. In fact, every student in this school is asked to sign forms that allow the adults to conduct all sorts of research and involve students without having to subject students to all of the distractions of dealing with the university institutional review boards with each new research project.

"At the same time, many of our LDSs go to the universities to contribute the knowledge of practitioners. Many LDSs also have reading groups, wherein they discuss books and alert each other to still more books. LDSs also pursue learning and degrees online, and we have two university courses in our main building each quarter. So that means six courses are offered each year right here in town. And, of course, many LDSs opt to take courses at the university. Tuition expenses for all of the university courses are always reimbursed 100 percent.

"As part of the induction of new staff and our many community partners, we pledge to them a high level of support in developing the capacity to fulfill these guidelines."

ARTS IN THE SCIENCES LEARNING COMMUNITY GUIDELINES FOR WORKING WITH STUDENTS AND FACILITATING LEARNING

Take time at the beginning of the course to get to know who your students are. Each student should give you a form called "Introducing Myself as a Learner." Be sure to review the student's information carefully and incorporate it into your interaction with the student. Ask students to tell why they took your course and how it fits into their life plan or purpose in life. Guide students in an inquiry of the whole concept of purpose in life. Ask students what they would like to get out of the course so you can use this information to make sure you can meet the needs that students express.

- Make a point of getting a sense of each student's ability level. This will help you develop appropriate expectations as you assist the student in getting to the next level.
- Do your best to let students know that you care about them in a deep way. Yes, you are the LDS, but don't make yourself the center of attention. Make the students the center of attention. Recall when you were a school student and things LDSs did that made you feel special and cared about. Recall the things they did that made you want to learn. Focus there. Such care and connection may also be developed via online chat rooms or other online community devices.
- As you plan your facilitation, try to make the class meetings about 30 percent facilitator talk, and dedicate the rest of the class to listening to students or to group activities. To whatever extent possible, try to facilitate students' experiencing your area of expertise instead of just talking about it or reading about it. In these situations you can give relevant demonstrations along with personal attention and guidance.
- Make your course challenge both the intellectual and emotional intelligence of the students. As students confront these challenges, ask them to reflect on how achievement in these areas will be good for them. Remember, at the end of your course, students will complete anonymous evaluations when you are not present. That eval-

uation will ask students if they learned important information and skills, information and skills that will make them ready for even higher levels of challenge.

Consider this learning core: Students ready for college or the workplace should be able to

- analyze information and the social conditions around them;
- consider a variety of perspectives in developing ideas: give it the social test;
- utilize and synthesize information from a variety of sources, including personal experience;
- interpret information and personal experience in creative ways;
- explain their thinking and the process by which they came to certain conclusions;
- explain the differences between mindless, automatic thinking and mindful, reflective thinking; and
- create compelling communications (speech, writing, video, drama, poetry, benevolent works) that apply their analyses and demonstrate synthesis of theory, research data, and personal experience.

For evaluation, it is recommended that LDSs avoid paper and pencil memory tests. Rather students' knowledge and skills should be checked formatively throughout the term by you in the context of how important information and concepts might be observed or applied in the real world. For example, if your course is on the role of trains in the twenty-first century, a student's knowledge and skills might best be checked formatively by submission of a project proposal that demonstrates how the student might use important concepts presented in your course and how the student plans to apply them in the creation of a model. Your final evaluation of the student's work would be focused on this final project, a project wherein you had ongoing opportunities to correct the student and give guidance toward a high level of achievement. Be sure to include the student in a significant way in this final evaluation. Students should be helped to make honest and realistic evaluations of their efforts.

Although your course will have the serious purpose of helping students to develop these core skills in the context of your subject expertise, you MUST make your course FUN and EXCITING. This means that you will have to apply some imagination to how you engage students in appreciating your field of expertise. As you consider this challenge, try to recall yourself as a school student and how some of your LDSs made things fun and exciting for you. Keep these guidelines in mind:

- Kids like to be active. They like to move around, do things, and go places.
- Kids like to be social. Provide opportunities for kids to work together or with you.

- Everybody likes novelty. Kids liked to be surprised with the unusual and unexpected.
- Kids are visual
- Kids like to be presented with irony and contradictions that invite them to think, be creative, and solve problems.

Special Note

Students who are taking a course with a community partner will be preparing their projects for inclusion in electronic portfolios. When a facilitator's course concludes, a student's learning artifacts will be placed in his or her electronic portfolio as evidence that the student has acquired competency in a given skill. Every community partner should be mindful of the students' need to prepare these artifacts for posting in their electronic portfolios.

Facilitate real-world experience of your subject. Take students to and involve them in the places where your field of expertise is practiced.

NEW ROLES MEAN NEW SCHEDULES

To fully clarify the new role of LDSs, Rena concludes by showing the candidate two examples of LDS schedules where the candidate can see the focus on learning facilitation, community facilitation, and professional learning.

Learning and Development Specialist One:

> 8:00 a.m. Meets with a group of students writing a play. In a 30-minute period the students present their progress to the LDS and discuss a couple of problems with ending the play.
>
> 8:35 a.m. Meets with a single student who is writing a young-adult novel. The LDS has already read the 70-page manuscript and spends time asking the student about what she feels are the strengths and weaknesses of the project. They come to some agreement on how to revise and proceed.
>
> 9:00 a.m. Meets with a team of students who are preparing an argument for a mock trial.
>
> 9:45 a.m. Meets with a pair of students who are preparing a dramatic reading for presentation during the talent show.
>
> 10:10 a.m. Goes to the research center, where he is giving a group of eight students orientation on using the center and choosing search engines. They do a number of run-throughs of mock searches and research problems.
>
> 11:00 a.m. Meets with a group of eight students who are reading the novella *Anthem*. They review a few literary terms and discuss vari-

ous concepts implied in the book. They conclude the discussion with consideration of possible follow-up projects.

12:00 p.m. Meets with a group of nine students in a combination course on Hemingway and creative writing. Today, three students who presented short stories to the group will be critiqued by the rest of the group.

1:00 p.m. Has an individual conference with a student who is writing a memoire about a summer trip to Europe.

1:30 p.m. Has lunch in the commons with students.

2:00 p.m. Holds ninety minutes of office hours for student and colleague conferences, prep work, and returning phone calls and e-mails.

3:30 p.m. Meets with other LDSs to discuss competency approvals for eighteen students.

4:00 p.m. Meets with university personnel and five LDS interns to begin introduction to online course administration.

5:00 p.m. Goes home for the day and will spend forty-five minutes reading student essays.

Rena adds, "Under certain circumstances, some LDSs can work entirely from home communicating with students by e-mail and conducting online instruction and courses."

Learning and Development Specialist Two

8:00 a.m. Goes to police headquarters to assist the community partner sergeant with the start-up of an oversized class on prevention policing. The class is conducted while walking on Main Street.

8:45 a.m. Goes to the research center, where she is giving a group of eight students orientation on using the center and choosing search engines. They do a number of run-throughs of mock searches and research problems.

9:30 a.m. Meets with a team of students who are preparing an argument for a group art show.

10:10 a.m. Meets with a pair of students who are preparing to debate each other during a Community Congress meeting.

11:45 a.m. Meets with five students who are writing a situation comedy TV script. The LDS has already read the thirty-page manuscript and spends time asking the students about what they feel are the strengths and weaknesses of the project. They iron out particulars about a live presentation.

12:30 p.m. Meets with a group of eight students who are reading a historical novel, *Thunderous Spring*. They discuss students' writing short stories that capture the early twenty-first century.

1:30 p.m. Meets with a group of seven students who sell produce at the downtown square on Saturday mornings. They talk about adding a new location and new wholesale vendors.

2:00 p.m. Has an individual conference with a student who is considering going Next Level before taking a trip to South America.

2:30 p.m. Has lunch in the commons with students.

3:00 p.m. Meets eight students in the research center for orientation.

4:00 p.m. Holds ninety minutes of office hours for student and colleague conferences, prep work, and returning phone calls and e-mails.

5:30 p.m. Before going home, stops by the local movie theater to check on arrangements to show three different versions of *Romeo and Juliet* for a special weekend course for students.

Rena concludes by saying, "LDSs are expected to devote approximately 50 hours a week to their professional activities. And they are expected to take 2 three-day weekends each month. Nine weeks of vacation should be taken periodically throughout the year as student needs permit."

In new schools, students and LDSs will have roles very different from those in industrial age schools. The scenes in this chapter helped in envisioning those new roles. Still, that vision is incomplete. It may also be different from readers' personal visions, if they have started to percolate. In any case, the incompleteness of the vision or how the author's is different from the readers' may be seen as a good thing.

The point of this book has not been to provide a final blueprint for new schools. Rather, it has tried to help readers to see why change is needed and how change might look. Now with this nascent vision, let's consider how early career teachers might start the process of change in their change-resistant schools.

REFERENCES

Ben-Shahar, T. (2007). *Happier: Learn the secrets to daily joy and lasting fulfillment*. New York, NY: McGraw-Hill.

Cook-Sather, A. (2002). Authorizing student perpectives: Toward trust, dialogue, and change, in education. *Educational Researcher, 31(4)*, 3–14.

Cook-Sather, A. (2006). Change based on what students say: Preparing teachers for a paradoxical model of leadership. *International Journal of Leadership, 9(4)*, 345–358.

Cushman, K. (2012). *Fires in the mind*. San Francisco: Jossey-Bass.

Dale, J. (1997). The new American school: A learning organization. *International Journal of Educational Reform, 6(1)*, 34–39.

Deming, W. E. (1986). *Out of the crisis*. Cambridge, MA: Massachusetts Institute of Technology.

Dewey, J. (1938). *Experience and education*. New York, NY: Kappa Delta Pi.

Fielding, M. (2003). Review of 'What Pupils Say' by Andrew Pollard and Pat Triggs. *Journal of Educational Change, 4(1)*, 38–39.

Goleman, D. (2012). *Emotional intelligence: Why it can matter more than IQ*. New York, NY: Random House.

Holcomb, E. (2007). *Students are stakeholders, too!* Thousand Oaks, CA: Corwin.

Joselowsky, F. (2007). Youth engagement, school reform, and improved learning outcomes: Building systemic approaches for youth engagement. *NASSP Bulletin, 91(3)*, 257–276.

Lave, J., & Wenger, E. (1991). *Situated learning: Legitimate peripheral participation.* New York, NY: Cambridge University Press.

Lieberman, M. (2013). *Social: Why our brains are wired to connect.* New York, NY: Crown.

Mezirow, J., & Associates. (2000). *Learning as transformation: Critical perspectives on a theory in progress.* San Francisco, CA: Jossey-Bass.

Mitra, D. L. (2004). The significance of students: Can increasing "student voice" in schools lead to gains in youth development? *Teachers College Record, 106*(4), 651–688.

Polanyi, M. (1969). *Knowing and being.* Chicago, IL: University of Chicago Press.

Rudduck, J. (2002). The 2002 SERA lecture: The transformative potential of consulting young people about teaching, learning, and schooling. *Scotish Educational Review, 34(2),* 123–137.

Rudduck, J., & McIntyre, D. (2007). *Improving learning through consulting pupils.* London & New York: Routledge.

Senge, P., Cambron-McCabe, N., Lucas, T., Smith, B., Dutton, J., & Kleiner, A. (2000). *Schools that learn: A fifth discipline fieldbook for educators, parents, and everyone who cares about education.* New York: Doubleday.

TEN

Guiding Step 10: Begin the Journey to New Schools and Happier Careers by Making Connections

The point of this final chapter is to prime early career teachers for leading change. It will offer concrete suggestions for getting started. The pathway will not be heroic or spectacular; rather it will involve the process that all change requires: baby steps, then bigger steps. It is important to remember that as teachers look to lead the evolution of teaching, they will want to take the profession to a more personalized and happier place. Thus, each suggestion offered will look to embrace personalization and the happiness it will bring our future communities of learning.

To this point, this book has offered compelling reasons for change, with a primary focus on professional learning and teacher fulfillment. The situation is clear: Unless our schools are changed, our teachers will be inducted into the assumptions and practices of industrial age schools. They will learn about schooling and learning from the perspective of factory design and management. This will leave them unprepared for effectively serving in the twenty-first century. In the face of this, early career teachers should take action and assert leadership to control their own destinies. Consider these guidelines in getting started and getting new schools for new learning.

ACKNOWLEDGE THE DIFFICULT CIRCUMSTANCES

Chapters 8 and 9 encouraged a vision of a different kind of school. It will be a small, caring community of learners, with new roles for students and teachers. It will employ a large variety of learning models and focus on personalizing and individualizing learning. It will move the focus from teacher-centered, teacher-talk instruction to developing students' desire to learn, using many learning models.

Readers might be thinking "This is exciting. I like the idea of using all of the cited new models for learning, and I like the idea of making everything about school more personal. I also like the idea of a heightened focus on professional learning and teacher fulfillment in these caring communities. I would really like to teach in a school where teachers were expected to think and be imaginative, not just follow dictates and directives from afar."

Then readers look up from this book, and there they are in an industrial age school. Most of the people around them don't even know what the term "industrial age school" means. On top of that, even though they are annoyed with their loss of control and the incessant focus on standardized testing, readers know that the educators around them are not thinking about dramatic change. They are thinking about doing the best they can, getting their work done today, and going home to live their personal lives, where they have some control.

Most of the adults in the public schools have accepted with resignation that they will be forever burdened with central authorities dictating what will happen in their classrooms. It's been that way for decades, and there is no relief in sight. They don't like it, but nothing in their environment suggests that they have other choices. Thus, they are resolved to do their jobs as best they can, collect their pay, and live their lives.

GOOD IDEAS FOR CHANGE

The suggestions that follow are ideas for starting a change process in a traditional school. These suggestions are offered as a primer. They will help readers to get started.

Make Sure You Know What You Think

À la Michael Jackson, change starts with the person in the mirror. If readers are considering how they might influence change, they must make sure that they know what they think and what they believe. As this book has tried to prepare readers for leadership, it has also tried to raise difficult questions that the teaching profession must face. Now readers may have more familiarity with the issues raised than most people do. Still, the decision to start speaking out and taking action to influence change should be based on the clarity of readers' thinking and beliefs. All of the readers of this book should make sure they know what they believe and why.

This is a very important point because in looking at how teachers have lost control of their profession, much of that loss may be attributed to teachers' beliefs. On the one hand many teachers don't really know what they believe. So, when a new dictate comes from the central authorities, they often don't react to it because they are not sure what they believe. They lack a professional philosophy, and without it, they hesitate to question authority. They lack the confidence to argue over why a dictate is good or not good or how it should be modified. To enter into such discussions, a person must have strong convictions.

On the other hand, there are many teachers who do have a strong education philosophy, but they do not use it. As a younger teacher, that would have included the author. Such teachers have put their philosophy on the shelf because thinking and debating among professionals is not a part of the culture in an industrial age school. It is not a part of life in an industrial age school to have teachers reflect on the assumptions and practices they use from year to year. In fact, what teachers learn in these traditional schools is that their ideas don't matter. What matters is complying with the dictates that come from authorities and getting the work done.

If this book has done its work, readers will not want to become like either of these groups. They will make developing their philosophy of education an important part of their life and use it when they assess or size up a school as a place where they might plant their careers. If they really want to move change, they must be able to tell others what they believe and why they believe it is best for youths. They must be able to tell others why they will be happier with change.

Assess Personal Motivations

Early career teachers must also get some clarity about the strength of their motivation to contribute to change. How important is change to them? Would they just like it, or do they demand it? Would they like to be the leaders of change, or would they just like to help the leaders? What do they envision themselves doing to get schools where they think they should be?

Having read this book, some readers may look at their schools and conclude that change there is really hopeless. If that is true, it would probably be better in the long run for those readers to seek another place to work and be guided in choosing another place by their philosophy and knowledge of what makes teachers happy. As they consider their motivation, they should equate their desire for change with their desire for a career that is humanly fulfilling.

If readers want the schools they work in to be learning organizations where they are encouraged to think and challenge the status quo, they should look for that place. If that is where they are now, that is great. If they are not in that place, they are left with questions for themselves: "How important is it to me to be in a school where I can be thoughtful and exercise my philosophy of education? Am I willing to uproot and take some risks to find that place?"

Assess Schools in Terms of Opportunities for Professional Learning and Fulfillment

One of the author's motivations in writing this book has been to help readers get the careers they want. Readers will be able to achieve that in a newly conceived school where everybody is encouraged to think and create change. Right now readers should consider how their careers will turn out if schools remain as they are or if they change and imagine how in 20 years it will be to look back if now they decide not to act. In this regard, readers may want to have some conversations with veteran teachers about how they feel about how their careers turned out.

When readers listen to these teachers, they should listen for resignation. Are these teachers telling readers that they did the best they could under the circumstances, where they had little control? Or, do these teachers talk about the three things that satisfy: having autonomy and control over their professional lives, being a member on a team of respected professionals who make decisions, and having careers of continual professional growth. Now is the time for readers to act to make themselves happy teachers.

Do More Reading

If readers feel highly motivated, they should do more reading and networking. Remember that the ideas in this book are ideas the author shares with other thinkers in education. There are a number of wonderful books the author would like to suggest that have to do with the need to change our schools. Each of these books will deepen readers' understanding of why change is necessary, how change will look, and how to create change.

Readers might want to start with a concise statement from Will Richardson's *Why School* (2012). Then Tony Wagner offers two works that really get at the concept of twenty-first-century learning: *Creating Innovators: The Making of Young People Who Will Change the World* (2012) and *The Global Achievement Gap: Why Even Our Best Schools Don't Teach the New Survival Skills Our Children Need—and What We Can Do about It* (2008).

Yong Zhao also offers two works that consider learning from a twenty-first-century perspective and point to actual alternatives: *Catching Up or Leading the Way: American Education in the Age of Globalization* (2009) and *World Class Learners: Educating Creative and Entrepreneurial Students* (2012). Gaining knowledge of real, on-the-ground alternatives is also assisted in *Breaking the Mold of School Instruction and Organization* edited by Honigsfeld and Cohan (2010), and *Trusting Teachers with School Success:*

What Happens When Teachers Call the Shots by Farris-Berg, Dirkswager, & Junge (2012).

In an especially timely work, Cathy Davidson brings to bear the science of neurology and how the twenty-first century invites a new understanding of learning in *Now You See It: How Technology and Brain Science Will Transform Schools and Business for the 21st Century* (2013).

Also, readers will also want to know that recently a seventeen-year-old named Nikil Goyal had a book published with ideas similar to those in this book and in those of the previously cited authors. He has achieved considerable fame as a result. His book is titled *One Size Does Not Fit All: A Student's Assessment of School* (2012). The author found this book to be a very meaningful read and believes that sharing it with teachers and students would be very helpful to the cause of change.

Share This Book and Others with Friends, Colleagues, and Students

Passing this book to another early career teacher would be a great way to start change. When offering it to another teacher, readers might say something such as "I don't know whether you have read this book, but it has a lot of surprising ideas about the career of teaching. I'd like to discuss them with you if you have time to read it." This small beginning could be the start of something important for each reader as an individual as well as for the school.

Readers should also know that this book has a companion book, *The Evolution of Learning: A Guidebook to School Change, Authentic Learning, and Leadership for High School Students*. The author explicitly states in both books that it is his intent to support leadership and get readers to start conversations about change.

In the book for students, the author employed a term, the "core scenario." The core scenario is a moment of action. It is when one person goes to another person and attempts to start a conversation about change. In the book for students and in this book, the term expresses the importance of agency, of an individual's taking action. In this case, a request is made to a person to consider some of the ideas in this book or to read this book for later discussion. If readers share this book with other early career teachers, they will have exercised the core scenario and started the change process.

All change comes out of people getting together to share new ideas. Teachers' sharing ideas makes them happier. Readers will learn from this process and then decide what new ways of self-direction and self-expression will make teachers even happier.

Form a Reading Circle

From just sharing this book with another individual might come the idea to share it with a group. A reading circle for this book or some of the others suggested would be a great start. It will make readers even happier. It will be an act of taking control.

Discussion would enable people to get thoroughly acquainted with the important ideas that point the way to new models for learning. If possible, a wide range of ages should be represented in such a group. It would also be important to include students and administrators if possible. This variety of perspectives would add a lot to the ultimate message that change can be good for everybody.

In consideration of a reading circle, it is important to remember that this book is being read by other early career teachers in other parts of the country. If readers are accustomed to online chatting, going to an online chat room to discuss this book might be a good start. Note that a chat room for the purpose of discussing this book has already been set up at www.owninged.com. Perhaps readers would like to chat online for a while before they try to start up a reading circle or discussion group at their schools. Or, if readers are unable to get a group together at school, they can always go to online chat rooms.

Readers should also note that if students in their schools have been given access to the book addressed to them, then they will be looking for teachers to help them. As with this book, their book also points them to forming a twenty-first-century school club and strongly suggests that they get adults to help them with their efforts. As readers look at the list below of what kinds of activities a club might perform, they will find working with students on this project very rewarding and a valuable learning experience. The student perspective on this issue of change will be mind stretching.

Join Organizations That Support the Evolution of Teaching

There are many organizations that identify themselves as interested in school change and new roles for teachers in schools. Some have already been mentioned, such as the Coalition of Essential Schools. It is likely that there are many more than the author knows about but readers should consider such groups as Edutopia, Educause, EdVisions, and Education Evolving, and The Center for Teacher Quality.

It is also true that some traditional teachers' organizations, such as the National Education Association, have committees that are dedicated to advancing innovative ideas about teaching. Farris-Berg, Dirkswager, and Junge (2012) reported on the NEA's 2011 report, *Commission on Effective Teachers and Teaching*, which charged "a group of twenty-one accomplished autonomous teachers and educational leaders from around the country" to "craft a new vision of a teaching profession that is led by teachers and ensures teacher and teaching effectiveness" (p. 186). Of course, the author would like for the commission to read this book, too.

Reach Out to Veteran Educators

In the preface the author explained that it was likely that many veterans would have trouble with this book because it invalidates much that they have done. Still, there will be those who will come to readers' support, anyway. It is in their nature to support younger people even if they don't fully understand or agree with what readers are trying to do. Readers should do their best to get these people out to a few meetings, share some of their reading with them, and make it clear to them how much they need their support.

Feedback to Teacher Preparation Programs

In the very near future teacher preparation programs should prepare teachers to go into traditional schools and change them, to advance school evolution and the evolution of teaching. In this regard, those involved in leading change should make an effort to bring in leaders from teacher education programs to talk with them about preparing teachers as change agents. The truth is that many school administrators also have a sense of feeling trapped in the traditional operations of traditional schools. They likely would be interested in prospective teachers who come into teaching prepared to start the change process.

Form a Twenty-First-Century School Club

Teachers and students working together should consider the following:

- Starting a club would help students who have read the companion book. Knowing that they have an adult to go to for help would add credibility to the concept of a twenty-first-century school and give the students a major morale boost.
- Forming a club is a way of bringing the issue of change into the everyday life of readers' schools. The author asks readers to imagine how they or anyone else would react if on morning announcements there was the message that there would be a meeting of the 21st Century School Club today. Certainly, people would wonder, "What does that club do? You mean there could be a different kind of school? How would it be different? What's going on at those meetings?"
- The formation of a club would educate administrators. It would require readers to advise the administration that people would be

getting together on a formal basis to discuss the need for a new kind of school. This should certainly be done gently and with great diplomacy, but at that point the administrators would likely become very interested in understanding what was going on. Readers might want to hand one a copy of this book.

- Use the club to educate the faculty and members of the community that change is a serious issue and there are new ways of thinking about schools. The club could have presentations. For starters, this book and the student edition come with a PowerPoint presentation available at www.owninged.com. This PowerPoint presentation may be used in the early days to give visitors an orientation to the basic concept of the club. A second phase might have members of the faculty, community, or students making presentations to get others to understand their unique perspectives on change. For example, maybe students could make a presentation on why they should have greater participation in the affairs of the school. Maybe parents could give a presentation on why schools would be more effective if they operated as small, caring communities. Perhaps teachers could make a presentation on the value of allowing teachers to invent their own courses. Readers should also consider the list of activities in the box, below all of which will in some way advance change.

- Get perspective on the issue of buy in. Change requires that a certain number of stakeholders buy in to an idea for change. When the change effort begins, most of the stakeholders should be supporting the change. If that is not true, the change effort will likely fail. Aware of this, very often school leaders abandon a change initiative because they cannot get most people to buy into the idea. This makes sense if they are trying to change a school of 1,000 or more students.

- Members of a twenty-first-century school club should not be thinking about getting everybody to buy into the idea of creating a twenty-first-century school. They do not need everybody. They need only those people who are truly interested. Readers of this book will not be looking to change a large school. They will not need everybody's buy in. The ultimate objective of starting a twenty-first-century school club would be to move away from the large, traditional school concept and toward a small learning community, such as the one described in the previous chapters. Starting such a community does not need the buy in of most of the faculty. It needs the commitment of about fifteen adult staff along with parents, students, and community leaders. That is much more doable. Textbox 10.1 provides ideas for club activities.

TWENTY-FIRST-CENTURY SCHOOL CLUB ACTIVITIES

- Pass this book and the student edition around so as many students and adults as possible have a chance to read it.
- Present the PowerPoint presentation and just talk about the important ideas.
- Invite students and faculty to get together and discuss this question: How should the schools of the twenty-first century be different from the schools we have now? Why? Find out who is motivated to start doing things, such as getting students more involved in course creation and all other aspects of school life. Good discussions can come from questions like these:
  - Would it be better if the twenty-first-century school provided for more active learning and less sitting and listening and textbook learning?
  - Would it be better if learning in the twenty-first-century school was more individualized and personally inspired rather than being one-size-fits-all textbook/curriculum learning?
  - Would it be better to have more learning through activity in the real world?
  - Should the school of the twenty-first century spend more time helping students explore and understand their unique, personal talents and aspirations in life?
  - Would it be better to have a broader variety of learning modes other than just reading and listening, learning modes that respect a broad array of unique, individual intelligences?
  - Would it be better to have more community- and world-service learning?
  - Could the school of the twenty-first century be a place where students talk and present as often as teachers do?
  - In the school of the twenty-first century, could students learn from a greater variety of adults throughout the community instead of just teachers?
  - Could every student in the school of the twenty-first century have a caring mentor to guide him or her on a daily basis?
  - In the school of the twenty-first century, could students be mentors?
  - In the school of the twenty-first century, could students teach classes and assist teachers in teaching classes?
  - Could the school of the twenty-first century be more than just one building, a network of learning that is happening all over town and beyond?
  - Could the school of the twenty-first century involve learning from all of the businesses around town, from the local deli to the corporate chemical giant on the edge of town?
  - Could the school of the twenty-first century be a place of routine experimentation in how people learn, which may include ways of learning we have not yet imagined?
  - Is it worth it to talk about all of these things, and how do we get started?
- Invite a guest speaker from a local college or university.
- Go on the Web to find videos from twenty-first-century schools.

- Develop a presentation on twenty-first-century learning that could be provided to various classes in your school or to the local PTA or PTO or to interested community members at the local library.
- Have members raise some issues within their classes about change and the failure of schools to change.
- Connect with other twenty-first-century school clubs to discuss strategy.
- Keep a history of your club. Collect all of the related documentation and minutes of meetings. This history will be more important than you know.

The following list of imaginary challenges likely will help the club attract the interest of students and staff. These imaginary challenges also could be used in poster ads in the hallways or on daily announcements. Readers might ask students to imagine the following scenarios:

- They are in schools where they get to choose or invent courses that really interest them.
- They are in schools where they can build their education around *their* strengths, talents, and aspirations.
- Their teachers take the time to understand them as individuals, their strengths, weaknesses, and dreams and aspirations.
- Their schedules might include classroom courses, online courses, group independent study courses, individual independent study courses, local community courses offered by local experts, community college courses, apprenticeships, alternative certificate courses, and more.
- They are in schools where students will be asked their opinions about how to improve learning and instruction.
- They are in schools where students will be frequently presenting the outcomes of their projects. It won't just be the teacher up front all of the time.
- Students and teachers are talking about how to change things all of the time.
- Students get credit for learning they do outside of school and during the summer.
- Students become teachers to other students when they have the expertise.
- Students who want to become teachers could become apprentices to some classroom teachers in readers' schools.

Finally, one of the primary goals of a twenty-first-century school club should be to expand its influence. As the club gets its bearings on how it affects the school, it might begin to invite people of influence and ask them to get involved, including other teachers, school administrators, and central office administrators as well as community members, such as city council members or the mayor. Readers should not overlook administrators of big firms or civic groups in their city who have taken an interest in education.

In the companion edition of this book for students, *The Evolution of Learning: A Guidebook to School Change, Authentic Learning, and Leadership for High School Students*, the author's presentation is slightly different. In that book the message to students is that the adults are deliberately denying students a new kind of school because they feel uncomfortable with change. As a result, the book explains that students are being denied a better education. In light of these circumstances, students need to take action.

As this book concludes, the author wants to remind readers that *The Evolution of Learning* book for students might soon be about early career teachers and how their unwillingness to change is holding students back. Unless early career teachers are actively working for change, they will fall into the ranks of the resisters to change who want to deny students a twenty-first-century school.

But, unfortunately, the deeper truth is early career teachers' unwillingness to change will also hold teachers back. The bottom line is that the lives and careers of teachers will ultimately be much happier if they join with students, lead change, and get new schools for new learning.

THE FINAL FANTASY

The author now asks readers to imagine they are now several years into their careers in traditional schools, doing traditional things; stressing over standardized testing, ever-changing standards, and unfair teacher evaluations; and feeling little control over their professional work. Recently, however, they have heard through the grapevine that a small school is being formed in their district and that it will include their preferred grade levels. A brochure for students contains the following description:

- Your learning involves a lot of fun and excitement, using many learning models.
- What you learn is relevant to your life now and in the future.
- You each have an individualized program of study.
- Your voice plays an important role in school operations.
- You get the individual attention you need and want.
- You routinely invent your study topics and even invent courses.
- Sometimes you work alone and sometimes in groups.
- You are an important partner in helping teachers improve learning/instruction.
- Most of your learning is active/project based (way less sitting and listening to teachers talk).

- Your school is much smaller, and there is a feeling of care and community.
- There is low drama and less competition and high emotional and spiritual support.
- Your learning is deeper than that in a traditional school, and you will be better prepared for college, work, and life.

Then, one day readers see the posting from central office. This new school is described as providing intensive site-based professional learning in conjunction with two university partners. It will be led by teachers, and teachers and students will be held responsible for the school's success. All of this gets them thinking about this book, Rena, and whether they will be willing to take a risk. The deadline for applications is the end of this week. They decide to . . .

REFERENCES

Davidson, C. N. (2013). *Now you see it: How technology and brain science will transform school and business for the 21st century*. New York: Penguin Books.

Farris-Berg, K., Dirkswager, E., & Junge, A. (2012). *Trusting teachers with school success: What happens when teachers call the shots*. Lanham, MD: Rowman & Littlefield Education.

Goyal, N. (2012). *One size does not fit all: A student's assessment of school*. Roslyn Heights, NY: Alternative Education Resource Organization.

Honigsfeld, A., & Cohan, A. (eds.) (2010). *Breaking the mold of school instruction and organization: Innovative and successful practices for the twenty-first century*. Lanham, MD: Rowman & Littlefield Education.

Wagner, T. (2008). *The global achievement gap: Why even our best schools don't teach the new survival skills our children need—and what we can do*. New York: Basic Books.

Wagner, T. (2012). *Creating innovators: The making of young people who will change the world*. New York, NY: Scribner.

Waters, R. (forthcoming). *The evolution of learning: A guidebook to school change, authentic learning, and leadership for high school students*. Lanham, MD: Rowman & Littlefield.

Zhao, Y. (2009). *Catching up or leading the way: American education in the age of globalization*. Alexandria, VA: Association for Supervision and Curriculum Development.

Zhao, Y. (2012). *World class learners: Educating creative and entrepreneurial students*. Thousand Oaks, CA: Corwin.

Index

accountability testing, xxx–xxxiii, xxxiv, 49
action research, 33, 80, 106, 147, 149
adaptive learning machines, 33, 80, 149
Aldrich, 28, 35, 87, 89
A Nation at Risk, 8, 9, 12, 19
annual yearly progress, xxxiii, 12
apprenticeships, 168
Assessing What Really Matters, 76, 77
assumptions, x, xii, xix, xv, xvi, xx, xxi, xxiii, xxv, xxxiv, 3, 11, 12, 21–34

Bandura, Albert, 88
blended learning, 33, 149
Breaking Ranks I, 9, 19, 37
Breaking Ranks II, 9, 19, 37
Breaking the Mold of School Instruction and Organization, 162

career satisfaction, xii, xvii, xx, 15, 43, 49
Carnegie, Dale, 127
certification, 24, 25, 106, 124, 126, 133, 134, 140, 141
Center for Teacher Quality, 164
change, more of the same, 9–12
cheating, 65, 94
classroom instruction, 11, 17, 22, 23, 25, 32–34
collective learning, xix, xxii, 16, 106, 112, 113
complexity, 13, 18, 71
community building, xxii
community partners, 121, 128, 129, 131, 143, 145, 146, 150, 152
compliance, x, xx, 28, 37, 46, 47, 48, 67, 88, 96, 102, 111, 112, 113
context, xi, xii, xx, xxix, xxx, 22, 23, 25, 41, 57, 63, 67, 72, 74, 94, 110, 112, 125, 148

control, ix, x, xi, xvii, xviii, xxi, xxx, xxxii, xxxiii, xxxv, 28, 33, 34, 35, 36, 44, 46–49
Council of Chief State School Officers, 102
Creating Innovators, 162
creativity, xviii, xxi, 28, 93, 94, 102, 103, 111
Csikszentmihalyi, Mihaly, 57
culture, x, xi, xii, xix–xxi, xv–xvi, xvii, xviii, xxiii, xxxii, xxxiv, 3, 18, 19, 39–49, 65, 67, 73, 106, 109, 112, 113, 120, 123, 151, 161
Customers as Innovators, 92
customization, 85, 87
cynicism, xxvi

data analytics, 84
Davidson, Cathy, 163
destiny, xiv
disengagement, 44–49
Drucker, Peter, xv, 39
Durham, Sherry, 62
Dweck, Carol, 28, 42, 64

educated consumers of educational experience, 94
Education Evolving, 164
Educause, 164
Edutopia, 164
Ed.Visions, 164
Eells, Rachel, xxviii
e-game learning, 33, 149
electronic portfolios, 85
emotional intelligence, 112, 143, 153
Esquith, Rafe, xvii
experience of learning, 50, 61, 104
evaluation, x, xvii, xviii, xx, xxx, xxxv, 17, 22, 24, 28, 67, 143, 145, 148, 153, 154, 169

Farris-Berg, Dirkswager, and Junge, xxxiv, 164
The Fifth Discipline, 10
Florida's Virtual School, 80
Flow, xxiv, 57
foundation funding, 82–83
free agent learning, 88
Fried, Robert L., 44
frustration, ix, x, xvi, xxi, 17

Gallop, xvii
game of school, xxxiii, xxxiv, 28, 39–49, 56, 62, 64, 65, 66, 94, 106, 112, 129, 151
The Game of School, 44
The Global Achievement Gap, 162
Goleman, Daniel, 143
Goyal, Nakil, 163

happiness, xvi, xvii, xxi, 132, 152, 159
Heath, Douglas H.,
Hebert, Durham, Silver, 62
Hebert, Terri, 62
High Stakes Teaching, 62
Hoenigsfeld and Cohan, 163
Horace's Compromise, 9
Horace's School, 9
how students learn, 22, 23, 25

implementation, xix, 10–11
Implementation Gap, 9, 10, 14
independent learning, 86
individualization, xxxiv, 34, 70, 73, 74, 76, 87
individualization as a premise for schooling, 69–70
industrial age: assumptions, xix, xvi, xxv; design, 3; school, xii, xix, xx, xxiii, xxvi, xxvii, xxxiv, 3, 4, 12, 22, 28, 34, 66, 67, 70, 72, 73, 80, 87, 94, 98, 103, 106, 112, 114, 120, 147, 152, 159, 160, 161; thinking, xvi, xviii, xxviii, xxxv, 15, 119, 120
innovation, xxxiii, 9, 17, 33, 92, 93, 102, 103, 107
instructional software, 16
intensity, 12, 33
intrinsic motivation, xxii, 16, 25, 67, 74
iTunes U, 86

John D. and Catherine T. MacArthur Foundation, 87

Kapp, 87
Kelly, McCain, and Jukes, 11, 16, 97

leadership, ix, xiv, xv, xviii, xxii, xxv, xxviii, xxxiii, xxxiv, 16, 41, 89, 97, 102, 110, 128, 140, 148, 159, 161, 162, 163
learning engagement, 55, 56, 57, 58, 61, 62, 66, 73
learning facilitation, 140, 144, 147–150, 152–155
learning focus groups, 146
learning how to learn, 113–114
learning models, 3, 17, 23, 26, 32, 33, 34, 81, 121, 130, 145–149, 159, 169
learning organization, xx, xxxiii, xxxiv, 15, 98, 101–111, 140, 143, 151, 161
Left Back, 9
Lieberman, Matthew, 143
Los Angeles Public Library, 87

Machiavelli, 47
MAP, xxviii
marketplace of educational experiences, xxxiv, 26, 76, 79–89, 91, 92, 101
Maslow, xvi, xxi
memorization, 28
mental models, xxxiv, 10, 11, 13, 98, 101, 108, 119
Met Life Foundation, xvii
mindset, 11, 18
MIT's Opencourseware, 86
MOOCS, 86
motivation, xi, xxii, xxix, xxx, 16, 22, 23, 24, 25, 40, 46, 67, 74, 111, 161, 162

Newell and Van Ryzin, 77
nings, 33, 149
No Child Left Behind, xxxiii
Now You See It, 90, 163

One Size Does Not Fit All, 163
online learning, 81
open courseware, 86
OpenCoursewareConsortium, 81, 86

open software, 82
open source movement, 81
organizational learning, xii. *See also* collective learning
owninged.com, 164

The Passionate Teacher, 44
Peer 2 Peer U, 86
personal, xiv, xvii, xxi, xxix, xxv, xxvi, xxx, 5, 12, 16, 25, 26, 28, 39, 40, 41, 42
personal commitment/investment, 40–44, 56–60, 67
personalization, 70
personal investment in learning, 46, 58, 64, 69, 139
Phi Delta Kappa, xvii
practices, x, xix, xvi, xx, xxiii, xxv, xxvi, xxvii, xxxiii, 3, 5, 27, 28; classroom instruction, 32
The Predictable Failure of Educational Reform, xviii, 9
private funding, 82–84
process of learning, 72, 74
product of learning, 72
professional development schools, xviii–xxi, xxvi
professional learning, x, xii, xvi, xvii, xviii, xx, xxi, xxii, xxvi, xxvii, 15, 18, 82, 89, 106, 113, 147, 152, 159, 160, 162
professional learning communities, xviii–xxi, 5

quality levels in learning, 63, 66
Quest2Learn, 87

Race to the Top, xxxiii
rebellion, xix, xxxi
reflection, x, xvii, xviii, 25, 26, 28, 67, 84, 92, 98, 104, 105, 106, 108, 110, 111–112
requirements, 26, 28, 67, 70–73, 82, 149
resistance to change, xxvi, 13, 14
resources, xxviii, 22, 23, 25, 109, 121, 128, 131, 136, 137
Richardson, Will, 162

Salin, 87
scaffolding, xxii, 16

Scherer, Marge, 37
Schlechty, Phillip, xviii, 14, 18, 62, 85, 108, 140
school reform, xxii, xxiii, xxxiv, 8–15
Schools of Hope, 76
Schools that Learn, xxxiii, 7, 9, 14, 136
self-determination, x, xvi, xvii, xxx, 42, 74, 136
self direction, 35, 102, 103, 111, 112–113, 163
self mastery, 104–105, 108–111
self-organizing, 19, 35
Senge, Peter, 108
signals, 64, 66–69, 67
Silver, Debbie, 62
Sizer, Ted, 9
Social: Why Our Brains Are Wired to Connect, 143
So Much Reform, 9
Spinning Wheels, 9
stakeholder membership, xvi, xvii
stakeholders, xxxiv, 28, 93, 99, 119, 130, 135, 139–140, 148, 166
standardized testing, x, xix, xx, xxx, xxxiii, 49, 62, 63, 71, 96, 103
strategic learning, 39–47. *See also* game of school
strategy, xv, 39
students as customers, 91, 98
student voice, xxii
Syms, Sy, 99
systems thinking, 109

teacher evaluation, 22, 169
teacher preparation, xi, xv, xxii, 15, 16, 19, 21, 31, 165
teacher proofing, xvii
teaching machines, 128
Teaching the Digital Generation, 11–12, 16–19
Thomke, Stephan, 92
Tinkering Toward Utopia, 9
traditional schools, ix, xi, xiii, xv, xxi, xxvii, 3, 4, 10, 11, 13, 21, 22, 23, 27, 34, 39, 41, 43, 46, 66, 70, 79, 96, 105, 106, 107, 114, 121, 130, 136, 160, 161, 165, 166, 169; teachers, xiii, 164
Trusting Teachers with School Success, vii, xxxiv, 163

TTWWADI, 11–12
twenty-first-century learning, 15, 104, 105, 134, 162, 168
twenty-first-century skills, xxxiv, 101–105, 108, 109, 110, 111, 112, 113, 114, 140, 143

value zone in learning, 62
Venture Capital in Education Summits, 86
von Hipple, Eric, 92

Wagner, Tony, 162
Wall Street funding, 83
what students learn, 22, 24, 25, 72
Why School, 162
Wikipedia, 82, 86, 114, 130
Working on the Work, xxiv, 62
World Class Learners, 162

Yong Zhao, 162
YouTubeedu, 86